Coach Me! Your Personal Board of Directors

Coach Me! Your Personal Board of Directors

Leadership Advice from the World's Greatest Coaches

Edited by
Brian Underhill
Jonathan Passmore
Marshall Goldsmith

This edition first published 2022
© 2022 John Wiley & Sons Ltd

The right of Brian Underhill, Jonathan Passmore, and Marshall Goldsmith to be identified as the authors of the editorial material in this work has been asserted in accordance with law.

Registered Office(s)
John Wiley & Sons, Inc., 111 River Street, Hoboken, NJ 07030, USA
John Wiley & Sons Ltd, The Atrium, Southern Gate, Chichester, West Sussex, PO19 8SQ, UK

Editorial Office
The Atrium, Southern Gate, Chichester, West Sussex, PO19 8SQ, UK

For details of our global editorial offices, customer services, and more information about Wiley products, visit us at www.wiley.com.

Wiley also publishes its books in a variety of electronic formats and by print-on-demand. Some content that appears in standard print versions of this book may not be available in other formats.

A catalogue record for this book is available from the Library of Congress

Paperback ISBN: 9781119823780; ePub ISBN: 9781119823797; Obook ISBN: 9781119823803.

Cover image: © Michael Nivelet/Shutterstock
Cover design by Wiley

Set in 10/12pt Warnock by Integra Software Services Pvt. Ltd, Pondicherry, India

B118011-140222

Printed in Great Britain by Bell and Bain Ltd, Glasgow

Profits from the sale of *Coach Me! Your Personal Board of Directors* will be provided to the Marshall Goldsmith Bursary at Henley Business School, United Kingdom, which is a special fund dedicated to training the next generation of worthy leaders from the developing world to become coaches.

To my beautiful wife, Julie. Eccl 4:12. – BU
To Katharine, Florence, and Beatrice. – JP

Contents

Foreword

A CEO's Journey through Coaching

Aicha Evans
CEO, Zoox, Inc.

Mark Thompson
World's #1 CEO Coach

When you meet world-class leaders whose talent is as extraordinary as that of Aicha Evans, you might not imagine her looking to executive coaches to be inspired and supported. However, throughout her remarkable career, she has tapped master coaches as strategic partners in building every great team, particularly in organizations facing massive growth and change. As CEO of Zoox, an Amazon company, Aicha is leading a mission as epic as a technological moonshot – autonomous driving – a radical redefinition of "personal transportation to make it safer, cleaner and more enjoyable for everyone," she says.

"My job, first and foremost, is to coach my team to become better leaders! And the biggest challenge every leader faces is to make yourself vulnerable to coaching as a role model of professional growth and personal transformation," Aicha smiled: "When it comes to change, you go first!"

As a CEO coach, Aicha's journey reminds me just how fortunate I am to learn from and support the world's most talented leaders. My mentor and friend Alan Mulally, the legendary former CEO of Ford and Boeing, often reminds me: "The secret to success as a coach is client selection!" When Marshall Goldsmith and I first met Aicha, we realized she was among the most gifted and compassionate technology leaders we would ever serve.

Whenever Aicha is challenged to break new ground or make change happen, "your first step must be to look in the mirror. You have to find your own growth story and help your team cross the chasm, cascading a culture of coaching throughout your organization," she said. "As you're promoted, your role as a leader obviously becomes less and less as commander and director, and more about coaching and cheerleading," she insists.

Growing up in Senegal, West Africa, "from the very beginning I thought I was going to be a fighter pilot," Evans said. "By the time I got to Paris as a student and bounced between Africa and Europe, I knew I wanted to be a technologist." Her passion revealed itself as she found herself compelled to disassemble and reassemble every electronic device in the house. As a teenager, her parents attempted to put a stop to her long-distance phone calls, which were racking up high international charges. At the time, phones had a dial, which her parents locked, but Aicha found a hack to run the dial tone code on the phoneline and continue her international calls anyway. "By the time I arrived in the US for college," she mused, "it was obvious to me that I'd be focusing on computers!"

At Intel, the world's largest semiconductor chip company, "I learned about one's responsibility as a technologist when it comes to society. I learned to be a leader at scale, to deal with press and media and investors. More importantly, I learned how to focus on people, but at a really massive scale, and coaching plays a big role in making that happen faster and better." Aicha believes that her focus on coaching individual executives and teams "helped me do really well at Intel. I was enjoying it and felt that I was working on something important."

At this point, she was a notable success and drawing considerable attention from corporate recruiters. "I had to have a one-on-one with myself and say, 'Okay, I'm happy here. What would make me think about something else?' And I answered, *transformative technology*." In other words, Aicha wanted to lead a company where she would "be there at the beginning where you get to participate in creating the wave, as opposed to riding the wave. And that's exactly what happened with Zoox. You have the opportunity to literally impact society."

Aicha never imagined still working at 50. She had envisioned that she'd be doing a different kind of coaching: "I thought that I would be teaching math in elementary school, middle school or high school, because I feel that math is not taught properly, especially to girls. Along the way, though, I've discovered what is called 'meaning' and how to have impact on people at scale using technology," she said. Aicha will likely never stop working and serving in some major way. "Frankly, I think that if I went home tonight and told my kids and my husband that I'm not going to be working anymore, they would say, 'You need to find something you're going to do between 9 and 5, because you're not going to manage us!'"

As a CEO, Aicha seems driven to help others find their highest and best impact on the world. Her best coaching advice for executives? "What I tell young people, particularly women in their twenties and thirties – and I'm even having these conversations with my 15-year-old daughter – *take a chill pill.*" She sighed and looked at me with that loving expression that comes from hard-won experience you would hope to get from your coach. "It's going to be okay," Aicha reassured. "Take the time to get to know yourself really well. What type of person are you; what really motivates you? If you find it, you'll know. Figure out what's important to you and then ride the different phases and waves."

And when things go wrong? "If something doesn't go so well, take a step back, have a one-on-one with your-self and talk to your support system, like your coach! I was fortunate to have CEO coaches Marshall Goldsmith and Mark Thompson to help me (and my team) see what really happened. You have to be willing to make adjustments, ask for help when you need it and, by and large, you're going to be fine." Evans insisted.

Coach Me! is a book about how coaching ignites hearts and minds to build better leaders. This book is a treatise on how we, as coaches, can discover and serve extraordinary leaders like CEO Aicha Evans – executives *who deserve to have impact* at every level of an organization in every community. With patience and love as a coach, you just might help them change the world.

Aicha Evans joined Zoox as the Chief Executive Officer (CEO) in February 2019. Prior to Zoox, Evans served as Senior Vice President and Chief Strategy Officer at Intel Corporation, driving the company's transformation from a PC-centric to a data-centric company. Previously, she ran the company's wireless efforts and oversaw a global team of 7,000 engineers. Evans is a member of the Supervisory Board of SAP and holds a bachelor's degree in computer engineering from The George Washington University.

Mark Thompson is a NYTimes bestselling author and the world's #1 CEO Coach ranked by the American Management Association and Global Leading Coaches/Thinkers50. Forbes described him as having the "Midas Touch" with clients including World Bank CEO Jim Yong Kim, Pinterest cofounder Evan Sharp, and Virgin founder Richard Branson.

Acknowledgments

We would like to begin by thanking the Thinkers50 organization for its vision in recognizing the top coaches in the world, which has since inspired this project. We are so proud to see how far this profession of coaching has come in its short existence.

Thank you to Kathy Vlietstra of CoachSource who handled the yeoman's work of tracking, reviewing, and organizing all of these chapters. We are also very grateful to all the fantastic people at Wiley who helped bring this vision to life, during a pandemic – Jake Opie, Monica Rogers, Christina Weyrauch, and undoubtedly many others.

We honor our families for their support of all our extra hours required to make a book happen. An enormous thank you goes out to our wives, with special acknowledgment for our families Julie, Jenae, Briana, Kaitlyn, and Evan (BU), and Katharine, Florence, and Beatrice (JP).

Without our 52 authors – and our Foreword guest Aicha Evans – and their thousands of years of combined wisdom, we would not have a book. Each author gave generously from their incredibly busy schedules to share learnings that were new, fresh, insightful yet timeless. We are so incredibly grateful for their participation. May their wisdom bless you on your leadership journey.

About the Editors

Brian O. Underhill

Brian O. Underhill, PhD, PCC, is an internationally recognized expert in the design and management of worldwide executive coaching implementations. He is the Founder and CEO of CoachSource, the world's largest purely executive coaching provider, with over 1,100 coaches in 100+ countries. Previously, he managed executive coaching operations for Marshall Goldsmith, the world's #1 coach.

Brian is the co-editor of *Mastering Executive Coaching* (Routledge, 2019), the author of *Executive Coaching for Results: The Definitive Guide to Developing Organizational Leaders* (Berrett-Koehler: 2007), and the author of numerous articles and blogs in the coaching field. He is an internationally sought-after speaker, addressing The Conference Board, ICF, EMCC, and many regional coaching events. He has been nominated as a Thinkers50 Leading Global Coach in 2019.

Brian has a PhD and an MS in organizational psychology from the California School of Professional Psychology (Los Angeles) and a BA in psychology from the University of Southern California. Brian is certified in the Hogan Assessments, Element B, Extended DISC and holds Advanced Certification in the Goldsmith Coaching Process. He is a Founding Fellow of the Institute of Coaching Professional Association at McLean Hospital – a Harvard Medical School affiliate. He was named a 2021 Fellow of the Society of Consulting Psychology (APA – Division 13). He is a Professional Certified Coach (PCC) with the International Coach Federation.

Brian resides in Silicon Valley, where he enjoys cycling, racquetball, plays music as a worship musician, and spends time with his wife, Julie, and their four kids.

Jonathan Passmore

Jonathan is senior Vice President at CoachHub, the global digital coaching company and also holds a professorship at Henley Business School, UK.

He has held board-level roles in government, not-for-profit and commercial sectors. He is a licensed psychologist, holds five degrees, and is an award-winning coach, author, and researcher. He has authored and edited over 30 books, including Top Business Psychology Models, Becoming a Coach, The Coaches Handbook, and WeCoach. He is also the editor of the eight-volume Wiley-Blackwell Series on Industrial Psychology. He has published over 100 scientific papers and book chapters on coaching, leadership, and change, and spoken at over 200 events worldwide. He believes in Open Science, sharing knowledge openly with other scientists and practitioners; thus, much of his work is available for free download from his website: jonathanpassmore.com, and the income from most of his titles is donated to charitable causes such as The Railway Children and Water Aid. He has received and been shortlisted for multiple awards, including Marshall Goldsmith Global Coaching Awards Thinkers 50, Global Gurus List, Association of Business Psychologists, British Psychological Society, EMCC, and Association for Coaching.

He has previously worked for PWC, IBM, and OPM as a change consultant and executive coach, with clients including government ministers, celebrities, and senior leaders in the public, private, and non-profit sectors.

He is based in the UK, and works out of offices in London, Berlin, and New York.

Marshall Goldsmith

Dr. Goldsmith is the author or editor of 35 books, which have sold over two million copies, been translated into 30 languages, and become bestsellers in 12 countries. His two other New York Times bestsellers are *MOJO* and *What Got You Here Won't Get You There* – the Harold Longman Award winner for Business Book of the Year.

In February 2016, Amazon.com recognized the 100 Best Leadership & Success Books in their To Read in Your Lifetime series. The list included classics and newer books – management and self-help books. Both *Triggers* and *What Got You Here Won't Get You There* were recognized as being in the top 100 books ever written in their field. Marshall is only one of two authors with two books on the list.

Marshall's professional acknowledgments include Harvard Business Review and Best Practices Institute – World's #1 Leadership Thinker; Global Gurus, INC and Fast Company magazines – World's #1 Executive Coach; Institute for Management Studies – Lifetime Achievement Award for Excellence in Teaching; American Management Association – 50 great thinkers and leaders who have influenced the field of management over the past 80 years; BusinessWeek – 50 great leaders in America; Wall Street Journal – top 10 executive educators; Economist (UK) – most credible executive advisors in the new era of business; National Academy of Human Resources – Fellow of the Academy (America's top HR award); and World HRD Congress (India) – global leader in HR thinking. His work has been recognized by almost every professional organization in his field.

Dr. Goldsmith's PhD is from UCLA's Anderson School of Management, where he was the Distinguished Alumnus of the Year. He teaches executive education at Dartmouth's Tuck School of Business. He is one of a select few executive advisors who has worked with over 150 major CEOs and their management teams. He served on the Board of the Peter Drucker Foundation for 10 years. He has been a volunteer teacher for US Army Generals, Navy Admirals, Girl Scout executives, and International and American Red Cross leaders – where he was a National Volunteer of the Year.

Introduction

Dear Leader,
Through your own leadership journey, we suspect that you can relate to at least one of these real-life examples. Or, perhaps you have seen similar situations with others?

> Steve was head of the oncology department at an established pharmaceutical company. For many who knew him, he was at the top of his game. He was the smartest guy in the room. Now, as CEO at a biotech, it was not going well only 6 months in. Why? Because he *had* to be the smartest guy in the room.
>
> (Chapter 12, Philippe Grall)

> Rosita's marketing ideas would revolutionize the company and increase revenue, but her blunt and directive style prevented her from enlisting midlevel global managers to execute on her concepts. Her communication style was preventing her from bringing her ideas to life.
>
> (Chapter 7, Lisa Edwards)

> The CEO of a marketing firm in China, Bruce, watched his business disappear overnight as COVID-19 spread quickly through his country – and the world. How would he save his business?
>
> (Chapter 34, Karen Wu)

> Marco, the possible future CEO of the largest manufacturing firm in the world, watched his most valuable person quit due to his management style. If Marco's fatal flaws are not fixed, he will not be promoted – or worse.
>
> (Chapter 13, Carol Kauffman)

> High-flying Arthur was promoted to the China COO of a major software firm when he began to struggle – badly – navigating this transition. His Regional COO said, "I'm disappointed, as he didn't function as the COO as we expected." His boss would replace him in 3 months if he could not improve.
>
> (Chapter 39, Cathleen Wu)

> Renee's nonprofit began with great excitement and high hopes. But, "Donations were scarce, human resources dwindling, and motivation running down" Would they need to shut down? Is this the end of the line for their mission?
>
> (Chapter 25, Magda Mook)

> Oliver was promoted from running one country to running many. And now his boss is saying, "ever since Oliver had taken over nine months ago, business in each geography was suffering." Oliver is befuddled, "It's as if all I've learned in the past isn't working for me anymore."
>
> (Chapter 21, Brenda Bence).

Coach Me! Your Personal Board of Directors: Leadership Advice from the World's Greatest Coaches, First Edition. Edited by Brian Underhill, Jonathan Passmore, and Marshall Goldsmith.
© 2022 John Wiley & Sons Ltd. Published 2022 by John Wiley & Sons Ltd.
DOI: 10.1002/9781119823803.cintro

Rick is stuck in between the conflict of two of his direct reports. His two department heads behave "like in kindergarten" – constantly blaming and pointing fingers at each other. How long can this possibly go on?

(Chapter 11, Christopher Rauen)

How about the CEO who was paralyzed by fear, too afraid to take risks…enough that the entire company behaved just like him. "We are not ready for big goals yet" – was the striking statement from a Senior Vice President. Will this company simply cower in fear and become irrelevant over time?

(Chapter 42, Oleg Konovalov)

No one said leadership would be easy, but you probably did not realize it would be *this* hard. Perhaps you can relate to one of these stories – either for yourself or you see it in others you work with (or work for!)

Perhaps you began your career deep inside a career specialty, such as accounting, engineering, biology, law, or any other profession. Somewhere along the way, someone suggested (or you actively sought) to take a new position managing others – and that was the beginning of your new – and never ending – leadership learning curve. You soon realized your training in your specialty did not include management or leadership skills.

Perhaps you then continued moving up the ranks – for some of you, you have reached near or at the top of your organizations. Your challenges have become more and more complex. At this point, hundreds or thousands of careers and lives are impacted by your decisions, untold amounts of wealth are hanging the balance regarding the products or services you may be overseeing, and indeed, the very future of your organization may be fully in your hands. The pressure can be unbearable.

But wouldn't it be great to have someone to talk to, to bounce ideas off of – an objective expert *outside* your organization to speak with confidentially, who will not tell others inside the company about your fears, hopes, and dreams. Some wise counsel, adept at understanding human behavior, organizational dynamics, and even your business itself. Perhaps, even a "personal trainer" who can help keep you accountable over time to do what you said you were going to do. Someone who can hold up a mirror and tell you the truth, even if no one around seems to be doing so. Leadership can be lonely, especially the higher you go.

This is exactly the role of the executive coach. And then some…

And we have gathered 50 of the world's top coaches to share their secrets with you – right here in *Coach Me! Your Personal Board of Directors.*

What Is Coaching, Anyway?

You may have heard of this field of "executive coaching" by now. Perhaps, only 40-ish years old as a profession, coaching has experienced meteoric growth over the past two decades. There are a now estimated 70,000 coaches worldwide. Various estimates place the industry at anywhere from $2 billion up to $15 billion per year (US dollars).

In the 1980s to early 1990s, coaching was initially used mostly for those "problem children" leaders who were in trouble as a last-ditch effort to fix them (or to pretend to try) before letting them go. Coaching was often done in secret, with the coach visiting surreptitiously (or meeting at an undisclosed location), with nearly no one knowing about it – even the coaching invoice line item description would be changed to keep prying eyes from noticing. One coach once told us she had a reputation as "the angel of death" – when she showed up, people knew her leader was on his/her final days.

Today, coaching is often seen as a badge of honor – a sign that a company wants to invest in your growth and development. Coaching for performance problems has actually decreased steadily in use throughout the years. In our (Underhill) 2018 study, 1/3 of coaches reported coaching for performance problems, which decreased to only a quarter in 2020. A 2007 Harvard Business Review study found that just 12% of assignments were used to address derailing executives.

Corporations, nonprofits, and government alike have increased their use of coaching multi-fold over the past many years. Many estimates suggest at least half to 75% of corporates use executive coaches to develop their leaders. In our (Underhill) 2020 research study, we found that 95% of those responding organizations planned to increase (or at least continue) their current use of coaching over the next 2 years.

Household name leaders – even celebrities – are working with coaches, and being public about it. Names such as Michael Dell, Larry Page, Cheryl Sandberg, and Steve Jobs (briefly) have been known to work with coaches. The late Bill Campbell, literally a former football coach, has been nicknamed the Trillion Dollar Coach by a book of the same name. Former Google CEO Eric Schmidt has said, "Every famous athlete, every famous performer has somebody who's a coach. Somebody who can watch what they're doing and say, 'Is that what you really meant? Did you really do that?' They can give them perspective. The one thing people are never good at is seeing themselves as others see them. A coach really, really helps."

What is driving this growth in the industry? Various studies have shown that attracting, retaining, and developing people have been one of the greatest concerns of organizations for the past many years (which is more acute in the post-pandemic world). Some firms are unable to grow effectively without more leaders in more parts of the world. Others are learning that leadership effectiveness is one of the most critical drivers toward corporate success. Yet, there is less time to send leaders off to traditional classroom training. Instead, coaching can be done *in situ*, on-the-job, in the moment, working on real-life leadership challenges. Studies show coaching creates much greater content retention than classroom training alone.

Popular belief is the word "coach" originated from the town of Kocs, Hungary, which in the 16th century was known for making fine transportation carriages, eventually becoming popular all over Europe. The purpose of the carriage was, of course, to take you from where you were to where you wanted to go. Today's term "coach" actually encompasses a countless range of professions, most notably sports coaches, but others including life coaches, career coaches, executive coaches, team development coaches, and the like. "Coach" has even been co-opted and used regularly by other professions, such as a "mortgage coach," "divorce coach," or our favorite: "nipple confusion coach." Popular TV shows have depicted (and very much misrepresented) "coaches" such as Wendy Rhoades from "Billions" or Denpok Singh, the spiritual advisor of Gavin Belson from "Silicon Valley."

Executive coaches are most commonly hired by an organization to help a leader grow in a particular area of development; 97% are usually retained to grow a leader in various competencies of leadership. However, during the course of this relationship, it is not uncommon for coaching to possibly explore various aspects of the leader's career path, or even their personal life at some point, as you will see in some of our chapters.

Coaching is best used for situations such as a leader transitioning from one role to a larger one, a super smart get-it-done manager who gets it done – at the cost of those around them, a leader who needs to act and portray "more like an executive," and an executive director who tries to do it all him/herself and fails to delegate; or for any of a myriad of situations usually under the banner of "leadership," "relationships," "communications," "influence," "transition," and much more.

Coaching is not well suited for situations such as someone who needs to get better at the technical aspects of their job (perhaps consider training, a consultant or mentoring), someone with deeper psychological concerns (therapy), and someone who has integrity issues (let them go), or – and incredibly important – coaching is not worth it for someone the organization has already given up on (let them go), or who personally has little interest in changing (see below).

So, how is coaching distinguished from consulting and therapy? To some extent, these professions may overlap, or could even be performed by the same practitioner, but yet they are also completely distinct. We see executive coaching as "the one-to-one development of an organizational leader" – its purpose is the development of the leader's skills within the organizational context (although in more recent years, coaching has expanded to teams and groups – beyond the one-to-one charter).

This seminal Harvard Business Review article on coaching from 2009 (https://hbr.org/2009/01/what-can-coaches-do-for-you) offers a great graphic to compare and contrast between consulting, coaching, and therapy.

Consulting	Coaching		Therapy
Paid to come up with answers	Advises individual leaders on business matters	Focuses on the future	Paid to ask the right questions	Focuses on the past
Focuses on organizational performance	Involves management in goal setting	Fosters individual performance in a business context	Tackles difficult issues at work and home	Diagnoses and treats dysfunctionality
Strives for objectivity	Based on organizational ethics		Focuses on individual behavioral change	Based on medical ethics
Provides quantitative analysis of problems	Paid for by the company	Helps executives discover their own path	Explores subjective experience	Paid for by the individual

Reprinted by permission of *Harvard Business Review* (Exhibit: "coaching borrows from both consulting and therapy"). From *What Can Coaches Do for You* by Diane Coutu and Carol Kauffman, January 2009. Copyright ©2009 by Harvard Business Publishing; all rights reserved.

Coaching is mostly future oriented, focusing on business matters within an organizational context, paid for by the company. In our view, the demarcation lines between consulting and coaching can and do blur some: some coaches are also consultants and vice versa. However, the lines between coaching and therapy are quite rigid; a coach will not profess to be conducting therapy (which would be unethical and illegal anyway) and said coach would instead refer a coaching leader to therapy when appropriate. A therapist is also never going to begin working with an individual patient as an executive coach, paid for by that patient's company.

Your Coaches – Your Personal Board of Directors

So, how did we select these 50 (actually 52) authors to write chapters for you contained within this book?

Since 2001, the London-based Thinkers50 organization published the first-ever global ranking of management thinkers. Every other year, an awards gala – the "Oscars of Management Thinking" (per the Financial Times) – would dole out distinguished achievement awards, along with the new ranking of management thinkers.

In late 2019, the Thinkers50 organization expanded its awards for the first time ever to include coaching. Thinkers50 queried one of us (Marshall Goldsmith) to nominate a list of the top coaches in the world, in an effort to crown the Marshall Goldsmith Distinguished Achievement Award for Coaching and Mentoring. In so doing, we had collected an unparalleled cadre of approximately 80 coaches on all inhabited continents, suitably named the "Leading Global Coaches." The top eight were nominated with a winner and then crowned.

We have then asked 50 of these diverse Leading Global Coaches[1] to share their best leadership advice for you, as a leader – to serve as your personal Board of Directors. Your Board will cover many typical leadership dilemmas you might possibly face – available to you right when you need them. Our coaches hail from 16 different countries, from Belgium to Zambia.

Coach Me! represents a virtual knowledge sharing from some of the top consultants in management to leaders everywhere – world-class executive coaching insights now available to all leaders, at a tiny fraction of the price it would take to hire one of these coaches! Assuming your organization paid something from the most extravagant $250,000 US dollars (for some of the world's most famous coaches, many included here) to perhaps a more reasonable $20,000 (a somewhat typical director level assignment) – taking a reasonable average of say $50,000 per assignment times 50 chapters means you are witness to $2.5 m in value within the pages of book. Not a bad deal.

Of course, we do not remotely profess to suggest that reading about coaching will give you the same benefits of actually growing through coaching. Each story is unique to each situation the leader found themselves in. Each leader has particular strengths and weaknesses that may not match your own. Each leader operates within an organizational culture with its own values, history, etc. Coaching provides each leader with transformational insights unique to their specific situations – along with an ongoing and built-in accountability structure, combined with feedback from those around the leader, all "on-the-job" in real time – all completely customized to the leader being coached.

And while no book can replace that, our aim is to let you be a fly-on-the-wall to learn from their stories. If only one insight here changes the story for your own journey, that of those who work for and with you, or for your organization or the communities you interact with, it will have been worth it.

In short, anyone in a leadership role in any size organization, whether nonprofit, for profit, government, or even informal groups benefits from the learnings. And, being a leader is not limited to hosting an official "leadership role" – leadership can be demonstrated at all levels of all types of organizations...from a volunteer on a committee of a small nonprofit to a CEO of a multinational corporation.

Your Board of Directors have offered you short chapters – just a few pages each – on purpose. So, you can quickly capture the learnings and move on. Nearly every chapter chronicles the real-life story of a very real leader (names and some identifying details changed, of course), so you can learn from their challenges.

About the Coaching Process

What actually happens in coaching assignments? What DOES an executive coach actually DO? Well, before coaching begins, you would need to select a coach – which is covered in the final chapter of this book. But, once coach selection is complete, most coaching would include some or all of the following characteristics/

activities (some of this content is also provided by the International Coaching Federation's list of Core Competencies for coaches - See Passmore & Sinclair, 2021):

Establish Rapport and Create a Safe, Confidential Space

First and foremost, a coach establishes strong rapport with their leader – a sense of chemistry and comfort. It should be noted that 97% of executives we surveyed (Underhill) named the "ability to build rapport" as the number one desired trait in a coach. A coach creates a safe space for silence, pause or reflection, while remaining curious, observant, and empathetic with the leader. Many of our authors talk about creating this safe place, such as Pamela McLean in Chapter 38, "we arrived at an important tipping point when John began to experience the value of our coaching work – a space where he felt respected and challenged to candidly examine how he was showing up."

Executive coaching is most typically contracted in a confidential manner, in that what the leader and the coach discuss is held privately between them. And, as most coaches operate outside of the organization, leaders can feel safe that what they are discussing is between them. Although the paying organization does usually want to know, (1) what the leader is working on through coaching (very high level), (2) when/how often coaching sessions are happening, (in some cases) (3) viewing the action plan generated through coaching, and (4) (in some cases) the coach's view of the leader's commitment to the coaching process.

Listen Actively

Listen actively is just what it sounds like – listening, actively. It is absolutely central to what a coach does in coaching assignments. Says our own authors, Morgan and Croft (Chapter 28), "it is the ability to listen and analyze that reaps the greatest return on the coaching investment." Listening is beyond just hearing what is said, but also discerning what is *not* being said, while considering all of it within the context of the system around the leader. Listening also includes summarizing what is being said (and verifying understanding), along with observing emotions, body language, tone, etc.

Collect and Share Feedback

Many of the authors will describe collecting 360 feedback, conducting interviews with key stakeholders and/or conducting additional assessments. 360 feedback is a written survey that goes out to all of one's key stakeholders – direct reports, boss, peers, and more – inquiring about the leader's strengths and weaknesses in various competencies. Interviews (or sometimes called "360 interviews") are the same concept, but the coach actually interviews each of these key stakeholders. In one example, Tom Kolditz (Chapter 23) shares his interview questions, which are a great example of this practice:

1. What are the leader's strengths?
2. What are the leader's challenges?
3. When is the leader at their best?
4. When is the leader at their worst?
5. If you were the leader's coach, mentor, or advisor, what advice would you have for them?

In addition, coaches may administer additional assessments, such as a Myers-Briggs, Hogan, DiSC, emotional intelligence tool, and countless others. Our own Jane Hyun (Chapter 10) used a cultural fluency assessment in her work with John, a leader who thought he was much more interculturally adept than he turned out to be.

The coach will then arrange to debrief all these findings with the leader, again in a confidential setting (sometimes the assessment results may not be confidential, worth making sure that this is clear with the coach and the organization ahead of time). This debrief can (to be very honest) be quite overwhelming at times ("When we met to review the findings, John was surprised by how his colleagues experienced him" – McLean, Chapter 38). Coaches are very skilled at presenting this feedback in a safe and empathetic manner, though it can still sting at times. Scott Eblin (Chapter 6) provides guidance on how to make the most of receiving feedback. Neuroscience studies, say Richard Boyatzis (Chapter 26), suggest that we tend to shut down when receiving feedback. Allowing time to elapse between receiving the feedback to then doing something about can make this easier.

Action Planning

Cited by 96% of coaches as part of their typical process, generating an action plan forms the structure of how the coaching would proceed for the coming months. Once a leader selects an area (or several) for development, the leader and coach co-create the specific steps on how to accomplish the coaching goals. Some organizations, and/or coaches, already have action plan templates from which to work. The various items in the plan may be one-time accomplishments (meet with my boss' boss to find out who I should better network with throughout this organization) or regularly occurring focus areas (how good of a listener was I today?). The best goals are often organized in the well-known SMART framework (Specific, Measurable, Actionable, Reasonable, Time-Bound).

Creates Awareness

Great coaches are incredibly curious, and they will ask just the right questions or make astute observations to create transformational insights for the leader. Coaches will seek to dive deeper into the leader's way of thinking, values, and beliefs – to get the leader to go beyond their current thinking on a matter. "A powerful one-to-one coaching conversation can help a person unblock his or her stagnation," shares Cara Juicharern (Chapter 30). Very often, leaders get stuck, and digging deeper into the blockage, creating awareness around it, and navigating how to move forward is part of the coaching process.

Coaches will also reflect what is being said, or even challenge the leader (gently) to help create insights, as is evident in many of these chapters. Arun was proclaiming that "family is my #1 priority" to us (Underhill – Chapter 44), but yet he was working often 16–18 hours per day. Politely pointing out this disconnect between what he said and what he was doing was necessary to help invoke change.

Coach Abdallah Aljurf (Chapter 36) tells us about Mr. Jones' great improvement as a great example of evoking awareness. "He did 97% of the work. My 3% was just being a catalyst who helped him as an executive coach to think loudly, arrange his thoughts, challenge his assumptions, beat his limiting beliefs, and make better decisions that saved him time, effort, and money."

Offer Advice

Surprisingly, most coaching generally does not come with loads of advice-giving by the coach. In fact, proffering advice is usually frowned-upon by coach training schools. Our own Howard Morgan and Ben Croft (Chapter 28) explain this well, "However, we suggest that for true growth in your coachee, it is more effective to help the person find the solution or decision themselves, rather than providing them with the answer – or advising that they do it your way." Neuroscience research is also showing this to be true – experiencing that "aha" by working through something is much more powerful than just being handed the answer.

Additionally, a coach does not have all the same context and information the leader has, but does have an objective, outside perspective for which to be a sounding board. A coach's advice may work well in one situation, but not in another. Notice Anna, who told her coach Marcia Reynolds (Chapter 48) she was turning down a job offer. Instead of advising whether this was a good idea or not, Marcia did something different: "I asked for her permission to explore her decision before she determined how best to turn down the job offer." Through the exploration process, Anna actually uncovered the deeper reasons motivating her decision…which she then realized she had made the wrong decision – and it was reversed. Marcia's advice or opinion on the matter would not have been as helpful and could have been detrimental.

After having said all this – and given that many coaches have extensive business experience behind them, and/or years coaching countless leaders in somewhat similar situations – a piece of key advice at the right time might be just perfect. But, usually, this is more of a later in the discussion type thing and usually done with permission of the leader.

Interact With Key Stakeholders

Most executive coaching is not conducted in a vacuum. Those around the leader are a vital component to helping the leader make permanent change in behavior. These individuals may usually be part of the initial feedback process, as mentioned above.

As coaching progresses, the leader and/or the coach will be interacting with some number of these key stakeholders along the way. Coaches commonly will conduct several three-way meetings with the leader and their boss to review the proposed area(s) for development, action plan steps, and evaluating progress as well. The coach may also liaise with human resources professionals internally regarding the same.

Following up regularly with the range of key stakeholders around the leader has been shown to produce measurable improvements in leadership effectiveness. One of us (Goldsmith) along with Howard Morgan (co-author of Chapter 28) found that the more often a leader follows up with those around them regarding progress on his/her area for development, the more likely those stakeholders are to notice behavioral improvement in follow-up surveys. Coaches will often facilitate these conversations between the leader and stakeholder and/or empower them to happen without the coach present. Some coaches may check in with these key stakeholders independently to see if they are noticing improvement.

Accountability

Coaching is usually contracted for several months or beyond (6 months is most common), which provides built-in follow-up and accountability. It is not uncommon for a leader to tell us coaches "I just did the homework we discussed last time because I knew we were going to talk today." This, of course, helps to get things done – simply, the presence of the coach makes this happen without much active intervention beyond that. For those leaders who are still procrastinating about accomplishing an agreed-upon objective, coaching provides an environment to explore what is getting in the way of making progress. Sometimes, the objective itself may need to be revisited, or the motivation behind the objective may need to be explored.

A leader and a coach can even agree on certain daily metrics to be shared with the coach on some regular basis (for example, "Did I recognize one of my direct reports at some point today?"). One of us (Underhill) had a leader who would rate his own listening skills on a 1–10 scale each day and then send the scores over before each session – the simple act of keeping track helped to keep this top of mind for this leader. Wearables, phones, and other available technologies bring an even greater layer of accountability to the coaching engagement: "Habit minder" style apps track certain behaviors we seek to start, stop, or continue – from which data can be shared and discussed.

Measure Results

Coaching is very measurable. First, many coaches or coaching firms will inquire about a leader's satisfaction with the coaching process, either verbally or through a written survey. More interestingly, stakeholders around the leader can be given a quick survey to see if they have noticed improvement in the leader's targeted behaviors since coaching began (as shown in Underhill, Chapter 44).

Some coaching assignments will endeavor to calculate a return on investment. Leaders are asked to estimate which business metric(s) would most be impacted by positive coaching outcomes and to determine what percent of the change could be attributed to the effects of coaching. This is compared against the costs of the coaching, any expenses, plus the leader's time invested in coaching, to determine what type of ROI was realized from the coaching effort.

Other Activities

Many more activities occur during coaching assignments. A coach may provide *homework* for the leader prior to their next session (for example, "meet with your boss regarding your progress to date"). *Experiments* encourage a leader to try out something new and report back the results. (Try to delegate two items to your direct reports that you normally do yourself. See what happens with the results you get.) An executive coach may even *shadow* the leader to observe them in action (live and/or virtually) that can yield some incredible observations. (I noticed in the team meeting that, when speaking, you would only look at Sally and no one else. What might that be about?) Coaches are also well-versed in *resources* that might be useful to the leader, such as books, articles, conferences, YouTube clips, and more. (Since you are working on time management, I highly recommend the book *Getting Things Done.* Would you like to read it and share your learnings with me?)

Organization of This Book

Our experience is common themes emerge. In research (Underhill and CoachSource) and a study by CoachHub and Henley in 2021 (Passmore, 2021) the following "themes" which have stayed fairly consistent in pre and post Covid times. Here are some of the top themes, from which we have organized your Board's advice:

- **Self-insight** – Knowing oneself: One's strengths, weaknesses, and personality.
- **Communication skills** – Communicating effectively, both written and verbal.
- **Interpersonal relationships** – Working effectively with others, networking.
- **Emotional intelligence** – Understanding and managing your emotions.
- **Empowering others/delegation** – Empowering others to do their best work.
- **Coaching others** – Providing coaching and guidance to others.
- **Managing change** – Assisting others to contend with change, both internally and externally induced.
- **Transition management** – Handling your own transition into a new role either within your organization or to a new organization.
- **Execution** – Getting things done, meeting/exceeding your objectives.
- **Career development** – Concerned with growing your career.

This is not a complete list of the most common areas for which leaders seek coaches (Also popular development areas: "executive presence," "vision & strategy," "fostering teamwork," "women in leadership," "decision-making"). And some areas a leader and their coach might work on will not be reported back to the sponsoring organization, which can be somewhat public within the organization (for example, "I need help getting along with my jerk boss!" does not get reported back to the sponsoring organization, nor the boss for which the leader wants assistance!).

The book will conclude with further details on how to select a coach. A short bio for each author is provided at the start of their chapter, so you can better understand who you are learning from. A longer bio for each author is provided at the end of the book.

And thank you for supporting a great cause. Profits from the sale of *Coach Me! Your Personal Board of Directors* will be provided to the Marshall Goldsmith Bursary at Henley Business School, United Kingdom, which is a special fund dedicated to training the next generation of worthy leaders from the developing world to become coaches.

Let's Get Started

In this book, you will see 50 stories of leaders who had to save their companies, save their careers, save key talent from leaving…leaders who had to (quickly) change their business models, change their organizations, change themselves…leaders who had to grow revenues, grow others, and grow within.

One executive we had met in an earlier study said, "If you have coaching done well, you change your life, and your life as a business leader. If you have the right coach with the right fit, he or she can make a tremendous impact, and a good coach can get you there."

And by the way, the stories end well for Steve, Rosita, Marco, and Bruce – and all the rest of them. Read on to find out how.

So, let us get started.

Note

[1] And we invited a few additional friends to join this compilation, who were not part of the original group of 80.

References

Passmore, J. (2021). *Future Trends: Global Coach Survey 2021*. Henley on Thames: Henley Business School.

Passmore, J. & Sinclair, T. (2021). *Becoming a Coach. The Essential ICF Guide*. Berlin: Springer Publishing.

Self-Insight

1

Great Leaders Are Confident, Connected, Committed, and Courageous

Peter Bregman

Sanjay (I have changed his name and some details to protect privacy) was founder and CEO of a technology startup that grew rapidly to $50 million.

Then it stalled out.

Sanjay had not previously grown a company past that stage, and he was unsure what was wrong. He was hoping his team would pull together and figure it out but that had not happened yet.

"I think I need to change out my leadership team," he said to me, in anger and frustration.

"Or," I countered, "maybe you need to scale your leadership in order to scale the company."

Sanjay had not, to this point, done much leadership development work. He had ideas, told people what to do, and micromanaged the execution. He was impatient, angered quickly, and not very trusting. Turnover was high, employees felt unappreciated, and even the leadership team was unwilling to take risks for fear of the consequences.

Which meant that Sanjay was out of the communication loop (nobody was willing to disagree with him or bring him bad news for fear of his reaction).

In order to lead, you have to get your most important work done, have hard conversations, create accountability, and inspire action. Sometimes – especially at smaller companies – leaders can do that in very autocratic ways. But that's poor leadership, and poor leadership does not scale.

To scale, you need to show up powerfully and magnetically in a way that attracts people to trust you, follow you, and commit to putting 100% of their effort into a larger purpose, something bigger than all of you. You need to care about others and connect with them in such a way that they feel your care. You need to speak persuasively – in a way that is clear, direct, and honest and that reflects your care – while listening with openness, compassion, and love. Even when being challenged.

In 30 years of working with leaders to do all of the above, I have found a pattern that I share in *Leading with Emotional Courage* (Wiley, 2018 Peter Bregman), consisting of four essential elements that all great leaders rely on to rally people to accomplish what is important to them. To lead effectively – really, to *live* effectively – you must be confident in yourself, connected to others, committed to purpose, and emotionally courageous.

Most of us are great at only one of the four or maybe two. But to be a powerful presence – to inspire action – you need to excel at *all four simultaneously*.

If you are confident in yourself but disconnected from others, everything will be about you and you will alienate the people around you. If you are connected to others but lack confidence in yourself, you will betray your own needs and perspectives in order to please everyone else. If you are not committed to a purpose, something bigger than yourself and others, you will flounder, losing the respect of those around you as you act aimlessly, failing to make an impact on what matters most. And if you fail to act powerfully, decisively,

---

Peter Bregman is the CEO of Bregman Partners. He coaches, writes, teaches, and speaks mostly about leadership. His sweet spot is as a strategic thought partner to successful people who care about being exceptional leaders and stellar human beings. He is recognized as the #1 executive coach in the world.

Coach Me! Your Personal Board of Directors: Leadership Advice from the World's Greatest Coaches, First Edition. Edited by Brian Underhill, Jonathan Passmore, and Marshall Goldsmith.
© 2022 John Wiley & Sons Ltd. Published 2022 by John Wiley & Sons Ltd.
DOI: 10.1002/9781119823803.ch1

and boldly – with emotional courage – your ideas will remain idle thoughts and your goals will remain unfulfilled fantasies.

Let's apply this to Sanjay and identify precisely where and how he was getting stuck.

Confident in Yourself. Strange as this may seem given how Sanjay presents, he actually struggled with this element. This might feel surprising since he seemed clear about what he wanted, micromanaged, and used intimidation to ensure his ideas were followed. But those things are not confidence, they're arrogance. Confidence is being secure enough to be wrong, to listen to other's opinions, and to be open to how others approach things. People who lack confidence always have to have their way. People who are confident can let others win and prioritize the best idea over their own idea. Sanjay obviously believed in himself – that's also part of confidence – but he wasn't confident enough to be vulnerable. He definitely had room to grow here.

Connected to Others. This was Sanjay's greatest weakness. He did not trust people enough to give them space to own things fully, and people did not trust him enough to tell him things straight. He showed little curiosity and quickly drew conclusions about others; once he made up his mind about someone, they would not get a second chance. He did have some strengths here: he was direct with people and did not procrastinate on difficult conversations. People knew where they stood with him. But he communicated so harshly that those attributes that could be strengths became weaknesses.

Committed to Purpose. This was Sanjay's greatest strength. He was clear about what needed to get done, and he was completely focused on the strategy and plan. He was clear about the small number of things that would move the needle and he was undistractable. And he had a reliable process for staying focused on the most important things, ensuring accountability and driving follow-through.

Emotionally Courageous. Sanjay had room to grow here, and it turned out to be an important element for growing his strength in the elements where he was weaker. Risks, by definition, make us feel vulnerable, and Sanjay avoided that feeling. He resisted the unknown and intentionally avoided uncomfortable situations. This made it hard for him to be open to other people's ideas and listen to their perspectives, especially when those perspectives differed from his. How could others feel ownership and risk offering innovative ideas when their leader was not courageous enough to listen and consider them?

So Sanjay's strongest element was "committed to purpose," which got him admirably far. But his weaknesses in "confident in yourself," "connected to others," and "emotionally courageous" were holding him, his team, and the entire company from achieving their ambitious objectives.

What we're seeing in Sanjay is actually fairly typical for aggressive and successful entrepreneurs. His commitment to purpose is inspiring to investors, employees, and other stakeholders. And it fuels his persistence through the inevitable obstacles every founder faces. Meanwhile, that irrepressible drive and focus prevent him from listening to others in a way that truly engages them, and his fear of failure (which is one psychological element that drives his commitment to purpose) diminishes his confidence. It takes tremendous emotional courage to let other people – and their ideas, perspectives, and disagreements – impact the baby to which Sanjay has given everything.

So I shared all of this with Sanjay.

Just knowing what was happening helped him immediately. We spent some time strengthening his emotional courage by taking small risks *while* feeling the emotions he had been trying to keep at bay. Each time he followed through, regardless of whether he succeeded, he obviously survived and also felt the accomplishment of addressing the risk itself, which, of course, built his confidence and helped him take bigger risks.

In a short time, he felt prepared (even though he may never have felt "ready") to be vulnerable with his team, apologize for the way he had been leading, and ask for their help in becoming a different type of leader so that they could become a different kind of team and, finally, scale their venture.

So Sanjay brought the team together. He was extremely uncomfortable going into the conversation – that's almost always the feeling you'll have when you do anything that requires emotional courage.

But using emotional courage builds your emotional courage. Sanjay emerged from the conversation with the team stronger in all four elements: he was more confident in himself, more connected to his team (as he listened to them without interrupting and without interrogating them), just as committed to purpose, and more emotionally courageous.

What's most important is how developing his own leadership impacted his team's leadership. They became more connected to each other (as well as to him) and far more committed to purpose than before. Their confidence and emotional courage grew as they brought challenges and obstacles to the team in a way that they were hesitant to do before. Which, of course, enabled them to address those challenges, as a team.

That is how you scale leadership. And that is how you scale a company.

Want to develop your own capability in each of the four areas? Here are four quick activities you can do – one for each element – that will have an immediate, positive impact and help you lead with emotional courage.

Confidence in Yourself. This is about staying grounded in the face of success, failure, ambiguity, complexity, or anything really. One of the best tools for growing your confidence is meditation – even just 30 seconds of it. Sit comfortably, close your eyes, take a deep breath, hold it for a second, and then exhale slowly, relaxing every muscle as you do. Repeat even for just a few breaths, and you will feel yourself more grounded. Try it now.

Connection to Others. People feel connected when they feel seen, heard, and appreciated. Choose someone with whom you want to be more connected, and consciously devote time to listen to them, reflecting back what you've heard them say. You don't need to solve their problems or do anything fancy. Just listen and let them know that they have been heard. Try it with someone today.

Commitment to Purpose. This is less about having profound vision and more about focusing your attention and activity on what's most important. So consider, for a moment, what's most important for you to achieve over the next 12 months. Don't think too hard – you can get lost in analysis paralysis – choose what seems right. Then use it as a filter for all your communications. Make sure your messages to everyone around you are clear – this is what is most important for now.

Emotional Courage. If you are willing to feel everything, you can do anything. In order to grow your emotional courage, you need to give yourself an opportunity to feel things. Find one thing today that feels scary to you – even just a little scary – and follow through on it. Go slowly and feel everything while you do it.

Curious about how you stack up? There is a free leadership gap assessment on our website at www.bregmanpartners.com that will help you identify strengths and weaknesses in each of the four elements. Once you take it, you will have a good idea of where you have room to grow.

2

Six Interconnected Perspectives for Coaching

Philippe Rosinski

An accomplished senior executive with international experience, Annie had been asked to lead the development of a promising invention: going through an extensive testing phase, obtaining the necessary compliance authorizations, and finally bringing the product to market. Most top executives in her organization had initially neither realized the great business potential in this invention nor believed it would pass the arduous testing phase. But after Annie had overcome the first hurdles with flying colors, she had been able to convince her boss Peter that this opportunity was too good to be missed.

As she was facing challenges on multiple fronts, Peter and John (HR Senior VP) called upon me to coach Annie, who welcomed my help. Our sessions were confidential, so Annie could be fully candid and make the most of our work together. We also had an initial session with Peter and John, during which they shared their expectations, and we all agreed on Annie's developmental objectives. We focused on objectives that would be beneficial for her and the company and its stakeholders (while agreeing that Annie would be free to also bring up other topics during our confidential coaching sessions). I encouraged Peter and John to subsequently share feedback with Annie regularly, both to applaud her progress and to identify areas where more developmental work would be necessary. Moreover, the four of us met again to review progress midway and at the end.

Annie's challenges were linked to the six interconnected perspectives for coaching, outlined in the book *Global Coaching* (Rosinski, 2010). The heavy workload and stress were taking their toll on Annie at a *physical*

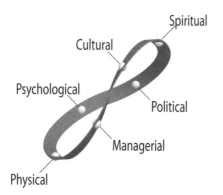

Figure 2.1 Six Interconnected Perspectives for Coaching. Source: Rosinski (2010, p. 247).

Professor Philippe Rosinski is the best-selling author of the groundbreaking books *Coaching Across Cultures* and *Global Coaching.* He is a world authority in executive coaching, team coaching, and global leadership development; the first European designated Master Certified Coach by the ICF; and a professor at BBT University in Tokyo. Source: https://philrosinski.com/ Rosinski & Company.

Coach Me! Your Personal Board of Directors: Leadership Advice from the World's Greatest Coaches, First Edition. Edited by Brian Underhill, Jonathan Passmore, and Marshall Goldsmith.
© 2022 John Wiley & Sons Ltd. Published 2022 by John Wiley & Sons Ltd.
DOI: 10.1002/9781119823803.ch2

level. Getting sufficient sleep, reengaging with regular physical activities (bicycling, power training, and yoga), and eating healthily became a part of Annie's developmental plan, who was currently running herself ragged.

At the *managerial* level, Annie needed to make a better use of her team. But, to do so, Annie had to learn to adapt her leadership style to various individuals and tasks to end up appropriately delegating much more than she had been. Being able to rely on her direct reports was necessary to free up time for more strategic tasks.

Despite her impressive track record, Annie confided in me that she was still lacking in self-confidence. Paradoxically, she was sometimes coming across as judgmental, know-it-all, and abrasive to her colleagues and superiors. At the *psychological* level, Annie had to become more confident (without arrogance) and assertive (calm and firm, without being aggressive and ironic). By developing her emotional intelligence, she would be able to build constructive and fluid relationships with others.

Annie's success also involved the *political* level: navigating the organization's matrix, getting various stakeholders on board, and building internal alliances with key decision makers. Annie did not have the direct authority to oversee the various aspects of her project. She was dependent on executives and professionals in other departments. Her ability to engage in what I have termed "constructive politics" (Rosinski, 2003, 2010) was crucial to reach her goals.

The *cultural* level was essential in various ways. As an American living in Europe, Annie still had to learn to adjust her leadership to a different context (e.g., becoming less direct and more particularistic). At a deeper level, Annie could benefit from revisiting some of her norms, values, and basic assumptions that had proven to be limiting and enrich those by leveraging cultural differences (Rosinski, 2003). For example, while her belief in control (i.e., life is what we make of it, we are in charge of our destiny, and we can achieve anything) had allowed her to be proactive and to obtain an impressive track record, it had also led her to fail to accept situational and personal limitations, to experience difficulties in letting go, and to be at the risk of burnout. This was exacerbated by a "time is scarce" outlook, which led her to be efficient (doing things right) without being necessarily effective (doing the right things). She could benefit from slowing down at times to regain perspective on what really matters as well as to relax and recuperate.

Finally, the *spiritual* level was not readily apparent in the initial mandate. And yet, existential questions of meaning and purpose were lurking below the surface and would need to be addressed for Annie to move resolutely forward.

In sum, although we did agree on a limited set of behavioral developmental objectives with Annie, Peter, and John, our coaching covered a much wider spectrum. It consisted in a *global* approach (i.e., integrated and multifaceted) suited to address Annie's complex situation for both helping her to define her success in a broad and sustainable fashion (the *what* question) and effectively enabling her success (the *how* question). We did not want to frame Annie's issues by excluding perspectives that would have been beneficial. Instead, we acknowledged upfront the advantage of viewing the six perspectives as interconnected and necessary for Annie to unleash her full human potential toward her important and meaningful pursuits.

The word *complexity* comes from *complexus*, which in Latin means "what is woven together." Complexity is a fabric of inseparably associated heterogeneous constituents. Many leadership challenges, and certainly Annie's, are like that today. To address the complexity, we need to enlarge our worldview, which is precisely what global coaching helps us to accomplish.

Annie's coaching lasted for a year. We met every month for three hours. In the initial phase, Annie examined her situation and set objectives, taking notably into account 360° feedback and personal assessments about her psychological and cultural preferences (using notably the Cultural Orientations Framework assessment) and exploring her desires (our very essence according to philosopher Baruch Spinoza), strengths, and developmental opportunities. In subsequent sessions, we would commend Annie's victories and address challenges along the way. For example, we would role-play delicate interactions with colleagues. I would play the role of Annie's boss, peer, or subordinate (based on her description) and she would attempt to be effective in the interaction. I would share some feedback, we would debrief the exchange, and she would try again. We might switch roles and do what is necessary for Annie to apply her insights and to practice. Between sessions, she would keep a learning journal with critical interactions, which we would refer to in the next coaching meeting. We would examine cognitive and emotional obstacles that might appear, and we would devise strategies (notably self-permissions and accessing buried emotions) to overcome them.

Among the various activities I proposed, I invited Annie to map out the various stakeholders in her organization, diagnosing her relational and strategic proximity (or lack thereof) with them. This allowed her to start building internal alliances in a systematic way. In another session, we used postcards as a vehicle to bypass logical thinking and examine unconscious motives to help Annie articulate and honor her sense of purpose.

Apart from the face-to-face sessions, Annie could call me to address urgent matters. She did so on several occasions, particularly before important meetings. She was preparing not only the content of her intervention but also the process: how she would engage with the various participants and manage the dynamics to reach a productive outcome.

In the end, Annie achieved a remarkable success and the new product she launched fulfilled its business breakthrough promise. She became more self-confident, less stressed-out, still demanding but friendlier and less judgmental in her interactions, more balanced (notably taking time again to exercise and be with her family), happier, and more serene. She was also better appreciated by her company.

While the global coaching approach proved particularly suited for this complex situation, it is fair to acknowledge that Annie deserves most of the credit: her engagement throughout the coaching journey, her courage to accept and act upon the feedback she had received, her openness to question her assumptions and move beyond limiting cultural beliefs, and her discipline to stick with the process made the difference. Her boss and colleagues also deserve some of the credit: the company offered the coaching engagement, and they helped through their benevolent feedback.

The alliance Annie and I formed, the quality of our relationship, between fellow human beings (beyond our respective roles of coachee and coach), also proved to be crucial. As much as I use models, apply tools, assess progress, and measure results, this never replaces my profound desire to truly relate and sincerely connect with my coachee. At times, Annie would ask me personal questions. I obliged whenever I felt it would strengthen our alliance and serve Annie's ultimate coaching goals. It has been a privilege to serve Annie and her organization and to be able to make a difference that will ultimately benefit many people.

Exercise

I invite you to assess your current situation from multiple perspectives and, if you notice gaps in certain areas, to devise the necessary actions to fill them. This will help you to achieve *global* success.

Physical

How can you increase your vitality and create the conditions for your optimal and sustainable performance? How can you promote wellness in your organization?

Managerial

How can you best adapt your leadership style (telling, coaching, encouraging, and delegating) to take into account the ability and willingness of the person you lead to accomplish a given task?

Psychological

How can you promote constructive relationships and foster healthy contact with your emotions?

Political

How can you increase your impact and leverage while serving others?

Cultural

How can you make the most of cultural differences for increased inclusion, unity, creativity, and effectiveness?

Spiritual

How can you find meaning, derive purpose, and best appreciate life?

References

Rosinski, P. (2003). *Coaching across cultures.* London and Yarmouth, ME: Nicholas Brealey Publishing.

Rosinski, P. (2010). *Global coaching.* London and Boston, MA: Nicholas Brealey Publishing.

3

Dealing with Your Demons as a Startup Founder

Alisa Cohn

Max, the founder and CEO of an AI data company located in Miami, came into one of our coaching sessions obviously upset. Now, Max is a pretty high-strung guy to begin with, and I had gotten used to his ups and downs, but this was even more pronounced than usual.

He got straight to the point: Sri, his brilliant CTO, had quit, and Marianne, the hot shot Chief Marketing Officer he had been trying to recruit, had declined the offer. All within the last 24 hrs.

This happens in startups – that's why the classic image of startups is a roller coaster.

But, when the downs of the roller coaster are happening to you, the founder, with all the other relentless pressure on you, it can feel like this is the end of all your dreams and hard work.

Even worse, these difficult moments can leak into your psyche, and you may wonder about your own capabilities, like Max did. In our session that day, he didn't want to talk about how he was going to replace Sri. He didn't want to strategize about how he would re-invigorate the search process for the CMO. He couldn't get over the difficult thought: maybe I'm just not cut out for this. "I have this recurring thought which I can barely admit to myself or to you," he told me, almost in a whisper. "What if I'm just at the end of my road? I can build this company up to here, but I'm not going to be able to take it from here. And everyone is going to find out."

Although Max thought he was alone, the truth is that feeling like you're a fraud and that you're about to get found out – known commonly as *imposter syndrome* – is a normal experience of many elite performers and, certainly, entrepreneurs.

Over my two decades of coaching founders as a startup coach, I've developed a set of tools you can use to if not overcome your self-doubt fully, at least stop it in its tracks, examine it, and give yourself the mental and emotional bandwidth to deal with it rationally and move forward. Here are three you can try:

Create a Highlight Reel

The problem with all forms of self-doubt is that many of your self-critical concerns are not real, but they sure feel real. So, you have to gather evidence of your actual competencies, not just what your inner demons tell you. Namely, you need to create a highlight reel.

In Max's case, we worked on his highlight reel on the spot. "I know that you're daunted by having these setbacks," I told him. "But that's not the whole story. You've had plenty of successes. Let's write those down."

After a little prodding, I wrested about a half dozen examples out of him. He had raised so much money that other founders came to him to ask him for tips for raising capital, and some people jokingly called him "the VC

Alisa Cohn, named "Top Startup Coach in the World" at the Thinkers50/Marshall Goldsmith Global Coaches Awards, has coached startup founders into world-class CEOs for 20 years. Author of From Start-up to Grown-up. She was named the number one Global Guru for Startups in 2021 and has worked with Venmo, Etsy, DraftKings, Mack Weldon, and Tory Burch.

Coach Me! Your Personal Board of Directors: Leadership Advice from the World's Greatest Coaches, First Edition. Edited by Brian Underhill, Jonathan Passmore, and Marshall Goldsmith.
© 2022 John Wiley & Sons Ltd. Published 2022 by John Wiley & Sons Ltd.
DOI: 10.1002/9781119823803.ch3

Whisperer." He had calmly guided the team through a massive product failure at a customer site and immediately gotten that customer to double their order, and the rest of the executive team (aside from the departing CTO) was excellent.

As we talked this through, Max calmed down. He even smiled. "This highlight reel could be a good thing for me to remind myself of every day," he said to me. Absolutely! Create a highlight reel for yourself and look at it a few times a week as well as moments when you are having a crisis of confidence. It will help you keep everything in perspective.

See Yourself through the Eyes of Others

When Max's critical voices got too loud, thought he was a terrible manager. That's why he was having this severe talent problem. However, I had personally talked to his team when I conducted 360 feedback, and the reality is that they loved his leadership. He was a sincere person they trusted implicitly. He was humble enough to admit what he didn't know, and he always painted an enthusiastic picture of the future, even when things were blowing up.

Did he have room to improve? Of course – we all do. But, overall, his executives saw him as one of the best leaders they had ever worked for and were enthusiastically and energetically working for him and the ultimate success of the company. His board was equally positive about Max's leadership strengths. I pulled out the 360 feedback report and reminded him of how people saw his strengths. I then asked him to role-play a few of his executives as if they were talking about him. Yes, he was embarrassed, but he couldn't help but see that he was his own worst critic by far. When you remind yourself how others see you, it automatically lets more voices into the committee in your head. The new positive voices can often stand up the negative voices and give you a better sense of how you really are.

Build Healthy Habits

The final tool in helping you deal with your imposter syndrome is to get on top of your state of mind by building healthy habits. A few years ago, one CEO I coach said, "It's not just lonely at the top, it's exhausting."

That's why, for the sake of the company, you absolutely must attend to your health – physical, mental, and emotional. Otherwise, even little things can knock you off your game. It is not just "eat your vegetables" because "eating your vegetables" somehow gives you the moral high ground. You do these things so that you can cope during difficult time, make good decisions under stress, and stay on an even keel when things get tough.

As Max and I talked, we did a checklist of the habits that he had built over the past year. Healthy eating? Check – he had signed up for a food delivery service that was working well for him. He had mostly given up alcohol. Fitness routine? Yes – he had a friend he ran with twice per week and a fitness trainer who came to him twice a week. Enough sleep? Ah…not so good. He had been working too late at night and it took a long time for him to calm himself down and then fall asleep. Because he was high strung, he woke up anxious in the middle of the night. To compound his problems, he often had early morning calls with Europe and late-night calls with Asia, which interfered with him keeping a regular sleep schedule.

I get it – it's not always easy to get enough sleep. But, as I told Max, you have to try. I asked him to explore his nighttime habits and see where he could improve. Perhaps, he could go to bed earlier when he didn't have late night calls, or maybe he could get off his devices and do calming things in the evening so that he didn't get so spun up right before bed. I also asked to add a day or two of fitness to his schedule if he could – we agreed that he slept better on days he worked out.

You need to diagnose your own habits to see where you need to upgrade, but I promise you this: if you upgrade your physical health, your mental health will follow.

As a startup founder, you have a lot of problems and pressures. That's normal. You may feel like an imposter or have some self-doubt. That's also normal. But, by intentionally putting in place these specific strategies, you will have a much better change of dealing with the darkness and accessing, much more often, your inner lightness.

4

Crafting a Grow-Forward Development Pathway

Didem Tekay

In my consultancy and coaching work, I observe leaders struggling to craft their own Grow-Forward pathway and put a plan in place. Many companies have performance systems that connect business outcomes with leaders' development plans and monitor the progress of leaders' mindset and skillset.

"I have many feedbacks and insights about myself; but I do not know what to do with all these, where should start?" Suzan, business director of a global healthcare company, shared with me in our first coaching session. She was frustrated; the company had supported her with tools such as a personal profile, 360 feedback, an engagement survey, and a leadership assessment. This was not the first development plan she was trying to craft; she had done a few plans in her previous roles, but they were mostly focused on corporate skillsets and unfortunately never worked. "They were – nice to have – plans I must confess," she said. She was with all these reports and trying to make a meaningful, relevant output to craft a development pathway for herself. When I asked her, what was different this time, she shared with me that till now she put daily work and jobs to be done upfront and just let go her personal and professional development. She was now aware that there is a gap between who she is and who she can be. Our first coaching session started to unfold with the question: What is the right mindset to create a development plan?

Most of the times, leaders focus on creating some tasks for development but do not deeply think about the right mindset and for them development is taken for granted by an unquestioned mindset. These assumptions are often underestimated or have not even been considered by many leaders. Their unexamined mindset leads them to focus on overcoming daily, weekly, quarterly, and annual business challenges and ignore what they need to work on to craft a Grow-Forward pathway they can practice. A Grow-Forward plan serves leaders as a pathway that they can review on a regular basis to ensure that they are staying on track and making progress in the overall shape of their careers and lives.

A Grow-Forward plan is essential for a person to progress. It is about intentionally and consciously choosing a path to follow, not leaving it to chance. Crafting a Grow-Forward pathway is a learnable skill, so I encouraged Suzan to practice developing a plan. We have explored some key beliefs to craft a development plan, and with the support of a seven-step framework, Suzan crafted her meaningful and relevant plan using all insights and visioning future.

Didem Tekay describes herself as a Grow-Forward Architect, curating development paths for leaders, teams, and organizations. She has been listed in the Forbes Global Forty Over 40 Women to Watch list. She is the author of the book *The Grow-Forward Manifesto*, which instructs leaders and leadership teams on how to foster personal and professional growth through co-creating Grow Forward pathways with relational practice.

Coach Me! Your Personal Board of Directors: Leadership Advice from the World's Greatest Coaches, First Edition. Edited by Brian Underhill, Jonathan Passmore, and Marshall Goldsmith.
© 2022 John Wiley & Sons Ltd. Published 2022 by John Wiley & Sons Ltd.
DOI: 10.1002/9781119823803.ch4

The Grow-Forward Pathway: Mindset, Key Beliefs to Craft a Plan

a) Think bold!

To craft a Grow-Forward pathway, I encourage you to think boldly in terms of setting learning goals for yourself. This plan is you investing in your future, so take time to step back and really think big. Visualize the progress you want to see in your life.

b) Stretch yourself!

A good Grow-Forward pathway consists of stretching components. It pushes you out of your comfort zone and presents you with a challenge. If your plan is too easy to do, then it is not supporting a Grow-Forward pathway.

c) Find your "Unique Presence"

Your unique presence is the key lens you need to see yourself through. Knowing who you are and being willing to create a better version of yourself is a progress mindset. Understanding self is also about developing an understanding of how you are seen by others, recognizing personal strengths and weaknesses, and identifying areas for specific improvement.

d) Be aware of your "Learning Style"

People learn differently, and we all prefer to learn in different ways. Know your learning style! There are lots of tools and frameworks out there to help you discover this! Once you know your style, you can craft your plan with learning processes and components that will work for you.

e) Take accountability for being a learner

You must take personal responsibility for your Grow-Forward pathway; you are the only person who can hold yourself to account for it. You need to be proactive and future focused; the time to focus on development is before it is needed.

f) Address your vulnerability

The Grow-Forward process gets you to face personal challenges and acknowledge the gaps you have (and which you will often have become very skilled at hiding). Learning and progressing is a challenging process. Make time to reflect and open a space to your vulnerability.

g) Create your allies

Who will be the allies you will need during this Grow-Forward journey? Ask yourself and list their names. Pay attention to who you are choosing and not choosing.

Crafting a Grow-Forward Pathway in Seven Steps

Step 1: What Do You Know about Yourself? Review and List

This step is intended to connect your internal self-awareness as well as your external self-awareness. Your inner self-awareness shows how aware you are of your values, passions, aspirations, and habitual responses. Your external self-awareness shows how aware you are of how others see you and experience your impact on them.

Step 2: What Is Possible for You in the Future? Dream and Visualize

Grow-Forward asks you to think about the possibilities that could serve you in the future to become your future self. The actions you take may be large or small, but as you take them you need to always keep in mind your current and future mindset. Taking the time really to think about and imagine your future may not be easy – and because it is never urgent (only important), we tend to postpone it or put it off when something comes along to distract you. It is crucial that you force yourself to get out of your comfort zone of busyness and immediate priorities and think about yourself strategically.

Step 3: What Is Your Grow-Forward Focus? Write It Down and Make It Visible!

Steps 1 and 2 provide a range of possibilities for you and your future. The Grow-Forward pathway gives you a focus to this range of possibilities. With Step 3, it is time for you to focus on your key assets and the points of progress you want to see. Part of what gives this step focus is the discipline of making these points visible by writing them down, establishing a constant reminder of what you are seeking to become and achieve.

Step 4: What Is Your Grow-Forward Plan? Execute and Monitor It

You are ready to use your learning style to choose and deepen your actions, tasks, and activities for your key progress areas. While choosing your relevant actions you need to keep in mind that for growth, progress is not going to be the same experience for you for every skill or progress area. For some, you will need to practice more and allow more time. It is crucial for you to seek out and find opportunities to try new skills and to overcome the anxiety that comes when learning something new (especially when you are used to being excellent in your established skill set).

Step 5: Who Are Your Allies? Share and Evolve Your Progress

Once you have your plan ready, share it with colleagues, friends, and thinking partners. Get their insights. Getting others involved always improves a plan. Although it may seem only relevant to you, you will be doing the work to progress in your relationships with others. Ask for real-time feedback and try to bring your curiosity when receiving it – seek to understand rather than explain or defend.

Step 6: Where Are You in Your Grow-Forward Pathway? Sit Back and Reflect

Journaling in all its forms is a great tool for establishing careful thought and reflection. Whether people do it through a daily or weekly written diary, or through voice messages to the self, or through art, poetry, and photography, journaling provides evidence for what is going on for a person and an audit trail of their commitment to grow.

The Grow-Forward plan covers a period of up to 18 months according to the specific needs of an individual. Within the plan, there needs to be explicit times set aside for stepping back in a deliberate fashion to reflect on where you are now with your plan and where you are heading. A Grow-Forward plan evolves over time and changes in response to circumstances. It is not a static thing, done once and set in concrete.

Step 7: How Will You Appreciate Your Own Grow-Forward Progress? Appreciation and Celebration

Appreciating your own growth and the growth of others is a Grow-Forward mindset attribute. You always need to focus on getting better at every moment. There will always be some obstacles in your way – some barriers that you never thought of before.

Appreciation comes in every moment that you recognize you have made progress, within yourself, and in the impact on others. Involve others in your appreciation and celebrate your growth. Feel the power of pride.

The process for Suzan started with the right mindset and followed with developing a skill and put some key actions around it. She chose three key learning objectives and crafted her plan around them. "I never thought I can focus on what to develop. Now I'm able to address areas for improvement confidently and there is a plan I can follow. This is a relief." The framework brought a structure and focus. The plan evolved, and she had reflected on her plan in each quarter. Suzan after working on her plan brought a collective approach, and six months later, she gathered her team to craft their development plans. One of her key focus areas for improvement was to develop others, and she reflected her experience, expanded it to her team, and demonstrated the skill.

5

In Pursuit of Identity and Inclusion

Priscilla Gill

The Talent

This chapter highlights Kenna's leader development journey through coaching. The coaching engagement was sponsored by Kenna's leader to help ensure strategy and relationship success as a senior-level, female physician leader in a large academic medical center. Kenna readily accepted the coaching opportunity with expressed interest in creating a strategic plan for her relatively new function and managing relationships vertically, horizontally, and diagonally.

For Kenna, stepping into the senior administrative leadership role was a "dream come true" as it aligned with her talents, strengths, and passion. Kenna was enthusiastic and determined to make a difference for her customers, meet role expectations, and demonstrate to her sponsors and stakeholders that they made the right decision by selecting her for the senior administrative leadership role. Her journey to this position included numerous successes in medical practice, contributions on the national and international level, leadership roles in professional organizations, and several honors and awards, along with significant family responsibilities and accomplishments.

In addition to the requisite technical knowledge, skills, and abilities needed for this new leadership responsibility, Kenna was competitive, creative, energetic, and socially active – a high extrovert with high standards. Kenna had many successes under her belt. She was highly driven, and by nature, Kenna was a winner and was focused on the end game.

Leader Identity

A few months after assuming the coveted role, Kenna received feedback from her leader recognizing her many endeavors and top-notch deliverables. There was also a perceived need for Kenna to get on the balcony to view the work environment and the people she interacted with. This remark was offered to help Kenna better facilitate open communication and lead effectively to consensus while designing a strategic plan for endorsement and funding. Although she acknowledged and appreciated the feedback, Kenna was concerned and felt the feedback was evaluative and less than favorable. Her leader's comments were particularly concerning because

Priscilla Gill, EdD, is passionate about helping leaders flourish and transform organizations to unleash the greatness of others. She currently leads Mayo Clinic's Workforce Learning enterprise function and previously led their Coaching and Mentoring Center of Excellence. Priscilla earned her Doctor of Education Degree in Organizational Leadership from Nova Southeastern University.

Coach Me! Your Personal Board of Directors: Leadership Advice from the World's Greatest Coaches, First Edition. Edited by Brian Underhill, Jonathan Passmore, and Marshall Goldsmith.
© 2022 John Wiley & Sons Ltd. Published 2022 by John Wiley & Sons Ltd.
DOI: 10.1002/9781119823803.ch5

Kenna knew interpersonal skills, relationship building, strategy, and execution were pillars of effective leadership, and she thought she was on target. This feedback challenged Kenna's leader identity – self-perception and self-expression (Skinner, 2015).

Kenna took a three-pronged approach to gaining clarity on her leader identity. First, coaching conversations helped Kenna begin to see feedback as a gift and an opportunity to learn what was helping and hindering her leader identity. Kenna began to take on the role of the actor and observer in her leadership encounters. She integrated communication tips into her day-to-day leadership and was simultaneously very mindful of how others responded to the different behaviors she practiced. Kenna further accepted the idea that developing and refining leader identity is a process of taking on a "learn it all" mindset to continuously bring her best self forward and fully step into her leadership to influence others to add value to teams, organizations, and communities.

Second, Kenna integrated journaling and yoga into her routine. These practices provided greater insight and self-awareness around who she was being and who she wanted to be.

Third, Kenna was very conscientious and made a conscious effort to consider the context of her new department and peers. With the context in mind, she began dialing back some of her strengths in areas that previously were wildly successful yet did not have the desired impact in the new context. To enhance her leadership effectiveness, Kenna began to intentionally create space for others to engage and to adapt her communication approach based on the different audiences and settings. Kenna's focus on her communication style also addressed her expressed interest in inclusion on the new executive leadership team.

Inclusion

The candid coaching conversations uncovered Kenna's strong need to bring her authentic self forward and her desire for inclusion – being accepted and valued. Kenna joined the team in the middle of major organizational changes, and there was little time for a full-fledged transition and onboarding plan. These changes presented Kenna and the executive leadership team with new and challenging demands that required a sense of urgency. The combination of changes and the need for quick deliverables from the executive team took priority over executive team development and the new leadership team member integration. Major changes typically challenge leader identity, so this created a layered impact on Kenna.

To address this paradox of identity and inclusion, components of a polarity map were discussed, and a SWOT analysis was conducted. (*Corporations often use SWOT analyses to understand internal business strengths and weaknesses along with external industry opportunities and threats. For personal development purposes, SWOT analyses help identify and maximize strengths and opportunities and minimize weaknesses and threats for the best outcomes.*) As a result, Kenna concluded that she would own her inclusion by putting her energy into what she could do to be effective at the executive table versus things others were or were not doing. Kenna took responsibility for creating her most preferred working environment. She decided to focus on building credibility and trust by "waiting" before speaking. This allowed her to be heard and to understand the interests and concerns of others by clarifying needs and potential points of intersection.

Kenna realized her decision to adapt her communication style would also facilitate increased credibility and facilitate needed conversations to advance her goals and the collective goals of the executive leadership team. She also knew trust was key to long-term success, so she began in earnest to build trust one person at a time. While she took advantage of public opportunities to acknowledge and appreciate others as appropriate, she also connected with her colleagues one-on-one to share her strategic plan that was being crafted during the coaching engagement. With input from colleagues, Kenna's strategic plan was further refined to better align with the overall department strategy. These intentional interactions also resulted in strengthened relationships.

The Process

As the coaching engagement matured, Kenna allowed herself to be more vulnerable on her development journey. She continued to fully engage in coaching and was open to a series of assessments to gain insight and awareness about her motivations, styles, skills, abilities, and behaviors that have an impact on leadership effectiveness. During the course of the coaching engagement, Kenna participated in personality assessments and 360° assessments. She identified a map of stakeholders including allies, potential allies, resistors, and potential resistors to get a full perspective of her strengths and opportunities for development in the context of the organization and her new role.

Kenna agreed to the Stakeholder Centered Coaching approach, which included an initial series of one-on-one stakeholder interviews, to provide actionable coaching feedback (versus evaluative feedback that can be an easy identity trigger) (Stone and Heen, 2014). As a result of the anonymous, in-depth qualitative feedback from stakeholders, Kenna determined that her primary coaching goal was to "optimize effectiveness as a leadership team member." The deeper coaching conversations uncovered the wish to strengthen her *leader identity* and to *be heard* at the executive leadership table.

Kenna sent thank you notes to respondents sharing her coaching goal and inviting them to serve as part of her team of coaches by providing periodic impromptu feedback and additional anonymous feedback via an online survey conducted at the beginning and conclusion of the coaching engagement.

The Payoff

Kenna's commitment to strengthening her leader identity and being included as a member of the leadership team was realized by following through on our coaching agreements and development strategies. Her success was demonstrated in the pre/post-online survey with quantifiable improvement in "effectiveness as a leadership team member" (*sign of increased inclusion*) and quantifiable improvement in "overall leadership effectiveness" (*sign of stronger leader identity*).

With increased self-awareness and reflection, Kenna flourished and was able to move her agenda forward with a noble intent to help the next generation of physicians. Kenna secured the executive team support and funding for her strategic program that has been endorsed for enterprise implementation and adopted by other national health care organizations.

The coaching engagement formally concluded after one year, and Kenna indicated that the focused attention on developing her leader identity allowed her to modify her leadership behaviors while being true to herself and better engaging her peers to meet her goal. According to Kenna, pondering the following questions was helpful along the journey:

- What makes you you?
- What is stopping you from expressing your best self?
- What impact would you like to have as a leader?

Summary

Many accomplished leaders find themselves at the crossroads of identity and inclusion – a desire to be a part of a team with a shared purpose while expressing personal inherent capabilities. This paradox of being the person you want to be and being included by the people who want something different can be difficult to manage in certain organizational contexts. It could be particularly perplexing for highly talented female leaders with a solid track record and a drive to succeed. Leaders, particularly women who tend to experience delayed leadership validation, are encouraged to focus on their intentions and personal development as well as the intention and development of others as shown in the Identity–Inclusion Loop (Figure 5.1) for the greatest leadership impact.

Identity – Inclusion Loop

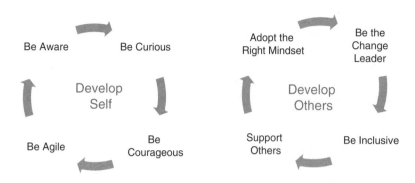

Figure 5.1   Identity–Inclusion Loop for the greatest leadership impact.

References

Skinner, S. (2015). *Build your leader identity*. Haberfield, NSW 2045, Australia: Longueville Media.
Stone, D., and Heen, S. (2014). *Thanks for the feedback*. New York, NY: Penguin Group.

6

Making the Most of Feedback

Scott Eblin

It was 30 min past our scheduled appointment, and Fred was nowhere to be found. I had been cooling my heels in the lobby of the Fortune 500 firm where Fred was a vice president. It had been a week since I had met with him to deliver a coaching report based on feedback I had solicited from his colleagues.

That last meeting had not gone so well. The verbatims in the report were tough; many of them could be described as brutally honest. When he read through the report for the first time, Fred discounted a lot of what he was reading and said that his colleagues "didn't get it." If he had to be the tough guy to make sure things got done and done right, then so be it. I wrapped up the feedback meeting by asking him to reflect on it for a few days and we would meet again in a week to discuss next steps.

So, seven days later, I was back and Fred was missing in action. The security guard in the lobby called Fred's number every 10 minutes and went to voice mail. I started emailing him from my phone trying to stir him up. No answer. After half an hour of pinging, I got up and headed for the parking lot. Just as I did, the elevator door opened and, lo and behold, there was Fred. "Oh, I'm sorry, he said, I didn't realize we had a meeting today and just got the message that you were waiting on me." My first thought was, "Wow, this is pretty passive aggressive," but I put that aside, shook his hand, and rode upstairs with him.

When we got to his conference room, Fred was stone faced. I asked him if he had had a chance to think through the feedback a bit more. He said he had. So, I asked him what he thought, and he said something along the lines of "Not much, really." I tried again with a different question and did not get anything I could build on or work with. This pattern went on for another 10 minutes, so I finally said, "Listen, I don't want to waste your time. It's clear you weren't expecting to meet with me today. I think I should leave, let you get back to your day, and we can talk again in a couple of weeks."

I was turning toward the door when I heard Fred softly ask, "Wait. Could you stay? There's something I want to tell you." Of course, I sat back down and asked what it was. "After you were here last time, I read through the report again and then took it down the hall to a friend's office. He's someone I used to work with years ago in a different company, and he's known me for a long time. I asked him to read through the report and then asked him if I was really like that. He said, 'You didn't used to be, but you are now. What the hell happened to you?'"

Tears were welling in Fred's eyes as he whispered to me, "I don't want to be that guy." I asked him if he had any plans for lunch. He said no, so we went to a nearby restaurant and spent the next 2 hours talking about his life. Fred did not realize it that day, but he had already taken some significant steps to making the most of feedback.

Research conducted by Richard Boyatzis demonstrates that receiving feedback can trigger the fight or flight response (Boyatzis 2011). Constructive (aka negative) feedback can prompt us to justify why we do what we do. That is a defensive mechanism designed to protect our self-esteem. The problem, of course, is that when you are the last person to recognize unproductive behaviors that everyone else is seeing and living with, you will eventually become ineffective.

Scott Eblin is an executive coach, leadership educator, and best-selling author of two books, including *The Next Level: What Insiders Know About Executive Success*, now in its third edition.

Coach Me! Your Personal Board of Directors: Leadership Advice from the World's Greatest Coaches, First Edition. Edited by Brian Underhill, Jonathan Passmore, and Marshall Goldsmith.
© 2022 John Wiley & Sons Ltd. Published 2022 by John Wiley & Sons Ltd.
DOI: 10.1002/9781119823803.ch6

Here, then, are some action steps to take when you are presented with colleague feedback:

Say thanks and keep going – Whenever you get feedback, the first thing you should do is say, "Thanks, I value your perspective and appreciate the time and effort you made in sharing it." It is not easy to give feedback, so you want to encourage it by expressing your appreciation. On the happy occasions when the feedback is positive, you can add to your thanks by saying you will do your best to keep doing that and by asking if your colleague sees other ways that you can leverage that strength or positive attribute for the good of the organization.

Say thanks and learn more – When one or more colleagues care enough and have the courage to give you constructive feedback, saying thanks is even more important. You want to encourage open and honest communications as that is the foundation for getting better. Look for the patterns in the feedback you are getting. While all feedback can be useful, one data point does not a trend make. If a significant number of your colleagues are all saying more or less the same thing, you have a trend on your hand. It does not do any good to argue with the feedback. My client, Fred, took an important step in overcoming this when he shared his feedback with an old friend to learn more about how he was perceived. You may or may not agree with the trend, but it does not really matter whether you do or not. Their perception is your reality. As you act on the feedback, remember that you are not just going to work on changing your behavior – you are going to work on changing people's perception of your behavior.

Choose a goal – This action step is about painting a positive picture of your future state, why it matters and the difference it will make for yourself and the organization. Getting that clear picture is a strong predictor of whether or not you will make the most of your feedback. Fred took an early and important step in this direction when he told me that he did not "want to be that guy." He was, at that point, beginning to get back in touch with what had made him successful earlier in his career and how he would build on that to lead in a more positive way in his current role.

Ask for help – The best people to help you make the most of your feedback are the people who see you in action every day. Ask them for their help. Share the goal you have set and ask them for specific actions you could take on a regular basis to move toward that goal. From that list of ideas, pick a few that you want to commit to doing regularly and ask them to watch for you taking those steps and let you know when they notice. You will have a built-in team of coaches and accountability partners. You will also be role modeling a commitment to self-improvement that will be an inspiration to others.

Follow-up – One thing I have learned in two decades of executive coaching is that perception change almost always lags behavior change. Let us say, for example, that the feedback you have gotten suggests you could be a better listener. You have asked colleagues for listening suggestions and have been consistently asking more open-ended questions in problem solving sessions and not interrupting people with your ideas as they are sharing their own. After a few months, you are the champ at both of those. And, if there's a multi-year story about you not doing those things, it is likely that a lot of people would not have noticed your changes yet. Keep going. Keep doing those things and keep asking your team for feedback in the moment about what they are noticing on your listening. You will eventually hear people saying "You've got it." That is when you know you have changed their perception as well as your behavior.

As for Fred, our work together focused on behaviors that could help him feel and show that relationships mattered to him as much as results. At work, he adopted behaviors that showed he viewed people as ends in themselves and not just as means to an end. He did a lot of things you would expect – asking about personal interests and families, going to lunch with co-workers and seeking consensus on the best ways to get things done. One of the most important things he did had nothing to do with work. When he started thinking about the value of relationships, he reached back out to old friends from his high school days and re-established connections that enhanced his life personally and, therefore, professionally. Fred is retired now, but in the 10 years following our work together, he was promoted and took on a bigger scope. Today, he is pursuing another passion in his work as a personal fitness trainer.

Ready to create a better future? Begin by asking for feedback and then making the most of it.

References

Boyatzis, R. (2011, January/February). Neuroscience and Leadership: The Promise of Insights. *The Ivey Business Journal* [online].

7

A Proven Technique to Ensure Your Leadership Measures Up

Lisa Ann Edwards

Rosita was a young marketing vice president of a well-known global brand who was known for her brilliant ideas and unique, creative flair. She also had a long-standing reputation for her brash, blunt, and off-putting communication style.

Rosita had marketing ideas that could revolutionize the company and increase revenue, but she often could not bring her ideas to life because of her communication style. Rosita's blunt and directive style prevented her from enlisting mid-level global managers to execute on her concepts. The impact was that Rosita's talent was wasted, and the company was unable to modernize its marketing strategies and fully capitalize on its product offering.

Experiencing frustration over her inability to lead her company in the direction she wanted to go, Rosita consulted an executive coach and began a reflective practice. She increased her self-awareness and began to reflect on what was getting in the way of her success. She realized that it was her leadership skills – she was confident her ideas were great, but she could not get buy-in from others to follow her. She began studying emotional intelligence, communication, and leadership styles. Over the course of a few years, Rosita became more attuned to the ways her direct and bullish communication style impacted others; she could see it was limiting her ability to get results. Gradually, Rosita began to find ways to soften her tone, ask more questions rather than directly tell others what to do, and invite others to share their ideas. Eventually, Rosita was able to implement one of her most revolutionary concepts to align marketing practices by enrolling global managers, one-by-one, to adopt her concepts and execute on her ideas.

So what does Rosita's story mean for you? On the day that I am writing this, economic uncertainty looms ahead due to a pandemic that has nearly stopped the world. Times of crisis always bring into focus those actions we wish we had put into place before the disruption began yet had put off until another day. And, while no one is quite sure how our immediate future may unfold, one thing is certain: *it's sure to be different than what we had planned!*

Whether the impacts of this crisis have long since passed, prosperity abounds and you are eyeing a possible promotion…

Or, you are facing a world for which you do not feel prepared and want to empower yourself to lead conversations that affect your career…

Or, you simply want a tangible record of your leadership that you can look back to and feel proud of how far you have come…

Putting into practice a way to pinpoint your specific leadership contributions today will equip you for what lies ahead tomorrow.

Before you start to think "but I don't think I've made any leadership contributions that are specific," or "leadership is just something that you know when you see it," or even "it's not possible to pinpoint leadership

Lisa Ann Edwards works with Executive Coaches to track and measure coaching ROI so that their client leaders can see how far they have come.

Coach Me! Your Personal Board of Directors: Leadership Advice from the World's Greatest Coaches, First Edition. Edited by Brian Underhill, Jonathan Passmore, and Marshall Goldsmith.
© 2022 John Wiley & Sons Ltd. Published 2022 by John Wiley & Sons Ltd.
DOI: 10.1002/9781119823803.ch7

contributions in practical, tangible measures," I want to assure you that nearly every leader I have worked with has expressed those very same concerns.

No doubt you have made significant changes and evolved in your leadership, too. You have likely impacted your team and organization in ways that you may not even be aware. Additionally, you probably have plans for your organization that would benefit from further development of your leadership skills. If your plans are ambitious, it is even more critical that you hone your leadership skills.

Research has shown that a model of leadership known as *transformational* leadership (as opposed to *transactional* leadership) (Bass, 1990) results in improved staff motivation (Johnson et al., 2014) and increased creativity (Dong et al., 2016) and organizational learning, innovation, and performance (García-Morales et al., 2012). Transformational leaders embody four skills: idealized influence (modeling what they want their followers to do), intellectual stimulation (challenging staff to learn and grow), inspirational motivation (sharing a vision that inspires employees), and individualized consideration (taking into account where each person is and meeting them where they are). None of these skills are realistically achievable without a reflective practice – each requires thoughtfulness, intention, awareness of self, and awareness of others. We can only become transformational leaders through *reflection* (Johns, 2004).

Take advantage of the time you have today to track your measures of success and then plan where you want to improve. While more sophisticated tactics do exist, it is often the hurdle of simply getting started that holds leaders back from measuring their efforts.

Start now and know that you can improve your measurement practice as you go. Here is a simple way to begin:

1. **Identify your top five areas of past growth:** Reflect on the top ways you have grown over the last 12 months. Narrow your list down to the top five areas of growth. The key is to let the ideas flow and not to over think it. If you find it hard to pinpoint how you have grown, think back to your most recent leadership experience and ask yourself how you approached that experience differently than you would have a year ago. Nuggets of insights about your growth are sure to emerge.

2. **Rate yourself:** By looking at your top five ways you have grown, rate yourself on a scale of 1–5 (1 = no change; 5 = significant change) on each of those areas of growth. The only person who will see your ratings is you. Your ratings are both subjective and relative, and in this case, that is perfectly fine. You are aiming to get a sense for yourself where you believe you have grown the most and where you still have opportunity to develop.

3. **Ask others for ratings:** Next, ask those you work with (manager, peers, or direct reports) to rate you on those areas of growth. Ask for examples of growth as well as opportunities for continued growth when you capture ratings to give your rater the opportunity to comfortably share why they assigned their ratings.

4. **Consider the financial impacts:** Once you have clarity about the practical tangible ways you have grown, consider how your growth has impacted your team and the organization. What you have been able to accomplish as a result of your growth? In what ways does that accomplishment lead to a financial gain or savings for your organization? Considering how your transformation has impacted your contributions to the organization in financial metrics is an important step of this process and will boost your confidence and sense of pride!

5. **Document:** Finally, it is easy to forget our successes. We often focus on the next challenge ahead and lose track of our achievements, growth, and successes as we dig into our current problem or goal. Document your leadership impacts, now. One day, you will look back to this historical record and be glad you had it.

You can repeat this process by identifying your goals, reflecting on how you can improve your leadership to achieve those goals, and identifying areas for future growth.

Rosita's transformation was slow, and at first, she was unaware of the new impact she was having. Only by taking time to slow down and *reflect* on her personal leadership transformation was Rosita able to see the impact. Rosita thought carefully about the specific ways in which she had changed, identifying what she believed were her top five areas of growth, and then rated herself on those changes. Without sharing her personal ratings, she got input from her manager on her manager's ratings of those changes. With comparative feedback from herself and her manager, Rosita's eyes were opened as she was able to clearly see the specific ways in which she had grown.

More importantly, Rosita's leadership transformation led to an organizational transformation. The organization was able to modernize its marketing strategy because 100% of the global mid-level managers adopted her concepts. Not only did the organization achieve new levels of revenue, but the company saved $1.3 million dollars in marketing costs due to the effectiveness of Rosita's plan!

When Rosita reflected on the ways her personal leadership transformation led to the financial gains and positive impact those gains had on the organization, she felt surprised about the impact and proud of the efforts she had made to grow.

All leaders want to grow and be known as a leader who makes a positive impact. We all want to make a difference in the world. That is why we are here. By tracking your progress and documenting your growth and impact today, you are prepared for whatever the future holds and assured you will measure up.

I hope you feel proud of how far you have already come, and I hope your reflective practice prepares you to rise to meet the challenges ahead.

References

Bass, B. M (1990). From transactional to transformational leadership: Learning to share the vision. *Organizational Dynamics*, 18(3), 19–31. https://doi.org/10.1016/0090-2616(90)90061-S

Dong, Y., Bartol, K. M, Zhang, Z. X, & Li, C. (2016). Enhancing employee creativity via individual skill development and team knowledge sharing: Influences of dual-focused transformational leadership. *Journal of Organizational Behavior*, 38(3), 439–458. https://doi.org/10.1002/job.2134

García-Morales, V. J, Jiménez-Barrionuevo, M. M, & Gutiérrez-Gutiérrez, L. (2012). Transformational leadership influence on organizational performance through organizational learning and innovation. *Journal of Business Research*, 65(7), 1040–1050. https://doi.org/10.1016/j.jbusres.2011.03.005

Johns, C. (2004). Becoming a transformational leader through reflection. *Reflections on Nursing Leadership*, 30(2), 24–26.

Johnson, W. B, Skinner, C. J, & Kaslow, N. J (2014). Relational mentoring in clinical supervision: The transformational supervisor. *Journal of Clinical Psychology*, 70(11), 1073–1081. https://doi.org/10.1002/jclp.22128

Communication Skills

8

The Highs and Lows of Communication

Hortense Le Gentil

Take Alexander, my client, and the CEO of a large insurance company. He was brilliant, with a clear vision of where he wanted to take the company. He also had a plan for how to get there, which involved changing the company structure and incorporating new technologies. He was spending a lot of time and energy turning his plan into reality, acting like an all-capable Superman – flying from meeting to meeting, solving crises, and pushing his reforms through while tending to clients. Busy as he was, he had little time to spend with his team, which languished. He could not understand why they were not putting in more effort, and he felt he had to make it all happen himself. He was exhausted and felt isolated.

The trouble was that he had never taken the time to explain his intentions, his plan, and the bigger purpose and vision behind them. Having made no effort to bring everyone on board, he had very little leverage. He was left trying to do all the heavy lifting by himself, and his impact was limited.

How did we help Alexander get his teams on board and increase his impact?
We worked on two main points:

1. Be aligned yourself.
   What I call alignment comes from rigorous self-examination. Thus, the first person you have to lead is yourself. Who are you and what kind of leader do you want to be? Ask yourself who you *really* are – in the present day, not who you were at the outset of your career. What is your dream? Who are your heroes? From there, flow several other questions: What drives you? What are your values? Your strengths? Your weaknesses? Does your inner purpose dovetail with the purpose of your company? How? As a leader, what do you want to be remembered for? Incorporate the answers to these questions into your outlook and you are well on your way to alignment.

   Alexander realized that he was acting like "Superman," his hero. He was "flying" everywhere to save the world alone. I challenged him to see the connection between what he was fighting for and the importance of getting followers to fight with him. One day he admitted, "I see now – a leader does not need to constantly run around trying to save the world single-handedly."

   Once confident of your personal and professional alignment, you can communicate to others your vision, inspiring them to follow your lead. The first task is to express yourself clearly. This may seem self-evident, but Alexander was not doing this – almost as if challenging team members to read his mind. No one is able to divine your motives and ideas if you do not give voice to them.

   So, go back to yourself.
2. Communicate clearly and explicitly.
   "The single biggest problem in communication is the illusion it has taken place." So wrote George Bernard Shaw, one of the history's greatest communicators. It is estimated that during his long life the Irish writer

---

Hortense le Gentil, author of the widely acclaimed *Aligned: Connecting Your True Self with the Leader You're Meant to Be*, works with decision-makers around the world to help them lead with authenticity by finding and closing the gaps between the leader they are and the leader they want to be.

Coach Me! Your Personal Board of Directors: Leadership Advice from the World's Greatest Coaches, First Edition. Edited by Brian Underhill, Jonathan Passmore, and Marshall Goldsmith.
© 2022 John Wiley & Sons Ltd. Published 2022 by John Wiley & Sons Ltd.
DOI: 10.1002/9781119823803.ch8

penned no fewer than a quarter of a million letters, this in addition to a staggeringly prolific literary and critical output.

Now, no one is asking you to be Shaw. Send that many emails and your team members will most likely rise in revolt. What is demanded here is a meticulous, humane approach to communication, one that combines alignment and a very healthy give-and-take.

a. When the warning lights of bad communication flash, roll up your sleeves and talk individually to team members.

First, Alexander had to adjust his communication style, he regrouped. He met with his top collaborators, one by one, and carefully took more time to explain his vision and purpose, and why he thought them beneficial to the company and its people. He worked to convince his team that he was genuinely interested in their opinion, and he made space to listen and asked for collective feedback. "What do you think of the plan? Can we improve anything?" he asked. No one peeped, except to make vague acquiescing noises. "Everything is perfect!" he concluded. Without knowing it, he had come across what Shaw identified as the biggest problem in communication – the illusion that it has taken place. So, he tried another question: "Where do we have problems?" The dam eventually broke. He got many suggestions and contributions, some of which pointed to problems he had not seen before. The discussions generated fresh approaches that improved his initial plan strategy.

b. Facilitate the collective alignment of the individuals who make up your team.

One of the managers I know initiated the company's redefinition by inviting every member of the executive team to share their "why" over dinner. Sometime later, store managers and other field leaders were invited to do the same during an "all in – what drives you?" retreat. In most firms, executives and managers can and should take their place beside the frontliners, those on the shop floor, retail space, etc. A good first question? The same you have asked yourself. "What is your dream?" Their answer to this serves as a means to determine their own sense of purpose and, in the end, align that purpose with that of the company.

Alexander, on his side, initiated a coffee meeting inviting his team to share their doubts and dreams about the future of healthcare. They opened up by sharing family and personal stories.

Times have changed. The old model of executives issuing top-down directives to be carried out by middle management no longer holds. The business world has been transformed: it is far more rapidly moving and volatile than in the past. Moreover, team members, especially millennials, do not like to be told what to do without sufficient explanation. They prize autonomy – and meaning: they like to know *why* they are doing things.

c. Foster a culture of psychological safety and invite your team to speak up.

Getting your team to this point requires effort. Above all else, your company culture should harbor what social scientists call "psychological safety" – a secure space and process devoid of the fear of ridicule or reprimand. Your team members should be able to speak their minds openly. They must know that their opinions and criticisms are valued. Google wholeheartedly agrees with this approach. For two years, the company conducted a rigorous internal survey into what makes their teams most effective. The number one element? Feeling safe to take risks and be vulnerable in front of one another – in other words, psychological safety. The qualifications of those on the team turn out to be far less important than how the team interacts and communicates.

Once Alexander understood the value of communicating with his leadership team and encouraging them to do the same with their teams, he realized that he did not have to do it all.

Not only did the benefits of connecting with people become self-evident, but the connection became something he authentically desired, rather than actively avoided. From there, he earned the respect of his team, who – finally armed with a clear sense of direction, cohesion, and the satisfaction of feeling valued – became far more dedicated, not only to him and to each other, but also to the common purpose they shared and now clearly understood. Conflicts became easier to resolve. More people wanted to join his team. Better able to share his vision and ideas, Alexander carried far more weight on the board. No longer a task master, he became a leader who inspired others.

The tangible result? His division's net profits increased by 10% within one year.

9

How to Develop the Authentic Leader in You

Nicole Heimann

I was invited to a meeting with two board members of a large industrial company to coach Paul, the CEO. Paul was described as a highly intelligent visionary, very strong strategically, possessing a great ability to deal with complexity, as well as a global and holistic thinker.

However, the Board of Directors had been alarmed by an employee survey. They were nervous because they did not want to lose this CEO, but there was a problem: he was hard to "get." His executive team "did not feel" him. The communication felt strange. People had reported to the board that they felt like exchanging information with a computer without any emotional reactions. They did not know how to connect with him. The absence of emotional expressions made his team members and the people in the organization feel insecure and lose trust. One colleague said, "Each time I try to build a relationship by starting with some small talk, he doesn't join in the small talk and says, 'Get to the point' or 'What can I do for you?'" Nobody seemed to really "know" Paul, and he was experienced as distant.

From Paul's perspective, he saw himself as a strong personality, able to carry heavy loads alone. He did not share many of his insights in order to protect and not burden his executive team members. He shared with me that he did not disclose anything private about himself because it was not relevant to the other leaders' jobs, and he did not want to waste their time with his private matters. He also assumed that it did not interest anyone. He was shocked and disappointed to learn of the perception people had of him and it was hard for him to understand.

The board communicated to me that they would like to keep Paul in his position because of his innate strengths and the value of his contributions to the company, but that he had to become more accessible to his coworkers.

The Unintended Impact: Losing Trust and Happiness

My clients are often "disconnected" from themselves because they think they have no other choice in order to "survive" in the corporate world. Being disconnected means not being integrated – and leading against one's own inner self.

All of us are born in full authenticity, but over the years, the conditioning of our environment makes us lose touch with (a part of) our authentic core. We tend to build up a protective wall of multiple layers. This wall holds many years of conditioning, stores our pains and wounds, houses ego-parts, provides a home to our disempowering belief systems, and holds adaptive behaviors, masks, and roles we play. The myth of the

---

Nicole Heimann is a multi-award-winning executive and executive team coach, taking executives and their teams from good to great. She is the author of the book *How to Develop the Authentic Leader in You*, keynote speaker on authentic leadership an leadership alliances, and biographer of Dr. Marshall Goldsmith in the documentary *The Earned Life*.

Coach Me! Your Personal Board of Directors: Leadership Advice from the World's Greatest Coaches, First Edition. Edited by Brian Underhill, Jonathan Passmore, and Marshall Goldsmith.
© 2022 John Wiley & Sons Ltd. Published 2022 by John Wiley & Sons Ltd.
DOI: 10.1002/9781119823803.ch9

protective wall is a construct that wants us to believe that it is there to protect us. In reality, however, it separates us from our true inner power – our authenticity. What happens over time is that we unconsciously confuse the wall with who we really are, and we lose touch with our true authentic power.

People do not want to follow a leader who is inauthentic. Inauthentic behavior creates mistrust and significantly reduces productivity and effectiveness in organizations. The people around us are looking to connect with our humanity. This humanity lies in our authenticity.

The biggest professional cost of not being authentic is losing the trust of our followers and stakeholders. The biggest personal cost of not being authentic is our own happiness.

This is what had happened to Paul.

The Seven Dimensions of Leadership Intelligence: A Process of Re-discovering, Re-connecting, and Integration

Working together with my clients to build successful and authentic leadership alliances is my mission. My passion and expertise are re-connecting leaders to the core of who they truly are. My coaching process and methodology are based on the belief that we already have all the resources we need to be successful and that there is a huge potential inside of us waiting to be unlocked. In my model, we rediscover and reconnect to "The Seven Dimensions of Leadership Intelligence":

- **Physical Intelligence** integrates the capacity of full-body awareness and taking responsibility for our well-being and health.
- **Emotional Intelligence** integrates self-awareness and awareness of others as well as self-management and managing our own emotional state.
- **Pragmatic Intelligence** integrates the combination of IQ and experience.
- **Communication Intelligence** integrates how we communicate skillfully with awareness of intended impact.
- **Heart Intelligence** integrates the wisdom and the qualities of the heart.
- **Neuroscience Intelligence** integrates the understanding of the brain and its neuroplasticity in order to learn, unlearn, and relearn new habits and behaviors.
- **Consciousness Intelligence** integrates the consideration of the possibility that something bigger than ourselves exists, beyond time and space.

No single dimension operates in isolation, and all seven dimensions are integrated with each other. This means that transforming something in one dimension always impacts the whole.

In Paul's case, the physical and pragmatic intelligence dimensions were very strong. He was very fit and had a discipline of working out at least three times a week. He had a healthy and conscious lifestyle. From the debriefing with the Board, I also knew that his pragmatic intelligence was very high; he was a keen strategic thinker who got things done. However, he was not using the resources available in the dimensions of his emotional and communication intelligence in order to be more accessible to the people around him. The coaching process would enable Paul to access these resources and tap into them in an authentic way.

The first step was to deal with the myth of the protective wall. We first focused on revealing all the limiting beliefs inside the wall, ego-voices, and saboteurs, the stories we tell ourselves. We then sharpened his internal awareness through observation and focus on himself. I worked with his strength, his strong *physical and pragmatic intelligence* to develop his inner observer, becoming more aware of the emotions going on inside his body and mind. Activating the inner observer means integrating being fully present in the moment, and at the same time, observing everything without judging. What we can "see," we can manage. Making the unconscious visible and transparent is an important part of the process. Without awareness, our subconscious issues and emotions steer us without us realizing it. With awareness, we can choose how to deal with these issues and emotions and especially gain clarity about the intended impact we want to have as a leader.

Once we were clear on his "inner map," we focused his awareness externally to his executive team. We also started strengthening his *emotional intelligence* dimension. Paul was an amazing individual, very much connected to his deeper meaning and his sense of purpose. Only, he kept it for himself!

As he shared with me what creates deeper meaning in his life, I was in awe and encouraged him to start talking about it. To Paul, this was very personal; he felt very vulnerable in doing so and courageously started talking about it, one conversation at a time. As he was doing this, he experienced only positive reactions from people. The conversations led to deeper and more inspiring discussions. Communication became more personal. This experience nurtured his self-confidence and encouraged him to share more. By opening up about himself, he learned a lot more about others too, and true bonding started to happen. As Paul was doing the inner work, we integrated more dimensions of leadership intelligence as we continued through the coaching process.

From the "Not Accessible" Leader to Cooperative and Trustful Leadership

Paul became accessible and easier to communicate with. He became comfortable with letting down his guard and showing emotions, and we worked on expressing them authentically. He had bonded with his executive team. He had also become interested in the individuals his leaders were, and this had a huge impact on the culture in the organization. Paul learned to differentiate between his authentic powerful self and his wall full of ego-voices, saboteurs, and defense mechanisms. In the process of developing authentic leadership, these do not disappear, but instead, we become aware of them and decide from which place to lead – from our authentic self or from the sabotaging behaviors. Paul experienced his leadership no longer in isolation, trying to protect everyone, but through sharing and communicating more, he had become a happier and more fulfilled person. His leadership impact and effectiveness had increased significantly.

Here are some questions based on the Seven Dimensions of Leadership Intelligence, which can support you in staying connected to the Authentic Leader in you:

Did I do my best to

1. listen to what my body is telling me?
2. honor my values through my actions and behaviors?
3. take actions to grow my vision?
4. practice deep listening and connect with myself and others?
5. be grateful and share something personal that matters to my colleagues?
6. unlearn and relearn a habit I want to change?
7. serve for the greater good?

Integrating the Seven Dimensions of Leadership Intelligence is an effective coaching process that develops authentic leadership. If we are separated from (parts of) ourselves, we are also disconnected from others and unable to lead in an inspiring way. Expanding and integrating more dimensions into our leadership brings us in touch with new aspects of who we are and helps us to become the leader we are meant to be.

10

The Culturally Fluent Leader

When Leading Across Differences, Your Style May Need to Change

Jane Hyun

Managing a diverse workforce is one of the greatest challenges and biggest opportunities for the 21st century. Yet, we observe time and again that a diverse workforce without culturally adaptive leaders will struggle to create the work environment that nurtures innovation. Increased skills in navigating cultural differences can drive higher sales, forge stronger partnerships with clients and suppliers, stoke greater engagement with employees, and, most importantly, spark innovation.

We know that with language fluency, we have the ability to express ourselves readily and effortlessly. Like someone who is fluent in multiple languages, a truly fluent leader is able to work and communicate effortlessly with people who are different from him or herself.

John, a US-based leader for a technology consulting firm, was appointed to a global role overseeing five regional offices scattered across the Middle East and Asia. After 19 years working and living in three different countries outside the United States, he thought he was adept at managing across cultural differences. He was a fierce advocate for women and for advancing ethnically diverse leaders in his organization. He helped sponsor various diversity councils, and he served as the executive sponsor of the Multicultural Employee Network in the United States. He has worked in Mexico, Shanghai, and Bangkok with employees from a variety of backgrounds.

Yet, in our one-on-one coaching session where he received the results of his cultural assessment, John was shocked to learn of the sizeable gap between his perceived ability to work effectively with other cultures and his actual ability. What was he missing? From piecing together the ideas he had gleaned from our meetings, he thought that merely being exposed to and having experienced different culture groups was enough to effectively do business cross-culturally. He also believed that he had more in common with his colleagues than not. As a result, he focused more on driving results while neglecting to actively seek out diverse viewpoints of his team members in decision-making, collaboration across functions, and succession management. With the best intentions, he believed that building trust and respect with team members through a single approach would work with all his colleagues, even those who were culturally different from him, as he had never heard otherwise. On the other hand, his colleagues were struggling with his style of communication, and yet they felt uncomfortable bringing this up with him. In our coaching, John commenced a 9-month-long process to determine how increasing his cultural awareness and making small adjustments to his management behaviors over time could obtain better engagement and increased motivation from his team members.

Jane Hyun is the leading authority in helping global organizations leverage culture and diversity to drive performance and innovation. She draws upon 25+ years of experience navigating change in high-stakes business environments. Jane is the author of *Breaking the Bamboo Ceiling* and co-author of *Flex: The New Playbook for Managing Across Differences*.

Coach Me! Your Personal Board of Directors: Leadership Advice from the World's Greatest Coaches, First Edition. Edited by Brian Underhill, Jonathan Passmore, and Marshall Goldsmith.
© 2022 John Wiley & Sons Ltd. Published 2022 by John Wiley & Sons Ltd.
DOI: 10.1002/9781119823803.ch10

As leaders, you are often charged with managing employees whose backgrounds or cultures differ from yours. If you are lucky, your default leadership approach may work. However, with a multicultural team, the approach you have used may be less effective or at times even offensive to others. When you lead global teams, the stakes are even higher. That is why, whether you are building multicultural teams in one country or you are the GM of a global business across multiple continents, it is critical to build cultural fluency in your leadership approach – which operates on the understanding that norms and expectations vary across cultures. Good intentions are simply not enough to drive behavior change, and often, when adapting across cultural perspectives, it is easier said than done.

One of the earliest insights we discovered in our coaching of US leaders was that each individual brings a unique cultural perspective to his or her team, but the leader tends to overlook this reality. Many default to overlooking cultural differences in pursuit of efficiency, or in favor of a path of least resistance that presumes more similarities than distinctions. How has your current style been influenced by your background and personal experiences? When might this mode be less effective and for whom? When working with employees from different cultures, think carefully about where your usual approach might need adjusting. By overlooking culture, leaders are not fully engaging the talent of all of their employees, and they may miss opportunities as a result.

How does this impact individual leaders? For the past 20 years, we have guided thousands of leaders to be more effective with increasingly diverse team members. When we work with leaders like John, the goal is to enable them to achieve their business goals in a global and diverse business environment by acquiring cultural fluency in their management style.

At our next coaching meeting, we examined John's approach, with a long hard look in the mirror. His own comments reflect his powerful "AHA moment." "There are deep influences that come from my own experience growing up, and in a large family where we just openly talked about difficult situations," said John. "We addressed the issue; you usually got yelled at, and then it was forgotten. If you had a problem, you brought it up. And you did it forcefully. Being quiet never got you anywhere."

We then spent a good part of the next hour zeroing in on his most crucial leadership challenge. For John, it was resolving difficult issues caused by delays when working with offices in different continents. One of his local leaders based in SE Asia was on the receiving end of John's feedback after a project got delayed. John spoke to him in his typically direct way, stating that the leader was underperforming and that he had better become more efficient with his local team. Unfortunately, due to the way the feedback was delivered, it took weeks for the local leader to recover from it and he was close to resigning from the company. John reflects: "I realize that I didn't fully appreciate the business constraints that my counterparts in SE Asia were facing and my direct approach didn't land well."

The process of transforming someone into a culturally fluent and effective leader begins with assessing the person's current awareness and abilities. We then use education, follow-up coaching, and situational debriefs to transform them into one who is flexible, fluent, and effective across cultures.

As John increased strategies to deeply understand the diverse perspectives of his colleagues throughout the global regions over the next few months, he improved his understanding of his cultural assumptions and biases as well. One skill that he practiced diligently is something we call Pre-Engagement Questions. It is an activity that enables you to understand and intentionally reflect on your own assumptions about the other party before giving feedback or engaging directly with them. When used consistently by yourself, or with your coach, it allows for a deeper understanding of the other party.

Pre-Engagement Questions – The Three Critical Questions*

If you find yourself in a workplace relationship with someone different from you and you would like to engage in providing feedback with the genuine intent to improve your interactions with him/her, there are three pre-engagement questions we recommend that you reflect upon before you start speaking. Making this a regular habit will enable you to keep an open mind about the person until you get to know them, and you will keep yourself from making hasty judgments.

Asking Reflective Questions

1. **What are they thinking?**
   What could be impacting actions? Are there cultural values, personality, or other factors that could be driving them? How are they different from mine?

2. **How should I connect?**
   How will I break the "ice" and build a stronger rapport? How will I express my true desire to better understand the individual?

3. **How can I put myself in the other person's shoes?**
   What can I do to suspend judgment and better understand the other party? What can I do differently as a result? How will I convey that I am willing to meet him/her partway?

By incorporating these questions as well as equipping John with multiple ways to resolve conflicts using a different approach, we built his confidence and increased his willingness to adapt his style. He no longer felt that the other "offices" had to fall in line with the way they did things in the United States. By the end of our engagement, he had signed up for one-on-one language classes to learn Mandarin in order to communicate more effectively with a local leader. He was willing to meet him partway!

Learnings from John

John learned that a more adaptive approach had a direct impact on how he was perceived as a leader. He also realized that using different communication approaches did not mean that he was giving up something of himself. He also asked for feedback frequently to ensure that he read the meetings correctly.

Working with a coach skilled in understanding and bridging cultural differences, and completing an assessment of your cultural competence, can be a helpful way to identify your blind spots and determine a plan for addressing them. Be willing to adjust your leadership style first; never assume that other people will adjust to you.

Notes

*Three Pre-Engagement questions – from: Flex/The New Playbook for Managing Across Differences, J. Hyun & A. Lee, HarperCollins Business Copyright 2014.

Interpersonal Relationships

11

The Five Basic Needs of Employees. How Leaders Can Recognize and Use Them

Christopher Rauen

Rick, CEO of a software company with 1200 employees, reports to his coach about constant problems between two department heads. Information is not passed on in time, and instead of seeking solutions, they blame each other for the problem. Finally, the situation escalates in an open conflict. Rick is annoyed by the behavior of his department heads. He is not really good at handling emotions. He is a matter-of-fact person and prefers rational solutions. In a joint discussion with Rick, the department heads promise to solve the problem, but the conflict continues behind the scenes. Rick has the impression that the two department heads behave "like in kindergarten." He wants to know from his coach how he can better deal with this situation.

Such conflicts between employees are a frequent topic in coaching. Managers have to be able to deal with these conflicts and – if possible – help their employees to prevent them. They can only do this if they understand what basic motives drive the employees. Without knowing the five basic needs, the employees' behavior remains incomprehensible to managers. Solutions can then be instructed, but these are not really implemented. A cycle of problems develops.

So, what are these five basic needs? All people strive to satisfy the basic needs of bonding, control, self-esteem, pleasure, and coherence (Grawe, 2004). Even though each person feels all these needs, they are usually at different levels. It can also happen that a basic need that is not sufficiently satisfied leads to another basic need being satisfied to a particularly high degree. The needs are therefore not independent of each other but interact with each other (Figure 11.1).

Bonding: For every human being, connectedness is an important basic need. This begins with the bonding between mother and child and never ends, even if a person lives alone. Then the need for connectedness can also be satisfied through other relationships, e.g., with animals or objects or in inner talks with internalized reference persons. People who have a problem with this basic need of bonding seem to be cold, hard-hearted, arrogant, and cynical to others, but also solitary, insecure, and sensitive to criticism. It is difficult to establish a relationship with them because they are not really open.

Control: The feeling of essentially having control over one's own life is another basic human need. This becomes very clear in situations where people lose control, which can lead to massive fears. The need to control oneself, others, and the environment can vary a lot. A high desire of control often goes along with low self-esteem (which is sometimes reflected in the fact that someone "puts on airs" unreasonably). People who cannot satisfy this basic need sufficiently often appear pedantic, obsessive, stubborn, and blinded to others, but also helpless and emotionally unstable.

Dr. Christopher Rauen, Germany, Senior Coach DBVC/IOBC, works as a business coach since 1996. He is the founder and CEO of the Christopher Rauen GmbH, Chairman Board of Directors of the International Organization for Business Coaching (IOBC), author, editor, and publisher of the Coaching Magazine and the Coaching Tools Series.

Coach Me! Your Personal Board of Directors: Leadership Advice from the World's Greatest Coaches, First Edition. Edited by Brian Underhill, Jonathan Passmore, and Marshall Goldsmith.
© 2022 John Wiley & Sons Ltd. Published 2022 by John Wiley & Sons Ltd.
DOI: 10.1002/9781119823803.ch11

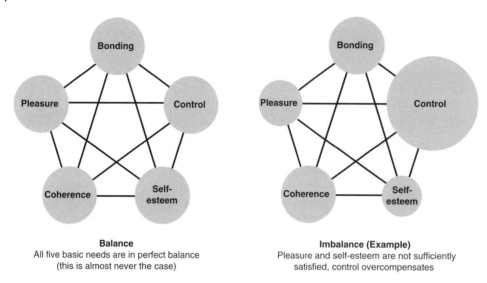

Balance
All five basic needs are in perfect balance
(this is almost never the case)

Imbalance (Example)
Pleasure and self-esteem are not sufficiently
satisfied, control overcompensates

Figure 11.1   The Five Basic Needs in Balance and Imbalance.

Self-esteem: Every person strives – at least in the long run – for increasing or maintaining his/her self-esteem. If this is not possible, an indirect increase in self-esteem is often pursued as a secondary strategy: humiliating others. People who have a problem with their self-esteem often seem like victims to others and seem to be suffering, whining, insecure, and self-pitying. If they can only raise their self-esteem by devaluing others, they also seem arrogant, self-centered, and boastful.

Pleasure: People strive to experience as much pleasure and lust as possible but use very different strategies. The pure hedonist wants "pleasure immediately" without taking into account the future. Hidden hedonists defer their urges in order to experience pleasure later on a higher level. They accept a limitation of their need, hoping for a reward on an even higher level at a later stage. People who cannot satisfy this basic need sufficiently often seem uptight, withdrawn, not very self-confident, with a high sense of shame, haggard, sometimes also stingy, and insecure. Basically, pleasure is a very strong need in every human being. People who do not show this need are in fact just hidden hedonists.

Coherence: Coherence describes the feeling of experiencing oneself and the environment free of contradictions. The more the coherence is perceived, the more the logic and cohesiveness seem to be in the world. Simplified conceptions of the world are often used in this context. In order to experience coherence, it is not necessary to be particularly intelligent. On the contrary, many very intelligent and sensitive people often develop only a little feeling of coherence, as they perceive themselves and their environment in a differentiated way and see contradictions. When we get older, the feeling of coherence usually increases, as perceived contradictions can remain unresolved next to each other so that we perceive them as less stressful. People who cannot satisfy this basic need sufficiently are often very intelligent but stand in their own way. They seem insecure and overly intellectual and try to understand everything down to the last detail and yet often cannot discover a sense.

The five basic needs strongly influence each other. For example, a lack of bonding can lead to someone having an increased need of control. A low self-esteem often leads to the fact that one can hardly feel pleasure. It is therefore necessary to always look at the big picture and not just at one of the basic needs.

In coaching, it is very helpful to explain the model of the five basic needs to the coachees. Unfulfilled basic needs of employees lead to problems. Good managers are able to recognize this in time. They help their employees not only to achieve their goals but also to satisfy their basic needs. This can have an enormously motivating effect. The prerequisite for this is to recognize unsatisfied basic needs. Then, it is important to give employees new tasks that challenge them:

- Lack of bonding: Give the employees concerned more opportunities for making experiences in the community. Give them a task that they can only accomplish as part of a team.

- Attention: The team members must like each other, and the task must be achievable. In doing so, you create a sense of community that enables a new level of performance.
- Lack of control: Give the respective team members a task that they can all handle. The task can be large and complex. The important thing is that the employees have the resources to accomplish it alone. Once they have reached the target successfully, their need for control is satisfied and they will feel less the need to control themselves or their environment.
- Lack of self-esteem: Never accept that employees humiliate others. Such behavior poisons the corporate culture and must be clearly sanctioned. Give people with low self-esteem a special task, a special assignment. It should be challenging but achievable.
- Lack of pleasure: Hidden hedonists are usually not a problem; they are used to endure difficult situations and look forward to a corresponding reward at a later stage. Problematic, however, are employees with very little need for pleasure who are already in a state of "inner resignation." Show them the playful aspects of work and the positive challenge of winning. Only people who have forgotten how to win have internally quit.
- Lack of coherence: Show your employees the meaning of their work and the purpose of the whole company. Which higher goal does it serve? What benefit does it bring to society? What benefit does it bring to the individual? Make it clear that they are all part of a greater cause.

In coaching with Rick, it turned out that the two department heads were unable to satisfy different needs: Department head A had a clear need for control. He constantly had the feeling of losing control. He thought the main reason was Department head B, his conflict partner. Department head B had a problem with his self-esteem. He was determined not to let A make him feel small. The conflicts between the two were repeated again and again. Solutions on the factual or intellectual level were not stable. What was helpful was a clarification of the problem on the relationship level. In coaching, Rick prepared a joint meeting where the two department heads developed new rules on how to deal with each other on the relationship level. This included arranging a weekly face-to-face meeting. After some time, the conflicts dissolved almost completely.

Ask yourself:

Which of the five basic needs are currently not well satisfied in your case? What behavior related to the basic needs reminds you of yourself? If you are a manager, which of your employees have you recognized reading about the basic needs above?

Literature

Grawe, K. (2004). *Neuropsychotherapie*. Goettingen, Germany: Hogrefe.

12

Steve: The Smartest Guy in the Room

Philippe Grall

Steve was head of the oncology department at an established pharmaceutical company. For many who knew him, he was at the top of his game.

Steve got an offer to become the president of a global biotech company in Japan. This new role gave Steve much more responsibility. It was his first time in a CEO role. His new company was much more dysfunctional, with the wrong people in many key leadership roles. Everywhere Steve looked, he said, there were "100 things that could be better."

About six months in, his boss pulled him aside. "Steve," he said, "You've succeeded in everything you've done in your life, and you've had to work hard for that. But for you become a truly successful President of this organization, some of the behaviors that you're exhibiting are working against you."

It was then that Steve decided to contact me to be his coach.

My Coaching Approach

My mission is to help great achievers to become leaders and, for those leaders, to become role models for everyone in the company. Steve was in a perfect position to get to this next level.

I believe that everyone has a diamond inside of them. Each diamond is unique. Each facet of your Inner Diamond represents your strengths and talents. These are the things you do best, with the most pleasure and the least effort. Knowing yourself means knowing your diamond. This is the first step to shining in business and life.

But there is a missing piece. Knowing who you are is not only about knowing your strengths. It also means knowing your weaknesses. I call this your "Shadow Diamond." These are the things that you want to change or transform.

When Steve Meets Mr. Spike

I set to work with Steve to help him discover his Shadow Diamond. As smart as he was, Steve was clearly out of his comfort zone as a first time CEO. He did not have to compete with anyone anymore.

As Steve put it, "You have to put your ego aside and be honest about not only what you *can't* see, but what you don't *want* to see."

Mr. Philippe Grall has coached corporate CEOs for more than 5,000 hours, and he has trained leadership teams in companies more than 1,000 times by using his original concept of the inner diamond. Mr. Philippe Grall mainly contributes to leadership improvement and human resource development for famous international organizations, such as L'Oreal, LVMH, Amgen, Richemont Group, etc.

Coach Me! Your Personal Board of Directors: Leadership Advice from the World's Greatest Coaches, First Edition. Edited by Brian Underhill, Jonathan Passmore, and Marshall Goldsmith.
© 2022 John Wiley & Sons Ltd. Published 2022 by John Wiley & Sons Ltd.
DOI: 10.1002/9781119823803.ch12

I started by interviewing Steve's main stakeholders face to face. They helped identify the shining aspects of his Inner Diamond:

- *Smart*
- *Logical communication*
- *Strategic thinking*
- *Quick understanding of business issues.*

These interviews also revealed his Shadow Diamond:

- *Impatient with some people*
- *Too demanding*
- *Tendency to disagree with his directors in front of their team. (In Japan, people do not like to lose face.)*

I had an idea of what Steve's issue might be but wanted to hear from him first. In one of our first coaching sessions, Steve shared his frustration: "I'm the only one who talks in meetings. When my team members do offer ideas, the level of their thinking is so poor... I don't know what to do."

I smiled at him and asked him, "Steve, what are you afraid of?" He was surprised by my question. He answered, "you know, I have to deliver results very quickly and need to make drastic changes as soon as possible. I don't want to fail. It is my first job as a CEO."

Steve did not realize it yet, but he was struggling with what I call the "Little Judge." The Little Judge is a part of yourself which originated at a very young age. When we are born, we are made of emotions: joy, hunger, fear, and sadness. Our parents want to give us all that they have. They teach us what they believe is right and wrong; what we should or should not do.

Our Little Judge is always in "reacting mode." You may also hear an inner voice saying, "You're stupid!" "You're wrong!" "You always make mistakes!" "You don't respect me!" or about yourself, "I'm not a leader!" "I'm not respected!" and so on.

When I explained this concept to Steve, he said, "I get it. My Little Judge comes in when I have the insecurity of feeling needed. Always needing to be the person who has the answer. Always being the center of the effort."

"Ok," I said. "That's your Little Judge's strategy. Tell me, if your Little Judge was a character, where would it be located and what is its name?"

Steve was quiet for a minute, eyes closed. "My Little Judge is sitting on my shoulder, and his name is Mr. Spike," he said. "He's telling me, 'You went to a good school, but it wasn't Harvard or Stanford. And you didn't go to business school. So you need to prove you're the smartest guy in the room.'"

This manifested in team meetings when Steve would say, "The answer to me is so obvious." This translated to his team as "You're all so stupid."

Steve was proud of his accomplishments. But Mr. Spike manifested himself as ego – which quickly became poisonous and destructive.

What he needed to realize was that, as a leader, he *did not* always need to be the smartest guy in the room. His job is to inspire his *team* to find the best answers.

I asked Steve to physically hold Mr. Spike in both hands, look at him, and say "Thanks but no thanks! I don't need you anymore!" Then, I asked him to physically throw Mr. Spike away. Steve laughed and did it with gusto.

He looked at me and said with a large smile on his face, "I feel much lighter now."

Steve's Shift: From Self to Others

Mr. Spike was the culprit, casting a shadow over Steve's Inner Diamond. When Steve truly understood this – and what to do about it – his path forward became clear, and he began to shine brightly.

Over time, Steve learned how to control Mr. Spike. He used to go into meetings unprepared and "wing it," relying on past experience and the wisdom of the moment, but it almost always backfired emotionally.

Now, he spends 15 minutes before each meeting asking himself, "What role do I want to play here? What mindset do I want to have and how can I inspire everyone to do their best work?" During meetings, Steve no longer feels the need to prove to the world that he is the smartest guy in the room. As he put it, "It's not about me anymore."

Three Steps to Shine in Business and Life

How can you connect to your own Inner Diamond and let it shine?

Step One: Discover Your Inner Diamond

Based on your life and business experience, list the talents and strengths that you believe you have now. These could be the following:

- **Physical qualities:** Health, strength, energy, rhythm, and even your fashion sense.
- **Inner state:** Self-awareness, intuition, openness, and observation. These are mindsets – different from emotions.
- **Intellectual capabilities:** Decisiveness, critical thinking, memory, and creativity.
- **Relationships:** How you interact with others (great listener, persuasive, team builder, and advisor).
- **Business skills:** Change maker, people developer, visionary, and marketer.

If you feel stuck, try thinking back to your childhood and what you most valued. It does not have to be related to business and your present self.

You can also ask three to six people you trust to tell you what they think your strengths and talents are. Ask them to reply by email. You may be surprised by the nice comments you receive. Their feedback will help you to enrich the image of your Inner Diamond.

Step Two: Face Your Shadow Diamond

Now, it is time to look at yourself in the mirror: Not only the light, but also the shadow.

To do so is very simple, list the attributes of your Shadow Diamond. These are negative attitudes, bad habits, and anything else that cloud over your true potential. Be honest and courageous: this part of the process is critical in order to let your Diamond shine fully.

Recall and make a list of complaints that your colleagues, partners, or family have about you: not listening, judgement, sarcasm, distraction, procrastination, etc.

Step Three: Illuminate Your Shadow and Shine

Create a character for your "Little Judge": a stone, a spiky ball, a little demon, etc. Let your imagination stretch, and see what comes to you. You can draw it if you want. Give it a funny name.

Extract your "Little Judge" from wherever it is: in your head, on your back, on one shoulder, etc. Place it in your hands in front of you and say: "Thanks but no thanks!" Then throw it away.

Check the difference in your body and in your mind.

Now, focus on your Inner Diamond and imagine how you want to shine in future business meetings. Take time to visualize showing your best self.

Caution: Your Little Judge will come back again, often invisibly, to reclaim its former position, especially when you are tired. Your only weapon is your awareness. You may need to throw it away again and again.

Before every important situation, meeting, presentation, sales talk, or interview, check if your "Little Judge" is there or not. Visualize your Inner Diamond shining in that situation. This technique is a powerful way for you to shine in business and life.

13

How Powerful Leaders Create Safety: View from Both Sides of the Desk

Carol Kauffman

When you are seen as powerful, people stop telling you the truth. As a CEO, you need to know the truth that others are experiencing. What can you do if no one will tell you? It can feel like you are on one side of the river and they are on the other. To connect and lead, simply walk over the bridge to where they are. If you can deeply understand them, they will follow you back over the bridge. This is so obvious, but why do not we do it more often?

Here are some lessons you can learn from a coaching engagement I had with a CEO. First, I had to walk over the bridge to where he was. Then, he walked over the bridge to his team. It was a small action with huge impact.

Marco was tapped to be the CEO of the largest manufacturing company of its type in the world. There was one condition, however. He had to be in coaching for one year before he could step into the role. It is a familiar story: brilliant results, the turn-around guy, and knew the business like no other. He was seen as a bully: steam-rolled people and did not listen, and people were afraid to tell him what was really going on.

Mandated coaching can be tricky, and this did not start out well.

After 4 months of excuses, we finally connected by FaceTime. I am not sure if he said hello first, but he did not sound happy to be talking with me. He quickly popped the question. "How long is this going to take?" I imagined him putting up his arm and flicking his wrist to check his watch.

"We'll figure that out together," I said. "I believe that coaching should orient around what you actually need, not that you fit into my structure."

"Well, what will we be doing?" I then shared a 2-minute description of options and ended with my usual opening question, "How could I be of the most service to you, right now?"

Lesson One: Cross over the Bridge

The first moments of our relationship he was on the far side of the bridge. It would have been easy to label him as bullying or "resistant," as others had. In this case, I could see his side easily. I would not want to be forced into coaching either.

What about you? You may have people that feel resistant to what you need to them to do. Before you react, see it from their point of view. Sounds easy? Try it 100% for a full day.

At the end of the day reflect: how many times did you reflexively defend or re-explain your logic before even thinking to ask a question? When you pushed or leapt into action, was it for the good of the organization, the long term or were you making your day easier?

Carol was ranked as the #1 Leadership Coach from the MG100 and in the top eight by Thinkers50. While on faculty at Harvard, she received $2,000,000 to launch the Institute of Coaching. She is a visiting professor at Henley Business School and a Senior Leadership Advisor at Egon Zehnder. Coaching leaders is her first love, and she has over 40,000 hours of experience.

Coach Me! Your Personal Board of Directors: Leadership Advice from the World's Greatest Coaches, First Edition. Edited by Brian Underhill, Jonathan Passmore, and Marshall Goldsmith.
© 2022 John Wiley & Sons Ltd. Published 2022 by John Wiley & Sons Ltd.
DOI: 10.1002/9781119823803.ch13

Returning now to the session I had asked, "How can I be of the most service to you, right now?"

After I had asked, "How could I be of the most service to you, right now?" Marco was silent for about one second, then leapt, rapid fire about his company. He talked and talked: high stress issues: reorganizations, volatile market, how he has to fix one region after another as they are developing a more globalized approach.

He then shifted to leading his upcoming executive team. "My major interest will be heading the top group. I want to get the most effective outcomes and find the thin line to cross in how I lead to make a difference."

Despite my desire to be on his side of the bridge at this moment I did an internal eye roll and thought, thin line? *Thin?* It is a pretty thick line. My reaction was based on extensive data I would have been given, the bullying, not listening, command and control... That said, it was crucial to let go of my preconceived judgments and reset my attitude. After all, how many multibillion-dollar global companies had I led? With training and practice flipping, your attitude back to the positive can become second nature.

Lesson Two: Find and Hit the Reset Button

People can feel when you do that invisible eye roll. Goleman (2006) and Boyatzis et al. (2005) show us how our emotions and attitude toward another person are contagious. Instantly, their neurological system kicks into the threat response. Focus narrows and heart pumps more blood to ensure survival. Big picture thinking, creativity, and interpersonal openness shut down in fight or flight mode.

Hitting the reset button can restore things quickly. Pull on your past successes with emotion regulation and mindfulness. Step into a growth mindset to change gears back to connection vs. judgement.

Happily, Marco did not pick up on my moment of negativity. "I can overdo things, and I don't want to lose people with potential. I might be doing things that disconnect people and take incentives away. But I have to get the slower members of the team engaged and if I don't lead boldly things won't happen. Like at the last team meeting, we had a big decision to make so I had to lean on people, hard."

"What happened?" I asked.

"My most valuable guy quit." For the first time in at least 15 minutes, he stopped talking.

"Would you like that to not happen again?" I asked.

He lasered in, "Yes."

"Can I give you a short tutorial?"

"Sure," he sounded interested

"There is something called Self-Determination Theory (Ryan and Deci, 2000). People want to feel psychologically safe and to be self-determined to feel they can have control over their lives. As leaders, we can help creative cultures and environments that address the three basic psychological needs. When these are met, they perform at more optimal levels. The acronym is ARC which stands for Autonomy, Relatedness, and Competence. In essence, people need a certain amount of freedom (not micromanagement) to feel psychologically safe and listened to and not have roadblocks thrown up that don't enable performance."

He interrupted, "But what if they can't have autonomy? We are in a free fall crisis here."

"Will that be forever?" I asked.

"No," he thought a moment, "I could let them know it's temporary. This is interesting, we have a board meeting coming up and they'll be there. Maybe I'll step back and give them more autonomy, after all, I'll know what they're going to say."

In the next session two weeks later, Marco taught me something I have used again and again. I think of it as "one CEO coaching others, through me."

"How did it go?" I had asked.

"Unbelievable! The board said it was the best ever. I decided that for their autonomy and relationship I should let them shine. They led the meeting and I sat back, and they did it incredibly well."

"Wow, what happened?"

"Before the meeting I remembered the safety thing. I told the team, do not worry about how you do at the board meeting. No matter what, I'll have your back. It changed everything. They looked more confident and one of the guys teared up. None of them ever had a leader say that to them before."

This CEO who was repeatedly labeled as a bully, who did not listen and had low emotional intelligence, in fact, was amazing. With very little input, he was able to access a part of himself that had always been there, but he had not tapped into at work. Many CEOs I have worked with who are labeled as bullies are not so at heart. They have been rewarded for being hard drivers and getting results.

Having a framework to understand what their people need and then flipping their power from pusher to protector pivot their style in a very positive way. Letting their team members know they will have their backs and being able to cross the bridge to understand their experiences unleash their power and talent.

References

Boyatzis, R. E, Boyatzis, R., & McKee, A. (2005). *Resonant leadership: Renewing yourself and connecting with others through mindfulness, hope, and compassion.* Harvard Business Press.

Goleman, D. (2006). *Emotional intelligence.* Bantam.

Ryan, R., & Deci, E. R (2000). Self-determination theory and the facilitation of intrinsic motivation, social development, and well-being. *American Psychologist.*

Spence, G. B, & Oades, L. G (2011). Coaching with self-determination theory in mind: Using theory to advance evidence-based coaching practice. *International Journal of Evidence-Based Coaching and Mentoring,* 9(2), 37–55.

Videos interviews with Richard Boyatzis, Dan Goleman, and Robert Ryan are available http://carolkauffman.com/videos

14

How "Face" Can Help You Manage Up

Maya Hu-Chan

Emma, a senior manager in the quality assurance and security area of a pharmaceutical company, was finding it difficult to work with her new boss, Marsha. Their communication styles clashed. Emma described Marsha as long-winded, meandering, and unclear, while Emma described herself as succinct, direct, and to the point.

"I can never understand what she wants," she said.

Emma complained that Marsha seemed to be desperate to assert her authority. This was especially frustrating for Emma, as she is a technical expert. She has been at the company for 10 years, while Marsha is brand new, and her background is not in quality assurance and security.

"She just wants people to know she's the boss," Emma said. "But she doesn't know the ins and outs, and she makes demands that don't make sense."

Emma enjoyed a different relationship with her previous boss. Their relationship was collaborative and centered on trust. She was hands-off, trusting Emma to work independently. Their communication styles were in sync.

When I started working with Emma, Marsha had been her new boss for just a month, but she was already at her breaking point. "I don't know what's the best way to work with someone like that," she said.

Understanding "Face"

As her coach, Emma sought me to help her "manage up" and figure out how to make this new, challenging relationship work. To do so, I first helped Emma understand "face."

Face is a universal concept beyond its origins in Asia. A person's face represents their dignity, pride, and self-esteem. When we "lose face," we lose some of that dignity. When we help someone "save face," we help them recover it. When we "honor face" for someone, we build them up and establish a relationship of trust.

I asked Emma several questions to help us to understand her new boss in terms of face and, ultimately, help her "manage up."

First, I asked Emma what kind of relationship she wanted with her boss. "I want her to trust me and to relax and let me do my job. I want her to give me autonomy. I want us to be able to trust one another and communicate openly to get things done," she replied.

I asked Emma to think about what is important to her boss. What does she value the most? "To build her credibility quickly within the organization," she replied. "To come across as someone knowledgeable with her peers, direct reports, and her boss. And to be able to start delivering results."

Maya Hu-Chan is a globally recognized keynote speaker, Executive Coach, and best-selling author. She is the founder and president of Global Leadership Associates, a global management consultancy. Maya is the author of *Saving Face: How to Preserve Dignity and Build Trust* and a columnist for INC.com.

Coach Me! Your Personal Board of Directors: Leadership Advice from the World's Greatest Coaches, First Edition. Edited by Brian Underhill, Jonathan Passmore, and Marshall Goldsmith.
© 2022 John Wiley & Sons Ltd. Published 2022 by John Wiley & Sons Ltd.
DOI: 10.1002/9781119823803.ch14

I asked Emma to put herself in her boss's shoes. What does she need from her? "I have lots of experience. I know the business. I know the field. I know the people, the stakeholders, and I have the technical expertise. She needs the support I can bring that can help her achieve her goals," she replied.

Through my coaching questions, Emma realized that Marsha needed someone to help her save face. Marsha was in a new high-stakes situation and felt insecure. She did not have someone on her side. Emma could become that person. If Marsha felt secure, she may eventually give Emma the autonomy she craved.

But first, Emma needed to earn Marsha's trust. Emma and I devised a strategy for "managing up," with honoring face, helping Marsha save face, and avoiding lost face as the driving forces.

These strategies for managing up are helpful to anyone hoping to establish a productive and positive relationship with their boss, with face at the core.

Face-based Strategies for Managing Up

- **Be proactive with support.**
Emma acknowledged that Marsha had gaps in technical and institutional knowledge, but that she was not able to ask for help or be open to admitting her shortcomings. To do so would mean losing face.

    To earn Marsha's trust, Emma would offer help proactively. As an example, two cross-functional departments approached Marsha directly to ask her to solve two different problems. Emma said, "I will work with you to take care of these." And, then she did – and let Marsha take credit. This helped Marsha to avoid losing face and achieve some of the credibility with her peers that she longed for.

    Proactively offering support helps managers avoid the often face-losing act of asking for it.

- **Ask for communication preferences.**
Emma used to have two monthly check-ins with her previous boss. She assumed Marsha would want the same. But after asking Marsha for her preference, Emma was surprised when she requested that their check-ins take place weekly. Marsha could eventually become comfortable with two monthly check-ins, but at this stage, more frequent updates would help her feel more secure and in control.

    Emma also helped Marsha feel more in control by providing her detailed timelines on projects so that she always knows what to expect and when. She would also take time to explain complex technical information in simple ways that Marsha, with her non-technical background, could digest.

    These steps helped Marsha feel more confident and secure in her role. They were effective ways to honor face.

- **Help your boss look good to their boss.**
Emma also asked Marsha when she has check-ins with *her* boss. She then offered to help Marsha prep for these meetings, giving her any information that she would need to make them successful.

    This helped Marsha go into these high-pressure situations feeling confident and prepared. This is honoring face.

- **Be sensitive to verbal and non-verbal cues.**
Before Marsha would have enough trust in Emma to communicate openly, Emma would have to read between the lines to decipher what her boss is feeling and thinking.

    Emma watched out for both verbal and non-verbal cues. For example, if Marsha seemed to be in a sour mood, she would politely ask, "Is there anything concerning you? Are you OK?" This communicated that she cared and was tuning in but was still respectful of Marsha's boundaries. When Marsha would share concerns or frustrations, Emma acted as a thinking partner to help her find solutions. Emma would also do this in private, never in direct view of peers or direct reports.

    Help your boss guard their sense of dignity by proactively anticipating their needs. When they trust you enough to reveal them, help them meet those needs.

- **Show them you have their back.**
Emma knew she wanted a collaborative, not adversarial, relationship with Marsha. So, when the opportunity came to save Marsha from a potentially face-losing situation, she acted without hesitation.

    Emma discovered that Marsha was about to make a decision based on incorrect data. When Emma caught the mistake, she scheduled a private meeting with Marsha and presented her with the correct information. Marsha was able to change her plans before presenting them in an executive meeting.

Emma showed Marsha that she has her back. What is more, she helped her fulfill one of her greatest needs: to appear capable in her role. Emma saved her from potentially losing face.

Show your boss that you are on the same team and that you can be trusted. When an opportunity arises to help them save face, or avoid losing face, take it.

After 6 months of enacting these strategies, Marsha began to trust Emma and see her as her right-hand person. Emma was pleasantly surprised to receive a positive first performance review from her new boss, and today, they have a positive and trusting working relationship.

Managing up is an often overlooked, yet crucial, professional skill. Though we cannot choose our bosses, we can choose how we approach our relationships with them. Focus on face – on maintaining respectful boundaries while proactively honoring face, on helping them avoid losing face, and on helping them save face when it is lost – and you will build the trust you need for a positive, productive relationship.

15

"The Payoff from Listening"

Frank Wagner

This story starts with an organization going through a massive transformation where they were reinventing how they did business. This transformation was due to the work the senior team had gone through to reimagine how they would match a new future picture based on a view that their industry was changing radically.

Every process, and every person, was looked at from the perspective of alignment with their new future picture. The leader chosen to head Sales for the entire country was promoted two levels from where he was before the change. Gabriel was relatively young and deemed the best choice to lead the sales organization into the future.

As part of this promotion, he was assigned a coach to help him in his first year. The external consultant who was working with the top management in the creation of their future picture, and the needed future conduct of their leadership, recommended me to be the coach to this new country sales executive.

In my initial meeting with Gabriel, I described the process we would be using to help him succeed in his new role. Toward the end of our first meeting, I asked him, "*What is the most important behavior you feel would benefit you the most by improving in order to successfully run the sales organization?*" It did not take him long to answer. He said, "*I think I'll need to improve in my listening.*" He then asked if the next step was to do a 360° assessment. I told him this would be customary, and I would check with the President regarding what was the best way for me to gather input.

The next day I had a call with the President to discuss how I would proceed. In our conversation, I asked the President the same question I had of his new direct report. His answered me with two words, "*Listen better.*" The country was a subsidiary of a parent company based in the United States. You may already be guessing what the Executive overseeing this country said when I asked him the same question. He was the most succinct. He simply said, "*Listening.*"

The methodology I use is called Stakeholder Centered Coaching*, where we use relevant people in the organization as internal coaches to support the leader in the actual change process. The most relevant stakeholders for this leader's goal were his direct reports who were the regional sales directors.

When I broached the subject of his stakeholders, Gabriel balked at having the most western of the Regional Sales Managers as one of his stakeholders. He told me that they had some history and neither one of them liked each other. He also said that this person was popular with his peers and their favorite for getting the top sales job. I told him that this person he wanted to exclude from the process was likely the most important one to include. What he said to me fell on deaf ears. And although Gabriel was set against it, I insisted this regional director being included.

Frank Wagner as a behavioral coach, Frank brings a broad base of experience working with individuals from mid-level management through C-level positions. Frank's specialty is leadership behavior, with an emphasis on commitment, teamwork, influence across organizational boundaries, and talent development.

Coach Me! Your Personal Board of Directors: Leadership Advice from the World's Greatest Coaches, First Edition. Edited by Brian Underhill, Jonathan Passmore, and Marshall Goldsmith.
© 2022 John Wiley & Sons Ltd. Published 2022 by John Wiley & Sons Ltd.
DOI: 10.1002/9781119823803.ch15

Once Gabriel had his goal and stakeholders, his next step was to let the stakeholders know what he is working on and ask for their support through ongoing feedback and suggestions. And the first task for the Stakeholders is to give two suggestions on how Gabriel could be a better listener.

It was like pulling teeth without anesthetic to get Gabriel to make his call to the West Coast. I did forewarn the leader that this regional director would not likely be helpful in any way on the first call. In fact, I predicted the call would only last 60 seconds or less. I asked the leader to call me after he had made is mandatory call to the Westernmost Regional Manager. And he did.

This is what he told me. "You were exactly right. All I got was silence on the other end of the phone and then an abrupt 'Not Interested.'" The next thing my leader asked was, "Can I stop checking in with him?" For our approach to work, it requires disciplined follow up with stakeholders for a leader to warrant a change in perception that the leader has improved in their eyes. So, I gave my leader the answer he did not want to hear. I told him, "No, he is one of your stakeholders as are every other Regional Sales Director. You will check in with all of your stakeholders every month."

The action plan Gabriel developed, without any help from the Westernmost Regional Director, was built off of the suggestions of his other direct reports. The key actions on how Gabriel was to improve his listening were:

- Ask questions with intention of proving someone else right.
- Paraphrase back your understanding of what someone said.
- Differentiate between the facts and opinions of what I and others are saying.
- Listen with the intent of learning something.
- Appropriately defer to someone else's point of view.

After a year, Gabriel was evaluated as significantly improving in his "listening" with every single direct report. And he had developed a genuine, positive relationship with the Westernmost Regional Director with whom he did not want to include in goal of becoming a better listener. Over time, he received many unsolicited comments about how he and this director were working so well together.

Gabriel was focusing on becoming a better listener. By working on this skill, other changes came with it. And these other changes were visible to the whole team. All relationships are a two-way street. The bad blood between Gabriel and the Regional Director who many felt should have got his job was well known. However, in the third month of the coaching engagement, a key breakthrough took place:

He called the Regional Director (who had not helped one tiny bit as a stakeholder). Gabriel called me after that call, and what he told me blew me away. He told me, "When I called him (the Regional Director out west), he told me that he thought I would go away and leave him alone. He told me that he still believes he should have my job and that he never had liked me." But the amazing thing is what the Regional Sales Director said next, "Kid, what I am about to say may shock you. I am beginning to respect you for not leaving me alone and continuing to call me about your listening...You know what, I think I need to work on my listening too."

From that conversation onward, the two of them both supported each other to become better listeners. And everyone on the sales team both observed this and benefited from it.

At the end of the engagement, where we debriefed of his results, Gabriel said that he became conscious that before choosing to work on listening, he used to listen to gather information in order to influence others to come around to his point of view. And he admits that he still does this on occasion. However, he was proud to say he is much more likely to use his new skill to learn something he did not know before. And he loves the result.

What Gabriel found was by "listening to learn," his influence came more easily and was more effective. What surprised him was how much more enjoyment he has in working with his direct reports. This was the most important learning Gabriel got out of all the hard work to improve as a leader. Listening was the means, while the real goal was learning. This coincides with the work of Jim Kouzes and Barry Posner in their book *The Truth About Leadership* (2010). Out of the 10 enduring truths about leadership, their research concludes that best leaders are the best learners.

What are the lessons from this example? There are two important lessons from Gabriel's actions and insights from working on his leadership. First, having the courage to work on improving yourself by including people who you are interdependent with yet do not get along with may lead to the best outcomes of all. And second, it proves to a lot of other people you have what it takes to lead.

My questions to you are: "Do you have the courage to work with others, and specifically your biggest critic? At least, are you willing to look for sources of help/support from unlikely sources? Do you have the humility to ask for their help, listen, and implement what these individuals suggest? And do you have the disciple to persist because it will not be easy and will take time for the relationship to change?"

The payoff is worth the pain to get there. You will be proud of yourself by acting like Gabriel.

Reference

Kouzes, J. M, & Posner, B. Z (2010). *The truth about leadership: The no-fads, heart-of-the-matter facts you need to know*. John Wiley & Sons.

16

The Necessary Reckoning of Corporate America

Terry Jackson

> *"There is a consciousness awakening and you cannot put it back in the box."*
> – Rev. William J. Barber II, president of Repairers of the Breach

What kind of country sees Black Lives Matter as a radical idea and Black suffering and death as unremarkable?

The necessary Reckoning of Corporate America begins by challenging all our assumptions. There are no sacred cows here. Everything is subject to challenge. This is not done to destroy them but to bring them into the light to look at them. We need to see if our assumptions are effective tools, skills, and means in today's reality, which will serve the purpose to which we must all dedicate our personal and collective power: that of recreating a commonly shared reality that provides a better quality of life for all members of the human race and paves the way for further and consistent development. It is based upon a recognition and celebration of the human spirit, something we all have in common.

We are at a pivotal time: a global pandemic and a multitude of social injustice issues. We are at the intersection of intellect and instinct. We need to be more human, and corporations need to be more responsive to the needs of society. It is the time for the necessary Reckoning of Corporate America.

We are at a time where organizations and individuals should be evaluating and re-evaluating their purpose. Purpose precedes the first step of every journey, both personal and organizational. To connect with purpose, organizations and individuals need to go within, asking themselves, "Why are we doing this?" When our purpose is about others – and the gifts of time, talent, and treasure that we give generously to others – it makes our "why" even more enduring. Leadership guru Daniel Goleman points out, to reimagine tomorrow, we need positive thinking, a strong foothold, and a deep sense of purpose. This is how we create meaning amid uncertainty as ambiguity abounds. This is how individuals and organizations begin the necessary reckoning so needed in our society.

The necessary Reckoning of Corporate America is mandatory. Diversity, inclusion, and equity have missed the mark since its inception in the 1980s. Gender pay issues, CEOs claiming they cannot find qualified African Americans to work with them one day and apologizing the next day, and LBGTQ challenges are testing the system, and Millennials have their own set of demands. Corporate America needs a necessary reckoning.

Dr. Eddie Glaude Jr., Professor at Princeton University, so eloquently put it, "We have a value gap" in this country. The idea that white lives matter more than the lives of others is a major issue. Sure, there are a few minorities in C-Suite positions in the Fortune 500, but these numbers are abysmal. At present, 38 women lead Fortune 500 companies. Only four African Americans lead Fortune 500 companies, and in the history of the Fortune 500, there have only been 18 African American CEOs. Talk about the needed Reckoning of Corporate America. When we examine the number of African Americans on the Board of Directors, we find that it gets worse because it is almost non-existent.

Dr. Terry Jackson is an Executive Advisor, Thought Leader, and Organizational Consultant. Terry is a Marshall Goldsmith 100 Coaches, was recently chosen by Thinkers50 as one of the top 50 Leaders in Coaching, and was chosen by Thinkers360 as a thought leader in the Future of Work. Source: Jackson Consulting Group.

Coach Me! Your Personal Board of Directors: Leadership Advice from the World's Greatest Coaches, First Edition. Edited by Brian Underhill, Jonathan Passmore, and Marshall Goldsmith.
© 2022 John Wiley & Sons Ltd. Published 2022 by John Wiley & Sons Ltd.
DOI: 10.1002/9781119823803.ch16

Blacks account for about 12% of the US population but occupy only 3.2% of the senior leadership roles at large companies in the United States according to the analysis by the Center for Talent Innovation (https://www.talentinnovation.org), a workplace think tank in New York City. Corporate America needs a necessary reckoning.

The "value gap" of many whites is rooted in fears. Laws cannot change fears. What can change those fears is getting close to that which is feared. In this case, human beings getting closer to other human beings.

All Roads Lead to and From Leadership

For those who serve in the capacity of teacher of leaders, executive coaches, and trusted advisors, this is a time of immense opportunity. A transformation of leadership is needed for the necessary Reckoning of Corporate America to be successful. Behavior change, perceptual change, and emotional intelligence (empathy) are all areas that can be impacted by yourself, the reader. This is a pivotal point in the leadership arena and all need to step up to impact the needed changes.

This is a call to arms. It is about finding and implementing solutions, not placing blame and shame for the problems. It is a movement that must begin deep within each of us to help societal problems such as diversity, equity, and inclusion instead of paying it lip service. This is a transformation of belief and thinking to solve the problems that we (not "they") have created. It is time to expand the parameters of our own perception and see each other as HUMAN. The necessary Reckoning of Corporate America is to tap into the power it possesses and only then, individually and collectively, can we successfully increase the quality of our reality, creating an environment that is conducive for sustainable personal and collective growth.

This should serve as a wakeup call for Corporate America. All must step up to the plate and claim their part of the responsibility for solutions. There is no hiding place and no excuses.

This reckoning must address all racial issues, gender issues, political issues, religious issues, and all those other barriers we have erected between the various segments of the human race. We are the ones who built the walls; it is up to all of us to expend the power necessary to tear them down and replace them with bridges of trust strong enough to support the truth.

This reckoning is a cry to corporate America to help improve our educational system. They should help revitalize our schools with positive energy and courses that teach our children real life skills. It is time to let go of what is no longer applicable and time to revise an archaic system filled with dusty ideas and false promises. It is time to replace old courses of the past with innovative, skill-based programs that teach people how to develop, according to their individual talents, a life plan that will bring them self-fulfillment and help them become positive contributors to society while being seen as human.

Money is power in our societies and nowhere is there so much of it as in the corporate world. It is time for corporations to give back some of the money and power they have earned or stolen from the people back to the very society and culture that has supported them. It is time for corporate leadership to become leaders and supporters within and outside the walls of their places of business, assuming a responsibility for helping to finance the rebuilding of our society. It is time to re-engineer more than just their processes to improve their individual bottom line profits but contribute their knowledge, skills, and resources toward constructing an environment that is safe, healthy, and conducive to the consistent and continuous improvement of quality for all human beings.

All of us have a role to play. We have seen the developments in this world, and we have either chosen to be a part of them or chosen to ignore them. Now is not the time for selective ignorance. It is time to broaden our perceptions and grasp the opportunity to make a difference; a difference in your own life and in everyone's life so that the next significant development will be the development of our personal circumstances, the development of our minds.

Is it time we all begin to assume the responsibility for improving the world in which we live? Is it time to recognize our differences as a source of increased perception rather than barriers? Is it time we all get off our butts and begin constructing rather than denouncing and destroying? Is it time to come together in a spirit of true communication, cooperation, and coordination? Is it time to build upon our strengths and develop our weaknesses? Is it time we recognize and celebrate the human spirit and tap into this incredible source of unlimited potential, redirecting our energy, time, and efforts toward more constructive and meaningful purposes? Isn't it time for a little transformational thinking?

By broadening our perceptions, we can begin to see what our potential really is. If we combine this potential by honestly committing ourselves to acting consistently ethically (principles), we can commit ourselves fully to a set of beliefs. As we learn about how we communicate and interact with others, we can include other people in our thinking and we can define our life's purpose and plan how to achieve our goals as well as create methods through which we can ensure our success. Finally, by not giving up and being open to change, we will be able to sustain our efforts and ensure that we are always headed in the right direction.

The nation has experienced startling racial and gender watersheds before, of course, and each time African American gains were stifled long before full equality was achieved. The time is now for the necessary Reckoning of Corporate America.

Emotional Intelligence

17

Managing Our Out-of-Control Feelings

Jonathan Passmore

Sameet called to ask me about a problem in his senior team. Sameet explained, "We have a serious problem on our hand. I can't have my team throwing staplers across the room at their staff."

Sameet and I had a good relationship after I worked as his coach before his promotion to Managing Director. Since his appointment, Sameet has been slowly restructuring the business, and in the last year, he appointed a new communications director, Steve.

Steve came with a record of success from his previous role, and the early months passed without incident. But Sameet noticed in several senior team meetings the generally collegiate engagement had become more bruising. If Steve held a strong view, he brought a challenging engagement style to the meeting, quickly losing his temper. But nothing had prepared Sameet for the message last week, when a senior colleague shared the details of a Zoom call where Steve's behavior was described as "threatening," "bullying," and "aggressive" before he finally terminated the online meeting for all participants. The human resources director had spoken to those on the call and unearthed a more worrying trend. "Oh, it's hell working with Steve if he does not get his own way." There were multiple stories of abusive and bullying behavior from his time in the office, including stories of items being thrown across the office or slammed down on desks.

Sameet rung me, as he and Jo, the HR director, discussed, "should he stay, or should he go" based on the evidence they had heard. In the end, Sameet asked if I could help. The answer was "may be." I would be willing to meet Steve if he wanted to explore his emotional outbursts and was committed to work on making a change. Without feedback, an awareness this was an issue and a commitment to change, coaching would not be the right approach.

Steve and I met online a few days later. Over the following hour, Steve related his frustrations regarding his colleagues but acknowledged that on occasions his anger led to behaviors that some people would find unacceptable. In his conversations with Jo, he also understood the stark choice: the behaviors stopped or he would need to leave. We met each week for the next month, exploring both the triggers and also mechanisms to manage these.

During the first two weeks, Steve had agreed to take some leave and was out of the office. He explained to his staff that he was stressed and would be taking a holiday. The time, however, provided a cooling-off period for staff after Steve apologized and some time for Steve to develop a new plan to catch these volcanic explosions.

My starting point as a psychologist was to help Steve explore the relationship between the activating event/ trigger for the behavior, his beliefs/emotions/thoughts, and the behavior that others saw. The ABC framework

Jonathan is editor-in-chief of the *International Coaching Psychology Review* and Chair of BPS Division of Coaching Psychology (2021–2022). He is Senior Vice President CoachHub, and Professor of Coaching and Behavioural change at Henley Business School, UK. He has published widely with over 100 scientific papers and 30 books. His latest titles include: *The Coaches Handbook*, *Becoming a Coach: The Essential ICF Guide*, and *CoachMe: My Personal Board of Directors*. He is one of the most cited coaching researchers worldwide, has won multiple awards for his work, and is listed in the Coaching Global Gurus top 20 coaches (2021).

Coach Me! Your Personal Board of Directors: Leadership Advice from the World's Greatest Coaches, First Edition. Edited by Brian Underhill, Jonathan Passmore, and Marshall Goldsmith.
© 2022 John Wiley & Sons Ltd. Published 2022 by John Wiley & Sons Ltd.
DOI: 10.1002/9781119823803.ch17

of (A)ctivating event, (B)eliefs, and (C)onsequences is a great way to help people better understand the connects between external events and how they behave.

While the model helped Steve recognize that it was his thinking which drove his behavior, he wondered whether he would be able to catch himself in the moment and really control his anger. This was a habit that had clearly got out of control.

We explored different scenarios – did he always act this way? As he reflected, he recognized that for public spaces where he did not know people, he may get angry but was able to control his behavior. However, the pattern of explosive behavior was present in his family relationships. Steve was better able to control his behavior with people unknown to him, as he thought "they don't know better," but as he became more comfortable with people, it was easier for him to misbehave.

We continued exploring the difference between righteous anger and inappropriate behavior. There are times to be angry, as anger is a helpful emotion (i.e., ensuring justice is done or the weak are protected). As Steve had earlier shared, he was a Christian, and we explored Jesus' anger in the temple: was it appropriate, what made it appropriate, and how did Steve's own behavior compare?

I introduced Steve to the ACCEPTS model (see Table 17.1) by describing the framework and its seven steps.

The seven steps are less of a linear pathway and more of a series of activities that place the individual in control of which best fits the specific situation.

The first is to reduce one's stress level by engaging in (A)ctivities he/she enjoys. Steve was quickly able to identify several activities he enjoyed: eating out with Grant (his partner), tennis, and jogging. He agreed to allocate time in the coming month for a weekly date night, a weekend tennis session, and two jogging 30 minutes time blocks before starting work on Tuesday and Thursday mornings.

The next step is (C)ontribution. This can be a contribution to the world, which creates a sense of connection, meaning, and purpose. Steve said that he had volunteered in the past, but job changes meant he had moved away from his hometown, but there were things he could do. He had read about the local school asking for people to come in and read with children. He contacted the school, and both he and Grant volunteered to do 15 minutes of reading weekly.

(C)omparisons aim to help people to recognize how fortunate they are. Certainly, many of us in the developed world are truly blessed with health, wealth, and choices about what we eat, where we go, and what we do. Reminding ourselves to recognize and value our blessings can be very rewarding. As Steve was a Christian, this was an easy step. He quickly realized that he should be counting his blessings, not thinking the world was against him. He suggested that his morning prayers would include thanks for his blessings, and he would focus on one thing daily that he appreciated and how the individual, item, or event blessed him.

Often individuals under stress find it hard to engage in the lighter side of life to laugh, joke, and be happy – to generate positive (E)motions. For Steve, his natural work orientation and serious manner hid a more playful side that over the years had almost disappeared, only on holidays did this side emerge. Steve reported in one session that Grant had said that it was the side he loved the best about him, so they talked about how they could together find times to add more humor and playfulness into their routine. The trips to the school, tennis, and date nights played a role in this, and they added the idea of a trip to theatre, comedy store, or a night out, where laughter would be part of the evening.

To (P)ush away is about putting aside events that cause anger. This is about directing our attention away from the issue and thinking about other things. This seemed less of a problem for Steve as his response was more in the moment, but beneath this was a wide-ranging belief that individuals "should do better." To replace

Table 17.1 ACCEPTS.

- **A**ctivities – engage in activities you enjoy
- **C**ontribution – to others and the community
- **C**omparisons – to others less fortunate, or comparison to worse situations you have been in
- **E**motions – engage in positive feelings and humor
- **P**ush away – put the situation to the side for a while
- **T**houghts – think about something else
- **S**ensations – experience a different intense feeling

these negative assumptions, I encouraged Steve to identify positive attributes in each of his colleagues: what did he like about them, what did they do well, and to focus on this.

Stressful times can lead to negative (T)houghts. We agreed on a tactic for managing these explosive moments, which was to not engage with the thought or situation, but to withdraw. Steve and I rehearsed a script using an empty chair of what he would say when he felt the sensations in his body beginning to change. Steve would simply withdraw, by going to the bathroom or outside of the office. Phrases included: "I will be back in a minute, carry on without me." This provided a 5-minute breathing space to refocus with compassion toward others, reconnect with his blessings, and put the issue in perspective by considering the other things he did in his life.

(S)ensation can be enriching, whether this is a spicy curry or a cold shower. I shared with Steve the benefits of cold showers, which include improved immune responses and reduced stress. Could he change his routine to add in a cold shower each morning? Maybe in normal circumstances, this may have been a step too far, but Steve was determined to try everything and committed to experiment for 10 days with a cold shower each morning.

As our coaching sessions came toward an end, we agreed to a review meeting in 3 months. Could Steve sustain these new behaviors and make them part of his new habituated behavior? For many of us, getting the plan is easy, but keeping going with reading, tennis, or a date night gets harder week by week for the first three months. To help with this, Steve identified a number of "stakeholders," colleagues, and friends, who he would ask to support him and hold him to account. These included Grant but surprisingly also a couple of colleagues in his team with who he previously had negative encounters.

With their support, a strong personal motivation to change and a set of tools to help, Steve's outbursts disappeared. I am sure Steve inside still feels the anger, but the range of tactics he learnt mean that he is now better equipped to manage his emotions and remain focused on the issue. I understand that his stapler has also remained in his desk drawer.

18

How to Deal with Deeper, Coaching-Resistant Behaviors

Ron Carucci

"Why do I keep doing that?"

This is a common lament of leaders whose troubling behaviors appear at the most inopportune times. With the best of intentions and effort, some leaders are not able to achieve or sustain changes to unwanted behaviors.

I worked with the division president of a global professional services firm. For the purposes of this story, we will call him Andy. He was gregarious and articulate, with an infectious energy that earned him high regard. But these positive qualities were counteracted by a stubborn need to be right, crave the spotlight, and talk incessantly. Andy said to me, "I really do care about my people. I want to inspire them. I want them to feel energized. But I just can't reign in my stubbornness, and it keeps getting me into trouble." One interviewee told me, "Andy's a great guy, but he'll never change. He can't listen, and if you suggest he's wrong, he'll talk non-stop, or belittle you, until you give in."

Some disturbing leadership behaviors are resistant to coaching, training, or other developmental activities. Despite well-intended efforts, leaders struggle to maintain new behavior and, over time, pressures and triggers drive regression back to familiar, though troubling, behavior. As Manfred Kets de Vries says in *The Leader on the Couch* (Jossey-Bass 2006*)*, "Organizations the world over are full of people who are unable to recognize or change repetitive behavior patterns that have become dysfunctional" (p. 17).

Science[1] tell us that change is such an incredible feat because it requires engaging two parts of our brain. The front of our brain, the pre-frontal cortex, is where cognition happens. It is the rational part of our brain that acquires new knowledge and skills. We use this when we are learning how to make a behavioral change. A separate part of the brain often referred to as the "reward system" provides us with motivation, or the "will" to change by releasing dopamine when we do something that feels good. You can think of this combination as the "will" and the "way." When routine efforts to learn new skills or form new habits fail, it is usually because they are only engaging one of these two areas.

But sometimes troubling behaviors are rooted in formative traumatic experiences that imprint on the part of our brains that senses threat.[2] These memories are stored in our amygdala. While memories live in the past, when our amygdala detects danger in familiar situations, we re-enact those experiences as if they were in the present and respond with self-protective behaviors that can have damaging side effects. When this happens, neither the will (motivation) or the way (cognitive learning) is sufficient to drive change.

When I confront resistant behavior that my clients have not been able to change, I work to access the deeper narratives shaping them using an approach I call "origin stories." By no means does this replace longer-term therapeutic work (sometimes it reveals the need for it). But it does provide a safe place for leaders to examine

Ron is the co-founder and managing partner at Navalent, working with CEOs and executives pursuing transformational change for their organizations, leaders, and industries. Ron is the author of nine books, including the award winning *To Be Honest*, a regular contributor to Forbes and Harvard Business Review, a two-time TEDx speaker, and a member of the MG100 coaches community.

Coach Me! Your Personal Board of Directors: Leadership Advice from the World's Greatest Coaches, First Edition. Edited by Brian Underhill, Jonathan Passmore, and Marshall Goldsmith.
© 2022 John Wiley & Sons Ltd. Published 2022 by John Wiley & Sons Ltd.
DOI: 10.1002/9781119823803.ch18

the origins of persistent, damaging behaviors. The process involves four segments that, when carefully curated, can unlock the origins of troubling behaviors and set lasting change in motion. If you are struggling to change chronic destructive behavior – anything from irritated outbursts to freezing up in high-stakes moments to asserting excessive control under pressure – uncovering your origin stories may help you break through where other approaches have failed.

Identify and Write Your Origin Story

I ask my clients to recall scenes from their formative years, usually between the ages of 5 and 21, in which the importance of the behavior in question started to appear.

Clients frequently choose formative scenes involving pain and conflict, which tend to be at the inception of troubling behavior. I have never had a client struggle to recall a scene to write about, but they commonly struggle to pick *which one* to write about *first*.

During a 4-day intensive, I asked Andy to write several formative stories about how he learned that being both right about, and central to, so many issues became critically important to him. My goal was to uncover what threat being wrong or on the periphery represented.

Choosing how to frame an origin story requires isolating the difficult behavior in a non-judgmental way and hypothesizing about what need that behavior is meeting. My hunch was that Andy only felt safe when he was talking and that having his views questioned triggered a sense of inadequacy and shame.

One of the stories Andy wrote was about the social struggles of changing schools when he was 10. Andy was both a severe stutterer and suffered with ADHD. His new school required him to attend "special education" classes. For two years, Andy's daily walk of shame passed jeering peers to the place they referred to as the "stupid classroom" filled him with defiance and shame. As he grew, those emotions eventually fueled the behaviors he now could not change. Though Andy's IQ was high, his disabilities made demonstrating his intelligence on standardized tests impossible. Andy learned that to prevent being seen as stupid, he needed to be likable, sound eloquent without stuttering, and prove he was smart. And, to him, smart meant being right.

Identify Learned Narratives

The origins of troubling behavior are always attached to well-formed narratives. These narratives serve as templates through which we make sense of the world. And, unless we re-script these narratives, we spend our lives re-creating conditions that reinforce them.

I asked Andy to write down in one sentence what he believed that vulnerable season of his life had taught him. The narrative Andy wrote was "Unless you can prove otherwise, everyone will see how stupid you are." His interpretation is starkly revealing. Andy did not believe he had to prove he *was not* stupid. He believed that he had to hide the fact that he *was*. Those years of ritualized public shame caused him to conclude he was inadequate and unintelligent, and therefore, he had to conceal that "truth" from others. The traumatic experience of believing he was stupid and unlikable was being re-enacted in his workplace. His abrasive behaviors pushed people away, replicating his childhood experiences of rejection. Consequently, he had to acquire others' acceptance and admiration using upbeat energy and brilliantly articulated ideas. Andy realized he had spent his entire life perfecting a cycle that, despite making him feel momentarily safe, yielded the very rejection he sought to escape. To counteract feelings of self-contempt and shame, Andy was determined to make sure others believed he was a smart, great guy.

Identify What Need the Troubling Behavior Is Serving

The anchor that holds troubling behavior in place is the need it serves. Andy's unconscious need to collude with his belief he was stupid and unlikable is what ultimately made him resistant to change despite cognitively understanding he should. That belief was rooted in the part of the brain that imprints trauma, setting in motion the repetitive pattern. The behaviors of verbosity and inspiration quelled Andy's feeling that others saw him as stupid and unlikable. The familiar cycle made him feel safe despite yielding the very rejection he wanted to escape. Until Andy recognized what drove him to these behaviors, no attempt to change could stick.

When I asked Andy to tell me what he ultimately wanted, he said, "I just want to feel like I belong just by being me." The problem was that he learned early in life that he could not both "belong" *and* "just be me." So, he chose to feel belonging by concocting a new version of himself. Andy and I discussed what this meant: to counter his feelings of self-contempt and shame and purchase others' acceptance, Andy made sure others believed he was an affable, articulate guy, especially at his place of work.

While he freely acknowledged the negative consequences of his behavior on others (cognitive) and desired to actually stop (motivation), the unaddressed pain of those formative years (trauma) was simply too formidable to be more than momentarily counteracted by his will or his acknowledgment.

Once you identify the deeper needs troubling behavior serve, no matter how irrational they seem, you can begin the process of change.

Choose a New Narrative and Alternative Behaviors

Identifying the origins of troubling behavior is an important step, but lasting change takes time. Sometimes, the work of a trained therapist is best employed for this phase since old narratives will not die easily. I asked Andy, "What would happen if you really were smart, and didn't need to purchase others' approval with your enthusiasm or your verbal mastery to appear intelligent? Do you think others would still admire you if you were quiet?" For his new narrative, Andy wrote, "I am liked, smart, and safe even in silence." The work of learning to embody that narrative will take time, but he is on his way.

The damage of troubling behavior is not excused because we learn it has deeper roots. But if we dismissed every promising leader whose behavior resisted common approaches to change, leadership ranks would be dangerously vacant. We have to dig deeper to help those struggling in leadership roles to change and flourish. We commonly dismiss formative experiences as merely part of our past. But a divorce, a loved one's fatal illness, being bullied, or surviving a natural disaster can leave lasting marks that shape troubling behaviors we struggle to change.

Maya Angelou said, "There is no greater agony than bearing an untold story inside you" (*I Know Why the Caged Bird Sings*, Virago, 1969/2010). If you are wrestling with persistent troubling behavior, perhaps it is time to excavate what untold story might be driving it. You will live a far more gratified life, and those you lead will be especially grateful.

Notes

1   Psychologytoday.com *Why Behavior Change is So Hard* Elliot T. Berkman, PhD. March 20, 2018.
2   Harvard Health Publishing, Harvard Medical School, *Past Trauma may haunt your Future Health;* February, 2019.

19

Coaching for Conflict Management

Gary Wang

Though still a fairly young industry with only about 12 years in existence, executive coaching is gaining increasing popularity in China, driven mainly by leading multinational companies with a serious presence in the country. A number of factors have been fueling the growing demand, including fast-growing businesses, terrifyingly low workplace engagement facing most organizations, shortage of qualified leaders, the conventional and dominant command-and-control leadership style (deeply rooted in Chinese culture), competing coach certification programs and positive experience companies have already gained from their coaching experiences. Due to rapid economic growth that calls for a solid leadership pipeline and strong bench strength, China is today home to some of the most stunning success stories for coaching interventions, and coaching-induced transformations on both team and organizational levels have been great marketing for the coaching profession, and we are never short of such inspiring success narratives. I am very happy to share such a case on the power of coaching, especially in trust and relationship-building context.

Case Study:

Let us call this client of ours, an American company operating in China – "WBA" – an alias to protect the privacy of the client. WBA is a technology and market leader in filtration materials for a range of industries including papermaking and food processing.

In 2009, WBA's Asia Pacific operations started to tumble, not from competition or other external factors but from uncontrollable infighting rooted in a deep conflict between John, an American executive and Managing Director for Asia Pacific, who had recently joined from GE Plastic, and Weiguo, Plant Manager for its Suzhou plant, a $50-MM investment and the only manufacturing facility in Asia Pacific, and the #2 person in the region. Weiguo was a Chinese national with 16 years' experience studying and working in Australia and a culturally-savvy senior leader. He joined WBA Suzhou 12 years ago as plant manager and had overseen the building and operations of the Suzhou facility. What is more, he had hired the 140 operation workers who all deeply respected him for his leadership and integrity.

WBA is a family business started in Ohio, USA, about 120 years ago, and its Suzhou plant was a crucial base supplying the company's Asian customers. The Suzhou plant Asia Pacific business was booming, thanks to the country's runaway economic growth.

John joined WBA as Head for Asia Pacific based in Shanghai, about one hour's drive from Suzhou. In his regional presidential capacity, John was in charge of manufacturing, operations, sales, marketing, finance, procurement, HR and legal. Weiguo and five other executives reported to John.

Based in Shanghai, **Gary Wang** is the founder and CEO of MindSpan, the market leader in executive coaching in China. With over 400 coaches, MindSpan serves 450+ global and local clients in 19 countries, including 136 Fortune 500 companies. Prior to MindSpan, Gary was a senior executive with DuPont and Sony.

Coach Me! Your Personal Board of Directors: Leadership Advice from the World's Greatest Coaches, First Edition. Edited by Brian Underhill, Jonathan Passmore, and Marshall Goldsmith.
© 2022 John Wiley & Sons Ltd. Published 2022 by John Wiley & Sons Ltd.
DOI: 10.1002/9781119823803.ch19

Prior to joining WBA in 2007, John had worked for GE Plastics for 12 years in both the US and China, which was a defining experience for him. He joined the privately-held company as a change leader, and apart from setting aggressive growth goals, he tried to introduce a GE-like performance culture. John was groomed in that culture and believed that this culture would help WBA gain more market share and be more successful in Asia Pacific.

Without being fully aware that he was a new leader to WBA, or trying hard enough to engage his direct reports for necessary communication and buy-in for his aggressive cultural shift, John was shocked to realize that half of his direct reports were not aligned with his change agenda. His Sales Director and Business Development Director, both hired by himself and Weiguo, were all opposed to John's performance system change.

In trying to get rid of a "nice-company culture" as he had noticed, John was determined to launch a new performance management system, which demanded that leaders fire their bottom 10% performers. Weiguo and the other two leaders were against John's plan claiming that he was too aggressive and he did not give the company enough time for reflection and communication.

The collective clash with John was so violent that the two executives hired by John had opted to quit, and Weiguo was thinking of leaving the company through an early retirement package. He and John disliked each other so much that they had stopped exchanging eye contact. But, at 52 years old, Weiguo was in fact too young for retirement. What's more, ending a successful career with WBA in this unpleasant manner just didn't seem right. He cared about the wellbeing of the company and his employees. He knew that if he quit, the consequences would be catastrophic for everyone. He was a great leader with a people focus and an engaging style, he was well respected by his peers, direct reports and front-line operators. In the Chinese environment, it was nearly impossible for the company to find an exact replacement of Weiguo. John was at a loss what to do.

In finding a quick fix to this trying situation, Rachel, John's HR Director, learned of coaching from a friend, whose company had worked with us for years. After a meeting with John and Rachel in their Suzhou plant, I recommended Bill as the coach to work with John and Weiguo.

After meeting John and Weiguo separately, Bill and I discussed the best possible program design for WBA. Bill suggested a 7-month engagement with monthly sessions of 1.5 hours. What made our proposal particularly unique was that the initial three sessions were joint meetings among Bill, John and Weiguo and the remaining sessions would be individual meetings.

In the first joint session, which was conducted in the client's office, Bill asked both John and Weiguo to have pen and paper ready. Both coachees were still avoiding eye contact and the environment was noticeably tense.

Bill began by asking his clients his first question: "Now as the two most important people for WBC Asia, if you continue your conflict, who suffers, and who suffers and loses the most?"

Bill encouraged John and Weiguo to list out all their answers. With no interaction or eye contact, both men started pouring ideas on the paper, "leadership team members, employees, families of employees, customers, suppliers, the HQs, Suzhou government." As the list got longer, both men began to realize that they themselves were people most negatively impacted.

As both gentlemen realized that the ultimate answer to Bill's question was themselves, a deep relief fell upon them. They now found the air in the room much less stuffy and straining.

Then, Bill continued: "When two of you start working together as a team, a real team, who will benefit and who will benefit and win the most?"

It almost took no time for the two men to discern that themselves would gain more than anyone else in the world if they collaborated as a team.

By the end of his sharp questions, Bill had paved a way for John and Weiguo to feel comfortable enough to accept each other. They renewed their eye contact and shook hands, something they had stopped doing for more than 6 months. Ice walls were falling apart, and warmth, hope and joy had returned to the office. Rachel was as delighted as John and Weiguo.

After the first joint coaching session, the weekly leadership team meetings started becoming more substantial and productive when John and Weiguo resumed their trust-building exercises. They showed up positive and inspiring in front of their people and declared to their leadership team that that they had misunderstanding between them, but now they had undone this misunderstanding.

As sessions went on, with John and Weiguo becoming more and more committed to their collaboration and success of the company, the atmosphere in the WBA office had taken a U-turn for positivity. It seemed like the world had been remade and everything was becoming more agreeable on every level. The quarterly sales quotas were hit again and again. Bill had become a welcome guest to WBA.

Nine months later, John was promoted to become the President for International Business based in the firm's HQs, and Weiguo became John's successor.

Before heading for Columbus, Ohio, for his new position, John told Weiguo to include Bill the coach as a permanent "fixture" in WBA's leadership development activities. He wrote an email to Bill and me, thanking us for our support: "This coaching engagement has saved our Asia Pacific operations."

We were thrilled to see this coaching engagement end as one of the most extraordinary successes in our company history. After the first engagement, we worked with WBA for another 3 years with an annual contract for 25 hours. Weiguo's direct reports could each engage Bill for 4–5 sessions in case of need.

The biggest takeaway from this amazing client success, I would say, is the sheer power of asking the right questions. The story is all about asking the right and powerful questions, and that is the soul of great coaching. And, in so doing, a most untenable conflict situation was beautifully resolved.

20

The Cavalry Isn't Coming

Caroline Stokes

Here's how to become an internal evangelist for creating an emotionally intelligent workplace.

I first met Scott, a program director in a satellite office of one of the world's most valuable US public companies, when I was invited to discuss emotional intelligence with him and his team. As I often do at the outset of large-scale coaching engagements, I took the team through the results of their workplace EQ (emotional quotient) diagnostic. It is a tool I created to enable organizations to assess their overall emotional intelligence level and see how they need to evolve to acquire and retain "unicorns" – those key hires who will help a company stay resilient and drive growth.

We wanted to find out: was Scott's company already a "unicorn magnet," demonstrating advanced emotional intelligence in the workplace? Was it on the verge of becoming one? Or was the company just getting its bearings and only now learning what it means to be an emotionally intelligent organization? The results would initiate a year of powerful, wide-ranging work with Scott and his team.

Using the EQ diagnostic, we learned that, despite the company's huge success, its management team was just starting to understand what it means to be an emotionally intelligent organization. The CEO's vision was to change the culture from a product-focused company to a people-focused company, but we also realized that it might take 10 years for this goal to filter through the whole organization. Headquarters was making the transition, but satellite offices, like the one Scott was in, were not embracing the shift. In fact, it seemed that many of Scott's colleagues did not even know about the CEO's vision.

That realization hit Scott hard. Technology companies need to constantly innovate. They cannot afford to wait 10 years for change to occur, otherwise they will fall behind the competition.

He suddenly understood that despite the company's huge success, the cavalry was not coming. No one at headquarters was going to ensure that everyone at the satellite office could interpret and implement the CEO's vision to focus on people, and not products, locally. Having reviewed the EQ results, Scott had the realization that he needed to be the internal evangelist and people leader for creating an emotionally intelligent workplace and pushing out the CEO's vision to the rank-and-file staff. All at once, he realized that it was his responsibility. It also fell on his shoulders to empower his colleagues to develop leadership skills that would enable the organization to evolve into an emotionally intelligent company.

Although Scott had held executive-level, production-solution roles at major digital entertainment organizations, and he was now leading AI programs focused on changing the future of work, this was the first time he had the influence and ability to be the driving force developing a new people-first, people-operating system within the organization. Suddenly, he was able to see how integral his role was as a leader to evolve internal

Caroline Stokes is the CEO of FORWARD, author of *Elephants Before Unicorns: Emotionally Intelligent HR Strategies to Save Your Company* (Entrepreneur Press, 2019), and podcast host of The Emotionally Intelligent Recruiter. She is an award-winning leadership coach, partnering with global teams and leaders throughout their career and leadership lifecycle.

Coach Me! Your Personal Board of Directors: Leadership Advice from the World's Greatest Coaches, First Edition. Edited by Brian Underhill, Jonathan Passmore, and Marshall Goldsmith.
© 2022 John Wiley & Sons Ltd. Published 2022 by John Wiley & Sons Ltd.
DOI: 10.1002/9781119823803.ch20

thinking and create proactive solutions, rather than waiting for HQ to provide direction. As companies enter the fourth industrial revolution, many will experience disruptions such as automation, robotics, artificial intelligence, and economic changes – and leadership coaching is paramount to its long-term success.

His company's best defense against these global – not just internal – forces will be to develop into an emotionally intelligent organization where all employees have a purpose and role related to the company's mission. But, to do that, employees need to understand the company's mission. An emotionally intelligent organization has a strong cultural philosophy that helps it to attract and acquire the right people who will make it stronger – people who have the mindset to collaborate, innovate, self-direct, and problem-solve on a regular basis.

Until I presented the EQ results to Scott and the organization, the souls in the satellite office had unintentionally drifted along exclusively on their ability to create products and profitability. Instead, the organization needed to involve all employees in how to evolve the company, the product and the outcomes with a strategy that enables everyone to feel connected to their role and their development within it to create long-term success. In the tech industry, designers and programmers work in "sandbox environments" to create and pilot products, yet they were not using their highly advanced, design-thinking skills to do this from a people perspective. That realization hit Scott between the eyes, and he embarked on a new approach to convert the product-company mindset to a people-company mindset.

Although Scott and I worked together for a year, it essentially took one report and one presentation assessing his workplace's EQ, and one powerful speed coaching session to kick off a new directive for him and the satellite team. Our first task after reviewing the EQ results was to bring together employees and stakeholders to discuss where the team wanted to be 6 months from now, how they wanted to create their own identity and systems internally that authentically added value to the CEO's vision. In addition, employees had to unlearn the impression that HR was solely responsible for leadership training and to instead develop a sense of accountability and social responsibility toward the environment they work in, contribute to, and collaborate in, and to innovate with confidence and transparency.

They had to learn that their voice was repeatedly important on all the issues of experience – ranging from colleague to candidate to employer brand and leadership – and to co-create an inclusive environment of innovation for technology and new product pioneers.

Through weeks of coaching, I helped Scott see beyond prioritizing profits and creating a culture of foosball and free meals. Instead, we focused on engagement and vision as the fundamental factors for each contributor's success. Each week we discussed a "big hairy audacious goal" and set out a timeline for each. We regularly examined executive presence, the dynamics of different personality types (even including employees on the autism spectrum), and conflicting priorities and influencing abilities. The end result was that the distinct boundaries between the products, the organization, and people leadership began to blend and become an EQ movement.

Because the company was accustomed to working on products in agile sprints, Scott adopted a similar practice with the employees and stakeholders. We would invite them to work together on a topic, from concept to delivery, three months at a time, asking them to design the approach that would work for their satellite office and to ensure its culture development was aligned with the CEO's vision.

The first month we focused on appreciative inquiry and how to develop the courage to ask powerful questions and to speak with care and candor while adopting a curious mindset about the CEO's vision and how it could be translated into something they could co-create and lead with. This created a new way of thinking and communicating for the employees. We also conducted emotional intelligence assessments so each team member could understand what was holding them back, how their behaviors might be perceived by others and what they needed to work on so that they could be better understood. Such insight enabled them to remove the obstacles in their way and move forward with curiosity and enthusiasm. As with all coaching engagements, there may be people, such as individual contributors who do not want to participate in this exercise. However, even the most cynical find value from being able to clearly articulate their thoughts, goals, and needs, and they will ultimately see it as a positive investment of time to create a new norm.

They split the second month in half, focusing on designing a new way of thinking about employee experience and accountability (to the mission), candidate experience (attraction and retention), and leadership development. The rest of the month brought people together to plan how to become an emotionally intelligent workplace. With everyone engaged to learn, an agreement to be adaptable, and accepting of ideas, it created agency and accountability and we started developing a new way of working. The rest of my coaching engagement term with Scott evolved into a pureplay coaching and observation role where direct feedback begins on how the team manages and curates it for their own organization, unique structure, and challenges.

Once Scott understood how to evolve the organization from a product-focused company to a people-focused one, he was able to take the necessary steps for employees to feel connected, committed, and engaged with their work – from developing transparent and caring language to growing a people-first company that creates a new style of impact for the product and the organization. Scott noticed his employees could escalate issues without fear and have informal feedback sessions to create faster solutions instead of waiting for quarterly review meetings, where product-company organizations are typically primed to focus on the negatives that impacted quarterly results. As a result, the team's overall level of engagement, morale, and pride improved.

For the technology leader laboring over the future product in the fourth industrial revolution, which will likely change the world, it is easy to be an ostrich and ignore the human connection element, or rely on HR to manage it. Don't.

We all know, but often forget, that it is the talent in the organization that gives your company brand its legacy. If you care about the longevity of your organization, take the workplace EQ assessment so that you can see the areas where you need to evolve.

Next, decide how you want to proceed and remember the words of Margaret Mead: "Never underestimate the power of a small group of committed people to change the world. In fact, it is the only thing that ever has."

Empowering Others / Delegation

21

The Importance of Leadership Agility

Brenda Bence

"I've always been the 'fix-it' guy, but I'm not sure how to fix *this*," Oliver said to me the first time he arrived in my office for coaching.

As the recently promoted regional head of a large European industrial company, Oliver had shifted from successfully leading one, very large developing country in Asia, to leading six countries spread across various sub-regions of Asia. While each of the six countries was at a different stage of development, there was one thing they all had in common: ever since Oliver had taken over nine months ago, business in each geography was suffering.

Oliver believed that he knew exactly what needed to be done to improve each country's performance. But, when he shared his suggestions with the country general managers ("GMs") who reported to him, Oliver felt they ignored him, particularly the leaders in the more developed markets.

"I've never encountered a problem like this one," he confided. "I've always been successful in growing businesses in this industry. It's as if all I've learned in the past isn't working for me anymore."

On the receiving end of increasing pressure from his boss, Oliver felt his position was in jeopardy. He needed to get results in *all* countries he was leading – and fast.

As a next step in our coaching process, verbal stakeholder interviews uncovered Oliver's key strengths: the most consistent words used to describe him were "persistent, determined, focused, and results-oriented." Highly skilled in engineering, technology, and R&D, he had a strong industrial background and a good knowledge of the industry and the company's history.

The feedback also revealed opportunities for Oliver to improve, with most comments related to team building – in particular that he did not trust his teams. "Oliver is quick to judge, blaming and pointing fingers when anything goes wrong." His direct reports felt that he lacked the ability to motivate and manage teams across multiple, diverse geographies.

What was standing in his way? To get to the bottom of the problem, Oliver and I explored four major leadership styles.

The "ABCDs of Leadership"

I shared with Oliver what I call the "ABCDs of Leadership" – four fundamental yet different leadership styles that he could use at any time, as appropriate, given the situation (Bence, 2014). We explored what each style meant and the pros and cons of each.

Brenda Bence is a top-ranked global executive coach and leadership branding expert who guides executives and companies to achieve transformational success. Also an author and a keynote speaker, Brenda shares engaging real-life stories and pragmatic approaches to help inspire positive and sustainable change in mindset and behavior – all delivered with a good dose of humor.

Coach Me! Your Personal Board of Directors: Leadership Advice from the World's Greatest Coaches, First Edition. Edited by Brian Underhill, Jonathan Passmore, and Marshall Goldsmith.
© 2022 John Wiley & Sons Ltd. Published 2022 by John Wiley & Sons Ltd.
DOI: 10.1002/9781119823803.ch21

1. *Autocratic Leadership.* This type of leader tells people what to do without seeking input from them. While it saves time and provides clear direction, it can foster low employee morale and engagement. It does not allow for multiple points of view nor for team ownership, depriving employees of important learning opportunities. It also encourages dependency on the leader in question. This style is most effective when urgent decisions have to be made in a crisis or when in high stress situations where team members are looking for clarity and strong direction.

2. *Bureaucratic Leadership.* This style involves using procedures and laying out a step-by-step written plan to achieve success. A process-driven way of leading, it minimizes errors and allows for quick decision-making. It provides clarity of the various roles in the process and offers better risk control, avoiding redundancy as well. But maintaining set procedures can be rigid. It limits perspectives, which can mean losing the big picture and sticking to the status quo – all to the detriment of the situation. This method is often less motivating for team members and does not build relationships within the team either. Still, if a project is particularly complex or technical, the precision of set procedures can be helpful, especially when the environment requires high regulatory compliance, such as in banking and insurance.

3. *Charismatic Leadership.* This style leverages personal energy and enthusiasm to keep employees motivated and moving forward. It can create positivity, momentum, and high engagement, mobilizing a team to be more innovative and creative. This method also promotes high levels of staff retention. On the downside, charismatic leadership can sometimes be short term, creating a blind, unthinking followership among employees. This style might result in lack of details and/or documentation, and it could take longer to achieve outcomes. Some leaders using this style may be perceived as superficial and end up more liked than respected. Nevertheless, this style can be especially useful when team morale needs a boost or when buy-in may be difficult, such as when the company or division is facing a major change.

4. *Democratic Leadership.* In this style, a leader asks for inputs from others before making a decision. Democratic leadership drives employee engagement, builds the team, and helps individuals learn and develop. Given that this style gets the team involved, it often results in higher job satisfaction and employee retention. It leverages team members' different areas of expertise and allows for many different opinions to be heard. Since it depends less on specific individuals for results, however, it can be more time consuming. It can also appear directionless on occasion, as a consensus may not be reached for some time. There can be a lack of ownership and accountability as well because the buck does not stop with any one specific individual. This style serves well when working with a group of team members who have good experience in the job at hand and can provide valuable input. It is also an excellent style when you are newly promoted and working with former peers who have suddenly become your direct reports.

Once Oliver had done a self-assessment of these four key styles, he realized that he relied heavily on the autocratic style of leadership. This had worked well when he ran the large developing country where hierarchy was respected and the team was more accustomed to autocratic leaders. There, he had simply told his teams what to do, and they carried out his directions.

But relying heavily on autocratic style was likely what was limiting his success in his new position. The goal of his current job was to support and help grow the local markets in the way they most needed, and that meant assessing which style would work best for each of the countries. From our discussion, it was clear that Oliver's new direct reports – in particular, the general managers in the more developed markets – did not respond favorably to an autocratic leadership style.

The solution called for leadership agility.

The Importance of Adapting How You Lead

This new awareness allowed Oliver to develop an increasingly important skill in the 21st century: *leadership agility.* Armed with understanding the pros and cons of each key style, he could adapt his leadership approach to the needs of the situation. As a result, he adjusted the way he led with each country, particularly letting go and allowing local GMs to drive more of the decision making in those geographies where existing leadership was strong.

For Oliver, the outcome of this new approach was dramatic. Within a few months, in the words of his boss, Oliver had "moved to the next level of leadership and maturity." He was being called out as a good people leader, and his team engagement scores improved as well.

In the end, not only did Oliver's teams grow the business in all countries, but within 18 months from when he began coaching, Oliver was handed additional responsibility for two more geographies, countries that were larger and even more important for the company.

What Are Your Style Preferences?

What about you? Which of these four leadership styles do you use the most, and how much leadership agility do you exhibit?

Estimate the percentage of time you use each of the four key leadership styles. Write your percentages here so that they add up to 100%:

Style	Current Time Spent
Autocratic Leadership Style	_____%
Bureaucratic Leadership Style	_____%
Charismatic Leadership Style	_____%
Democratic Leadership Style	_____%
	100%

Now, have someone ask your direct reports to complete this same exercise *about* you, assessing how they experience your mix of style usage as a leader. Do a straight average of all their responses and review the results. Which style do your subordinates feel you use most, second most, third, and fourth? Compare their answers to yours, and ask yourself:

- Which leadership style do you use most frequently, according to your team? What is your second most used leadership style?
- Are you relying too heavily on one or two styles?

Now, sit back and consider: what percentage of each style do you think is *optimal*, given your current position and your current team?

Write down your "goal" percentages for each style – the percentage of each style you feel is most appropriate for someone at your level and in your position. Use these as your new North Star in terms of embracing leadership agility.

Style	Desired Time Spent
Autocratic Leadership Style	_____%
Bureaucratic Leadership Style	_____%
Charismatic Leadership Style	_____%
Democratic Leadership Style	_____%
	100%

Being adaptable is a fundamental capability to have as part of your 21st-century leadership toolbox. Applying a one-size-fits-all leadership style in today's fast-paced global environment will most likely put you in the same position as Oliver, unable to adapt to the changes that are inevitable in the future.

As you move through your day, look for situations where you can try out a different style. Challenge and stretch yourself, and you may be surprised to discover the difference it will make in your ability to lead in today's increasingly diverse workplace.

Reference

Bence, B. (2014). *Would you want to work for you? How to build an executive leadership brand that inspires loyalty and drives employee performance.* Las Vegas, Nevada: Global Insight Communications LLC.

22

Coaching Perfectionists

Sally Helgesen

Vera was a talented private banker with a long list of satisfied clients, impressive technical skills, and deep knowledge of her industry. Fluent in four languages and a graduate of Europe's top MBA program, she also held an advanced degree in economics from Oxford and had been identified as a high potential from the day she had joined her top-ten rated New York City financial institution. The firm had a storied reputation along with a commitment to hiring and advancing talent pedigreed by the world's top learning institutions.

Eighteen years into her career, Vera was on the short list to head her firm's wealth management business, a highly visible and demanding position. She certainly had the right CV, yet the executive committee hesitated. Could her demonstrated skill in satisfying fiercely demanding clients translate into the ability to lead a highly individualistic team of colleagues, each with an impressive client list of their own?

Her peers and colleagues tended to think not. "ABV," they said when interviewed by the HR team charged with recommending a new leader. *Anyone but Vera.*

What exactly was the problem?

Vera was as talented as the executive committee believed her to be, but she was also a perfectionist, who held both herself and those who worked with her to punishingly high standards. "She drives herself as hard as anyone I've ever known," said one colleague, "and I admire that. But she has zero tolerance for even small missteps by her team. She creates a lot of stress, for herself and for the people around her. Under her leadership, I think morale at wealth management would plummet. And we'd all be so fearful of mistakes that our client work would probably suffer."

Perfectionism is one of the most difficult behaviors to change because perfectionists think in terms of either/or. Either something is perfect, or it is substandard. Either people perform or they do not. It is also a behavior, a mindset, that tends to serve people well in the early stage or mid-stage of their careers. As a result, perfectionists quite understandably come to believe that dotting every *i* and crossing every *t* are the surest possible path to success.

This was definitely the case with Vera. But the extreme diligence and ceaseless striving that had served her well early in her career and delighted her clients did not really translate into an effective leadership style. Like many perfectionists, her unceasing demands tended to undermine engagement and create a culture of chronic risk aversion. In addition, her focus on getting every detail right made it hard for her to see the big picture.

Perfectionism can be a particular trap for aspiring women leaders like Vera. As I learned while researching my book *How Women Rise*, co-authored with Marshall Goldsmith (Helgesen & Goldsmith, 2018), the chief reason that so many women rise to a certain level despite unhealed perfectionism lies in the fact that organizations tend to reward and promote women based on precision and correctness. By contrast, men are more likely

Sally Helgesen, cited in Forbes as the world's premier expert on women's leadership, is a best-selling author, speaker, and leadership coach. She is listed as Number 6 among the world's top leadership thinkers by Global Gurus. Her most recent book is *How Women Rise*, co-authored with Marshall Goldsmith.

Coach Me! Your Personal Board of Directors: Leadership Advice from the World's Greatest Coaches, First Edition. Edited by Brian Underhill, Jonathan Passmore, and Marshall Goldsmith.
© 2022 John Wiley & Sons Ltd. Published 2022 by John Wiley & Sons Ltd.
DOI: 10.1002/9781119823803.ch22

to be promoted and rewarded based on visibility, connections, and the perception that they are strategic thinkers. But, precision and correctness, while valued at the entry level and mid-level, are not generally viewed as leadership skills – unlike visibility, connections, and big picture thinking.

Vera, who put a premium on always being precise and correct, was practically a textbook case of how perfectionism can undermine a woman who seeks to ascend to a senior position. Yet, her high level of determination and commitment made her an excellent candidate for coaching. An initial meeting suggested she could benefit from three things:

- Getting more honest feedback from her present team
- Practice in letting go of details
- Taking measured risks.

We started with feedback, where the classic Stakeholder Centered Coaching template proved invaluable (Goldsmith, 2020). I asked Vera to identify three people in her team who saw her regularly and to enlist them in helping her change. She would do so by telling them that:

- She had become aware that perfectionism was undermining her ability to lead effectively.
- She was committed to changing her behavior.
- She knew that she could not do this on her own because her behaviors had become habitual and so constituted blind spots.
- She wanted their help in holding her accountable going forward.

This help could take the form of suggestions or direct feedback about how she had handled specific situations – for example, how she led a team meeting.

I also made suggestions about how to handle the feedback she received. She did not necessarily need to act on it. After all, maybe she did not agree with it. Or maybe she did but was not ready yet. All she needed to do was listen, commit to thinking about what she heard, and, most importantly, thank the person from whom she had solicited feedback. No quibbles, no objections, and no pushback. Just a simple *thanks*.

Making these requests was painful for Vera. As a perfectionist, she had worked hard to hide her vulnerabilities. Asking for help required humility, trust, and a willingness to practice a very new behavior. But Vera persevered. Listening to the feedback she received helped her catch herself in real time when she heard herself trying to enforce unrealistic standards or creating needless stress.

To accustom Vera to letting go of details, I asked her to make a list of everything her team was working and then code it: blue for what needed to be done to a standard of 80%, white for 90%, and black for 100%.

Vera was taken aback because she had always assumed that *everything* her team did needed to be 100%. So, I asked her to break the list down. What about early drafts of proposals for client recommendations, documents the client would never see? Her team had long complained that drafts were accorded the make-or-break importance of final reports, every detail perfect. And, how about requiring 100% attendance at every meeting? Weren't some more important for some people than others?

Once Vera had completed the coding, she shared the lists with her team, asking for their thoughts and suggestions. The back and forth helped her develop a more realistic sense of perspective and see things from her team's point of view.

Both these tasks got Vera out of her comfort zone and accustomed her to taking measured risks, which is essential for perfectionists who seek to move to a higher level. Because of their desire to control every detail, perfectionists typically become chronically risk averse. This undermines their capacity to make the kind of strategic assessments that are a hallmark of leadership excellence.

It took a few months for Vera to get comfortable with this approach. In the meanwhile, the executive committee chose another candidate to head wealth management. The old Vera would have been devastated, judging herself a total failure for not getting the job. But, armed with a freshly developed sense of perspective and confidence in her ability to enlist support, Vera decided it was actually for the best. She fiercely wanted to be a leader in her field but recognized she had work to do.

"Getting out of my comfort zone showed me that the most effective way of learning is being open to mistakes," she observed. "I'd always heard that, but I didn't believe it. To me, mistakes were a disaster. As a result, I wasn't very good at learning. I think my new approach will make me a much better leader and prepare me for whatever opportunity comes next. Better to prepare than to crash and burn."

If you work with a client who is a perfectionist – or identify as a perfectionist yourself – here a few practices are drawn from Vera's story that could be helpful:

- Ask for help! Perfectionists usually feel shame about any imperfection, while sharing your vulnerabilities breaks down the isolation that results from trying to keep up a façade.
- Get comfortable with the idea that everything does not need to be delivered to a 100% standard and then specifically identify items that will have limited impact if they fall short.
- Find opportunities to go outside your comfort zone and practice unfamiliar skills.
- Document exactly what you learned from mistakes in the past and keep a learning log going forward.

Perfectionists often insist that *their* field offers no scope or room for mistakes, but this is not really true. I learned this lesson quite publicly. In London, I was addressing a large audience of women on the topic of perfectionism. I talked about using the 80–90–100 rule to identify tasks that did not need to meet the highest standard. I made the rather casual observation that of course this might not always be useful – for example, none of us would want a surgeon deciding that 80% was good enough.

During the question period afterward, a woman in the audience stood and identified herself as the head of ophthalmologic surgery at the nearby Royal Hospital of Medicine. She wanted me to know that perfectionistic surgeons in fact had quite poor outcomes. I asked why. She said, "First of all, their teams are usually terrified of making mistakes, so it undermines their performance. They are unable to excel at the specialized tasks they do. Second, when you perform surgery, you always come across the unexpected and have to make real-time calculations based on what you learn. Perfectionists tend to be rigid and uncomfortable with the unexpected. They prefer to know rather than to learn."

This exchange taught me that perfectionism is never a helpful behavior. Coaches who help perfectionists heal do everybody a service.

References

Goldsmith, M. (2020). http://www.stakeholdercenteredcoaching.com

Helgesen, S., & Goldsmith, M. (2018). *How women rise: Break the 12 habits holding you back from your next raise, promotion or job*. Hachette Books.

23

Coaching an Executive Client Out of Micromanagement

Tom Kolditz

My favorite client, Riley (not their real name), has an enormously challenging leader role. A politician elected by a voter base of 5 million people, helping to encourage the commerce of 440,000 businesses, with full emergency management responsibility in a geographic area the size of Rhode Island. They have an employee structure of 22,000 and a budget exceeding $5 billion. Their strategic reach exceeds that of all but a very small handful of global CEOs. The sum of economic and political responsibility is roughly analogous to that of the Prime Minister of New Zealand.

Despite such weighty responsibility, this leadership role was the FIRST for Riley, who has an academically heavy background in public policy and law. Eager to be coached, they were a few months into the role when we had our interview and I agreed to coach them. Riley had two things that reinforced my decision to work with them. First, they were passionately driven by purpose, with no perceptible motivation other than engaging and representing as much of the citizenry as possible – regardless of political party. They had no obvious long-term political aspirations, no business interests, and no love affair with power. Second, they genuinely sought my help, without a hint of arrogance, presumption, or hesitation. I found Riley to be 100% authentic and 100% coachable. One of Marshall Goldsmith's truisms came to the fore: the secret to being a great coach is picking great clients. This is a great client.

This issue with this type of client – brilliant, inexperienced, and strategic executive responsibility – was predictable. Riley tried to do way too much, way too fast. Having moved from a Volkswagen role to that of a Ferrari, they had a heavy foot. Rubber was burning! The staff was already burning out. My client (single, no kids) never stopped working, so the staff never stopped, either. My client's intellect stayed well ahead of the staff, and so they tended to be heavily involved in the details of planning, giving too much guidance, too much information, too many demands, and too much detail: too much, too much, too much. My leader client was the least-experienced person on the team, yet the most directive. My client had to fix the operating tempo or find themselves in a mutiny from an otherwise committed and loyal team. The other obvious and necessary fix was for the client to remain at the executive strategic level, with less management, less meddling, and less hands-on running the show.

My first suggestion was that we take in some information from the team. I interviewed ten staff principals, for about 20 minutes each. I asked only five questions:

1. What are the leader's strengths?
2. What are the leader's challenges?
3. When is the leader at their best?
4. When is the leader at their worst?
5. If you were the leader's coach, mentor, or advisor, what advice would you have for them?

Tom Kolditz is a director at Doerr Institute for New Leaders at Rice University, named the top university by the Association of Leadership Educators. A retired Army general holding a PhD, he received the Warren Bennis Award for Excellence in Leadership in 2017, and has ranked among the top 25 global coaches for 3 years.

Coach Me! Your Personal Board of Directors: Leadership Advice from the World's Greatest Coaches, First Edition. Edited by Brian Underhill, Jonathan Passmore, and Marshall Goldsmith.
© 2022 John Wiley & Sons Ltd. Published 2022 by John Wiley & Sons Ltd.
DOI: 10.1002/9781119823803.ch23

The interviews reflected the issues framed above. As is often the case with this technique, there was repetition and convergence on the two key issues, in this case, excessive operating tempo and too much management by an otherwise strategic executive.

As I fed the anonymized information to my client, it was clear that they would find it difficult to modify both their tempo (thinking it was necessary) and the level of detail they gave to their team. I had to offer a specific method for them to use to issue general guidance. The method would need to encourage delegation and give initiative back to their work force.

To help fix the issues, I taught Riley to communicate in *intent statements*. An intent statement is a concise summary of guidance. Such statements empower employees without giving them so much detail that it spoils their creativity or stunts their initiative.

An intent statement consists of four parts:

- *Purpose*: The "why." Why are we doing this project, plan, initiative, or organization?
- *Method*: Specify any non-negotiable required tasks. Include only the most important tasks. Do not overdo this step.
- *Risk*: Specify how much risk you are willing to underwrite without your expressed permission. Capital risk? Risk of loss of a client? Also include any outcomes or actions that you do NOT want to happen.
- *End State*: Answer the question, "If we are successful in achieving your intent, what will the outcome look like? What will success look like?"

The intent should not include so much detail that it looks like a plan, usually one paragraph will do nicely. All the statement should do is define limits for clients' employees, and the rest of the ideas and the work should come from the employees themselves. I challenged my client to write an intent statement for every initiative or plan they were working and to use such statements going forward, rather than lengthy meetings where they tried to cover every detail with staff.

I would like to tell you that the intent statements resolved Riley's issues – and they did help. They stopped the micromanagement immediately. Going through the process taught my executive what strategic guidance looked like, and by contrast, what the micromanagement had been in the past. The problem, though, was their efficiency at writing them. My client could literally write one in the car while being driven to an event, or while walking down the hall at work. Operating tempo actually started to rise, rather than decline. With more traditional coaching, though, my client learned to choose what was truly important and only write intent statements when necessary. We were able to attach greater value to each statement, and over a short period of time, the client became more judicious about issuing intent.

In addition to empowering clients' employees and teaching a client to improve delegation and stop micromanagement, there is another powerful use for an intent statement. When coaching a mid-level client, they may receive a phone call or verbal guidance from their boss and need to sort out exactly what is intended. In that case, writing out what they think is their boss's intent, and sending it up for review, can add tremendous clarity to what might otherwise be an unclear request or requirement.

Try it yourself. The next time you are on a flight or in a waiting room, take out a single piece of paper and write an intent statement for a plan or project you have underway. Share it with a co-worker, a friend, or even a family member. Ask them if it is clear to them what your intention is, and if they could use the guidance to work toward a goal. You will be inspired when the answer is "Yes." And the richest reward is when a client tells you that one of their people made an excellent unprompted decision that helped the company or organization and said, "I did it because I knew it was within your intent." At that moment, you will know that you have taken your client beyond mere directive management to genuine leadership.

24

Establishing Overwhelming Presence as a Managing Director

Takahiro Honda

Mr. Inoue is a managing director of a major real estate company with abundant experiences and excellent track records. On the other hand, the president of the company questioned his management as it seems the one by an "Expert General Manager" rather than by a Managing Director. In other words, he is operating at a level below that of his title. The president had hoped Mr. Inoue to get out from the micromanagement to his people, have a bird's eye viewpoint, and achieve large business results suitable for a Managing Director. Thus, the president had requested me to coach Mr. Inoue, who sincerely accepted this as an "opportunity to change himself." We were able to build a good relationship from the first session, which allowed Mr. Inoue to speak out his real intention.

While we were working on six sessions in total, 90 minutes each, the following four issues were revealed:

1. A low sense of self-esteem
2. Unwilling to provide recognition to his subordinates
3. Lacking an ideal image while finding a comfort zone of staying at a General Manager level
4. Failing to motivate subordinates from inside themselves, only telling them the "How," not "Why."

1. **A low sense of self-esteem**

In spite that Mr. Inoue works harder than anybody else, he had always said, "People like me need to make more efforts." I gave him feedback, "Your attitude that no matter how much effort you make, never approving yourself unless you get more than enough results, makes you look painful to me." He responded, "You may be right. I, however, cannot help doing things this way since I'm not gifted."

Regardless of his position, Mr. Inoue had not really had sufficient self-esteem (a sense of security that convinces oneself satisfied with being as he/she is). He insisted on achieving results under his nose until obtaining a positive evaluation while expending time and energy to the very limit.

Then, I listened to him about how he had been promoted to the current position of a Managing Director. As we were reviewing his history, he gradually became relaxed. Finally, he said, "I would like to reinforce my sense of self-esteem, definitely." So, I gave the following pieces of advice:

- "Evaluating results" is one thing, and "acknowledging that you did your best" is another. "Acknowledging that you did your best" leads to improve self-esteem,
- Acknowledging the fact of actions such as "I did my best for this and that today" and record them every day, and
- Avoid denying such facts and efforts depending on undesirable results or responses by others.

Mr. Honda is an ICF Master Certified Coach (MCC). He has coached corporate executives in more than 2,500 hours of sessions, and he has conducted training in companies more than 2,000 times. Mr. Honda mainly contributes to leadership improvement and human resource development for SoftBank Corp, Panasonic Corporation, Nisshin Food Products Co. Ltd, The Prudential Life Insurance Company of Japan Ltd, etc.

Coach Me! Your Personal Board of Directors: Leadership Advice from the World's Greatest Coaches, First Edition. Edited by Brian Underhill, Jonathan Passmore, and Marshall Goldsmith.
© 2022 John Wiley & Sons Ltd. Published 2022 by John Wiley & Sons Ltd.
DOI: 10.1002/9781119823803.ch24

Mr. Inoue started to practice the actions above, but he had first struggled to stop denying himself. As, however, the sessions went on, he finally experienced the essence and changed his presence drastically. Until then, he had appeared somewhat lacking confidence. He, however, now came to equip great presence with a calming smile. Reinforcing self-esteem then worked as the key success factor to overcome the remaining three issues.

2. **Unwilling to provide recognition to his subordinates**

Mr. Inoue had applied the attitude of "Never provide recognition unless achieving results" to his subordinates as well. As a result, his subordinates had entered into a bad loop of becoming exhausted, decreasing motivation, and deteriorating performances. The paucity in self-approval (owing to lack of self-esteem) resulted in inadequate approval of others as well.

Then, I asked a question: "So far in your life, for whom did you work when you demonstrated your fullest potential?" Mr. Inoue replied, "A mentor once I had in my youth. He was always looking forward to and encouraged me regardless of achieving results," which suddenly inspired him to notice something important and essential.

Mr. Inoue tried to begin with creating psychological security by paying respect to his subordinates. Also, he started to pay attention to his members who had not been in a very good shape. Then, his men turned bright, their actions changed to spontaneous and confident ones, and they began to produce results.

3. **Lacking an ideal image while finding a comfort zone of staying at a General Manager level**

Mr. Inoue did not delegate his authorities sufficiently to his subordinates. Because he had thought that a person like himself should not impose his own job on subordinates. Also, he had tolerated inappropriate speech and behavior by his subordinates as he hesitated to give negative feedback to others. Furthermore, he stayed away from decision-making by holding down his real opinions and only coordinated the opinions of others. As such, his attitude had created a sense of distrust even among the subordinates who adored him.

Due to the shortage of a sense of self-efficacy (sound confidence that convinces oneself that he/she could do if tried), he unconsciously opted to stay at a General Manager level as he felt it a comfort zone. It was closely related to his lacking a clear image of an ideal executive.

With the recovery of self-esteem, however, his sense of self-efficacy was also reinforced, and gradually, he came to imagine the figures as an ideal executive: being calm and not affected with short-term results and reputation, really trusting subordinates' efforts and growth, being able to leave jobs to them, confidently giving negative feedback with affection when necessary, being able to take a risk and make a final decision decisively, and dealing with people with a broad eyesight for large-scale projects. In fact, Mr. Inoue started to proactively visit key persons outside the company and close large-scale projects that only the top executives could do.

4. **Failing to motivate subordinates from inside themselves, only telling them the "How" not "Why"**

Mr. Inoue became aware that all he had given to his subordinates so far were instructions of the "How," and that he had not discussed the "Why" sufficiently, because he had been eager for immediate results and evaluations. Mr. Inoue started to discuss the value in fulfilling the job, as well as the purpose of the job, with his subordinates. They were thus motivated from within themselves. Reinforced self-efficacy allowed him to have a broader perspective: what things in the mid-to-long term future should we achieve to make the company, employees, and customers happy? How meaningful a contribution will our current business bring about from a viewpoint of the overall industry and the world? and can't we find unexpected potential in our business from a more drastic paradigm shift? As such, he came to pitch pro-active and broader questions to his subordinates.

While Mr. Inoue overcame the issues and achieved many results, the key success factor was to reinforce his sense of self-esteem as mentioned above.

In the following illustration, the insufficient oil of self-esteem requires bringing oil of esteem given by others and filling the glass (Figure 24.1).

So, one appears somewhat lacking confidence and needs immediate results to obtain esteem given by others.

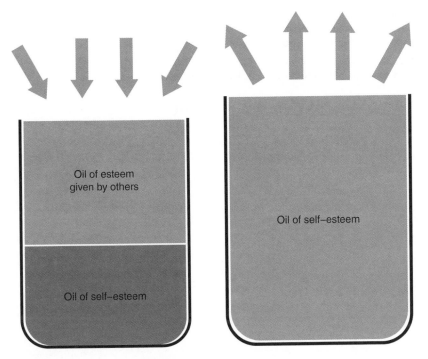

Figures 24.1 and 24.2 "Oil of Esteem".
Rule 1: The cup is oneself. Cup must be filled with oil of esteem.
Rule 2: There are two types of oil of esteem: Oil of self-esteem and oil of esteem given by others.
Rule 3: The two oils have different densities and do not mix. Oil of self-esteem is heavier and comes down.

Sufficient oil of self-esteem does not need oil of esteem given by others (Figure 24.2).

So, one creates a wonderful presence with a generous smile and cares for and appreciating others.

It allows one to vividly think of self-actualization and self-transcendence (= social contribution). Everything starts from there.

At last, Mr. Inoue stated as follows: "Just by changing one's mindset to 'I'm okay as I am' and reinforcing one's sense of self-esteem, people can change their lives as much as they want: maybe that is what I have learned. I encounter a variety of challenges every day, but I feel very fine and positive now. You may sometimes become negative. How can you laugh it away and turn it to an opportunity for growth? With that in my mind, I will keep on challenging from now on." I was deeply impressed with Mr. Inoue's seriousness, his utmost wonderful challenge to change his life.

Exercise

Reinforce the sense of self-esteem and self-efficacy

- May you be content with yourself just the way you are. [Mother Teresa]
- There is only difference; no better or worse.
- What have you achieved thus far? Why does the person who loves you love you?

Pay respect and create psychological security for your counterparty

- Everyone lives a life with ups and downs as the protagonist of his/her life.
- Cheer up his/her happiness sincerely.

Image an ideal figure lively with higher level self-efficacy

- If you had no restrictions, where do you really want to go?
- What would you really want to be?
- Where are people who realize things close to your ideal with high self-efficacy?

Articulate an attractive vision vividly

- What do you really want to do?
- What will you achieve to be smiling without regretting in only once life?

25

Letting Go: One Founder's Journey from Doing to Dreaming

Magdalena Nowicka Mook

According to the National Center for Charitable Statistics (NCCS), more than 1.5 million nonprofit organizations are registered in the United States. This number includes public charities, private foundations, and other types of nonprofit organizations, including chambers of commerce, fraternal organizations, and civic leagues. One out of every 10 people in the United States works for one of these organizations. Thus, the NGO workforce is the third largest among US industries, behind only retail trade and manufacturing.

Looking at the world, there are estimated to be over 10 million nonprofit organizations out there. John Hopkins University research suggests that if NGOs were a country, they would have been the fifth largest economy in the world!

Yet, few of the leaders of such organizations seek coaching although they often struggle to deliver on their mission, expand their reach and strengthen their impact. Some simply do not know much about coaching; others do not believe they can afford it; many conclude that they do not have time to engage in a coaching relationship.

This is where I met my client, Renee. She is an energetic, vivacious, beautiful woman with an infectious smile and a big mission she so deeply believes in. She is at helm of the organization that focuses on black girls and young women in a rough Minneapolis neighborhood. Their mission? Guiding girls to self-discovery without limits. When the organization first started, all people involved, including Renee, were volunteers, many of them able to support the cause with only few precious hours per month.

Renee has seemingly unlimited energy and for years has been running this organization with a good level of success, but not without a great personal cost. And the organization was not growing. It was time to scale or, sadly, stop all together. Donations were scarce, human resources were dwindling, and motivation was running down.

She was one busy woman! Running the educational classes, overseeing volunteers, writing a newsletter, and updating the website – the list of daily chores went on and on. But it was not sustainable. She knew what she was good at – fundraising, strategy, and inspiration. These things happened to be the greatest need for the program anyway, and she saw herself as the best person to do it. However, she was not spending enough time raising awareness and raising funds to support the cause. Not enough time, she would say.

We talked a lot about what held her back and the sheer busyness of all the things she was responsible for, which was overwhelming. So, step by step, we went through the list. We eliminated some things that were "nice to have" but not mission critical. Then came a difficult exercise of determining which of the remaining things she really needed to do, and which ones could (and should) easily be delegated. With limited staff, however, she was not sure how to do it. She felt deeply responsible for her staff and the success of the organization.

Magdalena Nowicka Mook brings experience in fundraising, coaching, and consulting and association management. She is the CEO and executive director of the International Coaching Federation (ICF), where she acts as a partner to the ICF's Global Board of Directors. Magdalena is a trained professional coach and systems' facilitator.

Coach Me! Your Personal Board of Directors: Leadership Advice from the World's Greatest Coaches, First Edition. Edited by Brian Underhill, Jonathan Passmore, and Marshall Goldsmith.
© 2022 John Wiley & Sons Ltd. Published 2022 by John Wiley & Sons Ltd.
DOI: 10.1002/9781119823803.ch25

Then came another realization for her – she was not recognizing all the resources that were in her reach! For example, she had a board of directors that represented powerful organizations and corporations in the area, though she never felt comfortable asking them to support the organization with corporate donations or in-kind support. Also, she never thought of tasking her directors with looking for candidates to eventually replace themselves. Furthermore, she never thought of asking them to fundraise on behalf of the organization.

One situation at the time, we managed to find many more resources that she could easily tap, creating more room for her to focus on strategy and vision.

The actual breakthrough came when analyzing her values as a leader. Always striving for excellence, she forgot to take care of herself! I pointed out to her that as a leader, she needed to pay attention to two things, beyond the mission of the organization:

- Growing and developing people she worked with
- Being a role model to the girls and young women she was supporting through her charity.

We examined the work on Self Determination Theory by Edward Deci and Richard M. Ryan (2012). Suddenly all pieces came together for her – she needed to let go and trust her employees and volunteers to do a good job – of course with a set of clear expectations. She understood that she was not doing her job when, at times of perceived crisis, she was jumping in and taking over. She noticed that what she considered her attempts at demonstrating care were perceived by others as control. Being a role model to black girls and women became her real "North Star," something she could always come back to, when in doubt. We also talked about the work of Tasha Eurich – Insight (https://www.insight-book.com) on self-perception versus how others see us and evaluate our effectiveness.

It was not necessarily an easy transition. We used several exercises, such as creating a list of things that only she could/should do and sticking to it. We went through an exercise of evaluating new ideas and projects against the agreed rubric, so there was no shame or guilt in saying "no." The brilliant work of Liz Weisman: *Multipliers: How the Best Leaders Make Everyone Smarter* (https://thewisemangroup.com/books/multipliers) really gave us a framework. We worked on developing a set of expectations for her employees and volunteers, applying the "reasonable plus" approach. "Reasonable plus" calls for a level of service and quality that any reasonable organization would offer, and any reasonable client would expect. And the "plus" part was a nod toward her strong drive for excellence and highest quality. This is the concept that I developed and utilized in my own work with my own organization – with good results. Reasonable plus made her very comfortable. And, finally, we worked on her having a trusted colleague who would offer honest and timely feedback, somebody that she needed to give full access and full permission to push back.

It has been a couple of years since I had a pleasure of working with her, and she is thriving. The organization she founded is thriving as well! She stepped down from the CEO role and now she now holds the position of Chief Executive Strategist – which is a Board-level position. She is a very passionate spokesperson for the organization, raising awareness and bringing powerful supporters to the cause. The organization now has seven full-time employees and an energetic board of eight individuals with diverse backgrounds and extensive networks of supporters. Most importantly, the organization keeps serving the very populations it was created to serve – your girls and young women of color, when they need it most.

Renee realized that by letting go of control she was not letting go of her dream, but rather she was allowing that dream to come true.

In other words, there are ways to make sure you concentrate on the right things for your own success and the success of the organization you are leading. Here are some suggestions:

- Make an inventory of everything you do during a typical week;
- Critically review the list and decide what can be done by you only, what is your passion and unique capability. Then see what others can pick up (employees and volunteers) (just remember, the fact that you CAN do something, does not mean you should!);
- Set clear expectations for your co-workers and volunteers; perhaps, Reasonable Plus is the approach that would work for you;
- Review your list at least every couple of weeks – are you sticking to what is yours to do?
- Ask a trusted colleague/advisor/mentor to give you direct feedback if they notice that you are slipping back into your old ways;
- Always stay focused on your vision and mission. You cannot go wrong!

References

Deci, E. L., & Ryan, R. M. (2012). Self-determination theory. In P. A. M. Van Lange, A. W. Kruglanski, & E. T. Higgins (Eds.), *Handbook of theories of social psychology* (pp. 416–436). Sage Publications Ltd. https://doi. org/10.4135/9781446249215.n21

https://www.insight-book.com

https://thewisemangroup.com/books/multipliers

Coaching Others

26

Motivating Others to Learn and Change

Richard E. Boyatzis

Let us open with a personal story – yours! Think of someone who helped you the most in your whole life to become who you are. Think of several people. For each person, remember a particular moment in which you learned something important or began a significant change – something that stuck with you possibly through today. In that moment, what did the other person say or do? How did they make you feel? Write some notes to capture the moment like you were going to write a script for a YouTube segment.

---

seriously, pause, and please do the reflection
write your notes in the margins

We have involved several million people around the world in this reflection. They most often tell us that the person cared about them, listened to them, encouraged them, and challenged them. Rarely, if ever, was the moment focused on completing a task or having them fit into a company culture. Nor was it instrumental for job performance. Instead, it was something deeper. And the impact is often still felt decades later. We call these moments *coaching with compassion.*

In our new book with my colleagues Professors Melvin Smith and Ellen Van Oosten, *Helping People Change* (Boyatzis et al., 2019), we review our 39 longitudinal behavior change studies, 3 fMRI (functional magnetic resonance imaging) studies, and 2 hormonal studies of the internal mechanisms of helping or coaching people to learn and change. They point to a clear message that coaching with compassion invokes an openness to new ideas and possibilities. It extends the durability of any learning and change effort.

Sadly, most leaders focus on the tasks and problems at hand. Then, they attempt to motivate others by increasing the pressure or incentives to change and improve their performance. We call this approach to helping and coaching, *coaching for compliance*. You are trying to get someone else to change (or learn) in a direction *you* want. You are trying to get them to comply with your image of what and who they should become. Besides decades of accumulated experience, we now have the research to show that this approach, although well intended, does not work.

Coaching with compassion activates the psycho-physiological state called the *positive emotional attractor*. Coaching for compliance activates what we call coaching for compliance. The chart illustrates some differences between these two attractors. Both are necessary but result in dramatically different sustainable efforts at change and learning.

An example from our book describes how this occurs. It is similar to conversations occurring in offices between leaders and their subordinates. This is about a young high school soccer player. She had been groomed

---

Richard Boyatzis is Distinguished University Professor, professor in the Departments of Organizational Behavior, Psychology, and Cognitive Science at Case Western Reserve University. The author of more than 200 articles, his books include *The Competent Manager*, the international bestseller *Primal Leadership* (with Daniel Goleman and Annie McKee), and *Helping People Change*.

Coach Me! Your Personal Board of Directors: Leadership Advice from the World's Greatest Coaches, First Edition. Edited by Brian Underhill, Jonathan Passmore, and Marshall Goldsmith.
© 2022 John Wiley & Sons Ltd. Published 2022 by John Wiley & Sons Ltd.
DOI: 10.1002/9781119823803.ch26

since adolescence by her parents and coaches to play soccer (the US version of World Association Futbol). The family included a number of great soccer players. Her high school coach had been noticing, however, that she really did not seem to have a passion for the game. After practice one day, he asked her, "Why do you play soccer?" She was puzzled by the question and said, "Because everyone in my family plays soccer. And because I am good at it." Then the coach asked, "But do you love it?"

Somewhat dejectedly, she said, "No, I don't…It was fun when I was younger, but now it feels like something I have to do…I don't want to let my family down." Her coach had noticed something else in her behavior and asked her about it. This resulted in a revelation for both her and her coach. She loved running, but no longer felt the same about soccer. She changed sports and became a phenomenal long-distance runner! Her parents and siblings were using *coaching for compliance*. Her coach was using *coaching with compassion*.

Another example is a VP of IT in a mid-sized company. He was doing quite well and even had an IT consulting business on the side. But he was not feeling as excited or challenged as he had in the past. As part of a leadership program, his coach (one of the authors) asked him to reflect and write a several-page personal vision about the life he dreams he might have in 10–15 years. The essay was all about a social advocacy movement in which he was involved. He mentioned nothing about his work, his relationships, or himself. The coach jokingly said that it was a great vision as long as he had a large trust fund. He laughed and said no, he had worked his way from a very rough neighborhood. The coach worked with him through a dozen reflective exercises and kept hearing what seemed more like an escape than a dream.

Finally, the coach asked him to picture a Friday night returning home. He feels really good about what he did this week. He pours himself a single malt (his favorite drink) and is smiling. The coach then said, "What happened this week that felt so good?" He immediately answered that he had helped a group of inner-city teens learn how the computer was a way to a better life, not some nerdy thing. The coach asked why he did not pursue that. He could not afford his lifestyle, helping his ex-wife and daughter on a teacher's salary. The coach asked if he could spend a half day a week doing a workshop at a local high school, or a day a month at a community college. His eyes lit and his energy returned. Within four months, he was teaching special courses at a large, local community college. In subsequent years, he began mentoring programs for "new-hires" at his company, and then in another company he joined. He was doing his work and pursuing another dimension of his life dream! This is how coaching with compassion can unlock the energy and deep sense of purpose in people. The coach helped this executive to find his dream and make it happen.

Coaching to one's dreams and deeper sense of purpose invokes the positive emotional attractor. Our published research studies show how this psycho-physiological state activates neural networks and hormonal systems that enable a person to be open to new ideas, other people, and emotions. It brings forth a renewed energy that is contagious to others and increases the amount that a person can accomplish at work, at home, and in other settings.

Another C-level executive at a large bank was amazed while going through a leadership program. His coach (one of the authors) asked him to develop his personal dream. It was the single most transformative experience in his life. Later, he said that he was surprised that the company would invest in him, not just his performance. Within 8 months, he lost 100 pounds and kept 80 of them off. He was exercising regularly, running marathons with his wife, and enjoying life at a new level. He began using the technique of coaching with compassion with his subordinates. They were excited and motivated. Within a few years, he was enjoying the developmental activity so much, he asked the CEO to shift him from VP of Audit (which he excelled in) to VP of HR.

The ultimate challenge for leaders is how to motivate people to learn and change. It starts with themselves. Do they feel excited about work and life? Then, it extends to others either directly through coaching activities or through emotional contagion, which happens in thousandths of a second regardless of what emotions the executive is feeling. When activating the positive emotional attractor through coaching with compassion, the renewed excitement and curiosity spread to others.

Most people want to develop, adapt, and explore novelty. By focusing on problems to be solved or tasks to be completed or goals to be achieved, leaders actually turn others off to other possibilities. It is a major contribution to the frighteningly low engagement scores in most organizations. Adding another metric or goal is not motivating. We have shown that it is coaching for compliance. Even if a subordinate complies and makes a change or begins to learn something new, the effort is short lived. It lacks the durability needed because it is a defensive response to a demand from another person. As an obligation, it lacks the self-sustaining neural, hormonal, and emotional state to renew and revitalize.

Leaders can get there. They can inspire others to be open to new ideas and change. But it takes what may seem a counterintuitive approach. Focus on the other person's dreams and their sense of purpose and values. Work on developing resonant relationships characterized by shared vision (purpose), shared compassion (caring), and shared energy.

Reflective Exercises and Conversation Guides (from *Helping People Change*, 2019)

1. Think about a coach or someone else who brought out the best in you. How did you feel about what you were doing and why you were doing it?
2. It is fifteen years from today. You are living your ideal life. You are living in a location that you have always dreamed about. You are living with the people with whom you most want to be living. If work is part of your ideal image, you are doing the type and amount of work you love.
3. What type of coaching do you observe most often in your organization – coaching with compassion or coaching for compliance? Why do you think that is the case? What is the collective impact of this on the organization?

Comparison of Positive and Negative Emotional Attractors (from Boyatzis et al., 2019)

	Positive emotional attractor	Negative emotional attractor
Neuro-endocrine	PNS arousal, empathic neural network	SNS arousal, analytic neural network
Affect	Positive	Negative
Ideal self	Possibilities, dreams, optimism, hope	Problems, expectations, pessimism, fear
Real self	Strengths	Weaknesses
Learning agenda	Excited about trying	Should do performance improvement plan
Experiment/Practice	Novelty, experiments, practice to mastery	Actions expected, things you are supposed to do
Relationships	Resonant	Dissonant or annoying

Reference

Boyatzis, R., Smith, M., & Van Oosten, E.. (2019). *Helping people change: Coaching with compassion for lifelong learning and growth*. Harvard Business Review Press; Boston, MA.

27

The Leader as Coach

Lance Secretan

When Stephanie was promoted recently to the role of CEO, she was thrilled and also felt like a deer caught in the headlights. "What exactly am I supposed to do?" she wondered. "Where do I learn how to be a great CEO?"

I worked with Stephanie to help her move out of her ego-centered fear (will I be effective, admired, successful, etc.?) and instead focus externally on the needs of others (they will quickly tell you what those are!). There is no sophisticated model needed for this. Just (1) what is the most effective and caring way to effectively **listen to** those I lead? (2) Once I identify their needs, what is the best way to meet them? (3) What does it take to inspire others to personal fulfilment and performance? (4) Do we share a dream?

I recently conducted a study of business literature and management journals to discover the most-often referenced "top qualities of a great leader" (Secretan, 2018). Here, alphabetically arranged, is a composite list of what I found. A great leader, it is said, must be:

CEO: Ideal Characteristics

Accountable	Delegator	Intuitive
Adaptable	Diligent	Motivator
Committed to goals	Focused	Positive
Confident	Good communicator	Results oriented
Creative	Honest	Visionary
Decisive		

This is deeply embedded in our business culture and is the default place that most leaders go to, in the absence of any formal training, as they attempt to practice the presumed characteristics of an ideal leader.

I also researched the top qualities that individuals ascribe to their partners in a great relationship/marriage. Here, alphabetically arranged, is a composite list of what I discovered:

Dr. Lance Secretan is one of the world's top authorities on inspirational leadership; a trailblazing teacher, mentor, advisor, and leadership coach (ranked 4th in the world); and a world authority on corporate culture. For his 21 books about inspiration, corporate culture, and leadership, he has received numerous teaching, writing, and humanitarian awards. He is an expert skier, kayaker, and mountain biker, and divides his time between Ontario and Colorado.

Coach Me! Your Personal Board of Directors: Leadership Advice from the World's Greatest Coaches, First Edition. Edited by Brian Underhill, Jonathan Passmore, and Marshall Goldsmith.
© 2022 John Wiley & Sons Ltd. Published 2022 by John Wiley & Sons Ltd.
DOI: 10.1002/9781119823803.ch27

Romantic	Ideal	Characteristics
Affectionate	Honest and ethical	Open-minded
Empathetic	Interesting	Passionate
Forgiving	Intimate	Playful, adventurous, and fun
Generous and serving selflessly	Loving	Respectful and independent
Good listener	Makes you feel special	Trusting
Growing together	Mature	Vulnerable
		Patient

Note how different these lists are from each other. It is as if we are expected to behave as two different people – as a leader on the one hand, and as a spouse, parent, or friend, on the other. Of course, this is an illusion – as if it were possible for us to wake up in the morning as Doctor Jekyll, go to work as Mr. Hyde, and then return as Doctor Jekyll!

The Leader as Coach

Many CEOs assume that the first list is the blueprint for great leadership. However, if we truly want to grow and inspire the people that work for us, we will need to tap into the second list more than the first one. It is the second list of characteristics that has the most powerful and inspirational effect with others. When CEOs really understand the power of creating an inspiring and emotional connection with the people they lead, it becomes clear that the CEO has two roles – coach and leader. Inspiring those we lead requires us to coach others, leaning heavily on the second list of characteristics. A symbolic first step would be to redefine all senior titles as "coach." Thus, the Marketing SVP would become the Marketing Coach, the CFO would become the Financial Coach, and so on.

Leadership theory and thinking have changed a lot in the last 40 years. The invaluable lessons we learned from studying luminaries, such as Peter Drucker, Tom Peters, Warren Bennis, and others, gave us the intellectual platforms on which we built our consulting, coaching and leadership practices. But "management" has given way to "leadership" and "motivation" to "inspiration." What we now understand so much better is that effective leadership is another name for effective coaching, and the heart of effective coaching is inspiration. Our colleagues and clients, like us all, will do the things that inspire them, and, just as importantly, they will not do the things that are uninspiring.

I describe motivation as, "Lighting a fire **under** someone" – it is based on fear – and inspiration as, "Lighting a fire **within** someone" – it is based on love. The underlying (and outdated) principle is that if we "bribe" someone with compensation, bonuses, titles, etc., we will *motivate* them to higher performance. Equally, the other side of this coin is that if we threaten them with a punishment for any failures, this will lessen their occurrence. Most modern leadership and human resource policies are founded on this outmoded carrot-and-stick philosophy.

The leader's role is to build inspiring relationships with others – internally and externally – customers do business with organizations that inspire them; employees love working for organizations that inspire them. Inspiration is the reason we do everything – or not. If our New Year's resolutions do not inspire us, we will not get them done. If our leader does not inspire us to achieve great things, they will not happen. So, our teachers and mentors today are more likely to be the models of this new thinking such as Satya Nadella (Microsoft), Mark Benioff (Salesforce), Ajay Banga (MasterCard), and Jack Ma (Alibaba).

Everything Is Connected

A very successful entrepreneur asked me to be his "leadership coach." After a few weeks of coaching together, I realized he had three major challenges: (1) he had not paid his taxes in years, (2) he was living in barren domestic relationship that he was afraid to end, and (3) he was in a codependency relationship with his addicted son. I explained to him that we needed to tackle these three subjects in order to accelerate his leadership capacity. He turned me down point-blank, arguing "I hired you as my leadership coach and that's all I want to work on." This shows the fundamental misunderstanding we have about the interdependence of all the moving parts in our lives. There are no specialties in coaching. We may speak of "lifestyle" coaches, "executive" coaches, "leadership" coaches, etc., but in reality, none of these aspects are separate parts of our lives.

In my estimation, there are 11 essential aspects of one's life, shown below, all of which must be considered in the relationships we have with our employees or our clients, and each of them must be fully functional in order for us to live to our full potential.

I call this, "The Whole Human® Coaching Model®."

If you touch one of these tightly integrated aspects of our lives, all of the others will be affected too, not just some of them. This is the nature of the human condition.

If your health is at risk or you have domestic strife or financial worries, it is impossible for you not to bring these to work. It is also illusory to believe that none of your colleagues will notice your pain or that you can perform at optimum levels, while your life is in turmoil (can an Olympian athlete achieve a world record after receiving a text that her partner was leaving her?). Each of these unaddressed pain points will drain one's energy, diverting positive energy that could have been invested into high performance.

This change in thinking updates the way we approach people at work. In the past, we used to say that our emotions should be left in the parking lot and that people's personal lives were not any of our business in the workplace. Now, we realize that the opposite is true. We do not have "workers" reporting to us, they are "people" who have joined our community, and they are looking for meaning, fulfilment, purpose, inspiration, and fun. And, these people have multiple aspects to them, all of which they want us to embrace, support, and inspire if we wish to help them grow and become their best selves.

Today, as I coach leaders, my priority is to update their perspective and help them manifest the necessary courage to deal with all aspects of the humans with whom they interact daily. A valuable starting point is to see

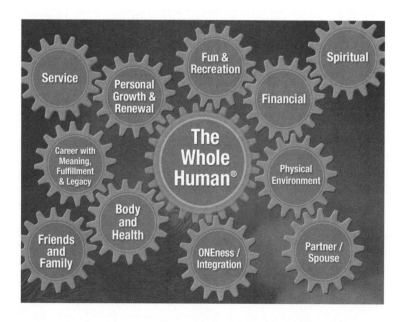

their own personal roles principally as a coach to others, and only secondly as a functional expert, and that inspiring people is undertaken at their level, not ours – the Whole Human. With these realizations, we can change everything – even the world.

Stephanie realized that listening closely and being empathetic, and loving and forgiving helped her connect with and inspire her team more than being accountable, results oriented, or decisive. An old Iroquois saying reminds us, "It takes a strong man to be gentle." The qualities that endear us to human beings will also endear us to those human beings we are privileged to lead.

Reference

Secretan, Lance (2018) *The Bellwether Effect* (pp. 15–17). The Secretan Center Inc.

28

The Five Most Important Qualities in Coaching Your Employees

Anywhere in the World

Howard J. Morgan & Ben Croft

One of the most challenging responsibilities that a leader/manager must do is to effectively coach their employees. Much has been written on the coaching process in the last twenty years, but little has focused on identifying the critical elements for success.

At first glance, many believe that being an effective coach should be inherent or instinctive to a leader. This is untrue for most leaders. For example, Bob, a senior leader with a chemical company, was promoted into a role that required him to lead a 10-person team scattered around the world. His question, given the cultural differences and geographic challenges, what were the key things he needed to do to establish an impactful relationship? To begin, being an effective coach takes intention: it requires the leader/manager to treat coaching in a different manner than most of their other management-focused skills and competencies.

If you have been lucky enough to have experienced a great sports coach as a child (or with your children), you have had exposure to what being a good coach can mean. As with coaching children, it is about encouraging the growth and development of people to help them accomplish goals/levels they thought impossible. After all, we are historically rewarded for providing the answers. In today's high-speed, information, and change-intensive world, however, "having all the answers" is an impossible task.

In our work around the world, a question frequently asked is: "What are the critical things for a leader to understand to be a good coach?" The five coaching qualities below are those that we recognize as having the most applicability for leaders, globally. Many also apply to "mentoring" relationships.

Establish Expectations

When working with someone within your organization, you should anticipate that there may be concerns about the motive behind "coaching" and that the coachee must believe that (s)he can trust you as a coach. Therefore, if you take the initiative to deal with this potential "challenge" proactively, it will lead to greater results. It also protects you from any confusion between your leader role and your coaching role. What does this look like? It means having an upfront discussion with the person that you want to coach and explaining how you would like to help them. Then, determine if they are open to your help. If there is one thing guaranteed not work, it is trying to coach someone that has no interest in either being coached or being coached by you. Recognize that coaching is a gift that you are willing to give, and if they are not willing, just move on. If they are interested, clarify the two roles that you will play. The first is as their

Ben is a multi-award-winning entrepreneur who specializes in executive and leadership coaching. He is the founder of WBECS (World Business & Executive Coach Summit), the world's leading professional coaching event that hosted more than 49,000 attendees this year. He is also the co-founder of The Global Team Coaching Institute, ACE, and five other active companies.

Coach Me! Your Personal Board of Directors: Leadership Advice from the World's Greatest Coaches, First Edition. Edited by Brian Underhill, Jonathan Passmore, and Marshall Goldsmith.
© 2022 John Wiley & Sons Ltd. Published 2022 by John Wiley & Sons Ltd.
DOI: 10.1002/9781119823803.ch28

manager/leader, and the second is as their coach. Indicate that you will mention that this is a "coaching moment" prior to having the discussion. Also, clarify that these discussions will not become part of any evaluation unless progress on the identified area(s) is not visible.

This Is Not about You, It Is about Who You Are Coaching

In many traditional leader/employee relationships, the focus is on you "as leader" and what the employee needs to do to achieve your and the organization's expectations. All reward systems are based on meeting/exceeding goal expectations. However, when engaging in a coaching relationship, there is a more impactful consideration: the personal and professional growth of the coachee. So, as a leader/manager, your lens must shift. It becomes about helping the person achieve clarity about what they want to achieve – in all aspects of their life – and then working with them to create a plan to get there. It is about challenging them to grow/develop to allow them to be more effective performers or even, having more satisfying lives. In our experience, great coaching results in coachees attaining levels that they did not believe possible. The true value of a coach is about recognizing what a person wants and is capable of and then galvanizing them to realize it. Hence, the reason that your leadership lens must be focused on the coachee. Their growth – professional and personal – is your reward. Set the path, monitor progress, and then celebrate success.

Avoid the Advice Trap

Most of us have grown up in the corporate world of leaders who are effective at providing decisions and advice. However, we suggest that for true growth in your coachee, it is more effective to help the person find the solution or decision themselves, rather than providing them with the answer – or advising that they do it your way. It is so critical, our friend Michael Bungay Stanier published a book entitled *The Advice Trap*. We have all heard the Confucius proverb: "Give a man a fish and he will eat for a day. Teach a man to fish and he will eat for a lifetime." Even if the coachee is looking for your specific answer, they will be better able to handle the next issue that arises, if you take the time to coach them through the solutioning process. While we are all driven to solve problems (it is faster, after all), it is more important to identify what the person really needs. If it is to get advice, great. If not, ask questions to bring clarity and to determine the best direction.

Listening and Asking Questions

Being a great coach is about having the ability to listen and ask questions to achieve clarity. Many coaches believe that they are being hired to give opinions and suggestions. This is true, in part. However, it is the ability to listen and analyze that reaps the greatest return on the coaching investment. There is a reason that "listening" is a common action item on leaders' "should do it better" lists. Most of us are action-oriented and feel impatient when we "just" sit and listen. It should be noted that listening is more than just paying attention to a coachee's words. It is about understanding the issue and urgency of what this person is saying and then asking questions and deploying active listening techniques to validate that you have heard and understood these issues. Then and only then, can the two of you come to the best outcome. It is inherent in all human beings to want to be heard. As a coach, leading the coachee to discover and reflect to build conceptual skills and cement learning should be the objective. Listening is also one of the critical signals of your respect. Yet, perceived lack of listening remains one of the main reasons that leaders/managers fail to make great coaches.

Follow-up

We have saved the most important quality for last. A key activity that you should deploy in both your leader/ manager and coaching role is to follow-up. Following up ensures that timelines and deliverables are met, and surprises are kept to a minimum. In coaching, follow up is also critical. No matter what the task/activity, follow-up dramatically ensures a favorable outcome. Likewise, coaching without follow-up will likely lead to disappointment. Following up on issues that have been surfaced in coaching sessions demonstrates that you are committed as their coach and as their leader. It is extremely frustrating when requests/issues disappear into a black hole – never to be resurfaced unless done so by the person.

To ensure that there is a cadence established for follow-up, we recommend that leaders/managers always set a date for the next coaching session at the end of the current one. Also, assign the coachee a "homework" assignment during each session and calendar in the specific items to be revisited. It is also important to keep the coaching follow-up sessions separate from the leader/manager regular updates. You can combine the sessions into one but keep a clear separation on the part of the session that is being used for coaching. Remember, like listening, designated time for professional and personal growth demonstrates genuine care and acknowledgment that commitment to self-improvement is both vital and valued.

So, what are the important questions to ask to ensure that you are embodying the most important qualities?

1. Have I been clear on the expectations for myself, the coachee and the objective?
2. Can I turn my focus to the coachee and their needs?
3. Can I shift into listening mode rather than instructing mode?
4. Am I willing to hold the coachee accountable for their commitment – and am I committed to see it through?
5. What is my plan to put follow-up structure in place?

For the leader, Bob, at the global chemical company, incorporating these qualities did not guarantee success, but given the international and virtual challenges, it did ensure that a foundation was established with his team – and the engagement did not fail. Establishing an intentional process at the start of the coaching relationship allowed Bob and the team to focus on success factors rather than letting cultural differences become the focal point. As Bob continued to become more skilled at deploying the coaching qualities, he established trust with his team, and they performed and were engaged – despite geographic and cultural barriers.

By incorporating these coaching qualities into our leadership behaviors, we will have the opportunity to see our employees thrive – and be rewarded by the leadership legacy we are creating as coaches.

Reference

Stanier, M. B. (2020). *The advice trap.* Box of Crayons Press.

29

The S Curve of Learning

Whitney Johnson

> *"Change is the only constant in life."*
> Heraclitus

It is not just us, and it is not just now; Heraclitus checked in about 535 BCE and checked out about 60 years later, so change has been our fellow traveler and a defining feature of human life for a long, long time.

As a coach, I have worked with many people, especially managers and top executives, who are resistant to change, especially the inevitable changes that occur in the workforce. This is counterproductive; learning to effectively manage change – rather than being managed by it – is Job One. The most important question facing us is "How do I calibrate my organization to at least survive, and ideally thrive, in changing circumstances?"

I will call him John. He was a frustrated and worried high-level executive of a mid-sized firm. One of the top talents on his team was dissatisfied, suddenly underperforming, and the usually accurate rumor mill strongly suggested that this employee was not just casually surveying other opportunities but was deeply engaged in a serious new job search. This was not the first talented team member John had lost; in fact, he felt that these painful personnel disruptions and the effort and expense required to recruit, hire, and integrate replacements was an almost constant irritant undermining the efficacy of his division.

As John and I discussed this common challenge, I asked him, "Why is [your employee] unhappy in her job?" He did not know and had not inquired.

It is astonishing how many otherwise responsible leaders are not having critical conversations with their employees, particularly around the issues of job satisfaction, career ambitions, and next steps. It is as though having expended the aforementioned efforts to onboard a new team member they believe the employee will be content to age in place with them – forever.

Human resources are just that – resources. They demand a thoughtful strategy of long-term investment and development just as other types of business resources do. You need highly engaged, passionate people bringing their best ideas to work for you every day and you need to be *consciously* developing that kind of person. If you are not proactively managing your people for *their* learning, growth, and adaptability you are creating a revolving door through which your best talent will exit.

I laid out for John the S Curve of Learning strategy that I advocate for human resource development. The S Curve was popularized by E.M. Rogers in the 1960s, who used it to model the diffusion of new technologies through the marketplace. We have adapted it to illustrate the process of human growth, as individuals surf their personal *S Curves of Learning.* It helps model how people grow and respond to change.

Whitney Johnson is the CEO of Disruption Advisors, a tech-enabled talent development company, one of the top ten business thinkers globally (Thinkers50) and the #1 Talent Coach – Marshall Goldsmith's Leading Global Coaches. Johnson wrote the Wall Street Journal bestselling book Smart Growth (Harvard Business Press) and hosts the popular Disrupt Yourself podcast.

Coach Me! Your Personal Board of Directors: Leadership Advice from the World's Greatest Coaches, First Edition. Edited by Brian Underhill, Jonathan Passmore, and Marshall Goldsmith.
© 2022 John Wiley & Sons Ltd. Published 2022 by John Wiley & Sons Ltd.
DOI: 10.1002/9781119823803.ch29

An *S Curve of Learning* has three primary phases: a low end, or launch point, where a lot of learning needs to be quickly acquired and yet it can feel like progress is slow. Then follows an ascent up the steep back of the curve. Basic competency has been achieved, and growth is rapid while learning can be exponential. This is a sweet spot of high engagement and greatest productivity. The curve flattens again at the top, mastery has been achieved, and learning and growth decrease as the potential of that curve is being exhausted. Complacency and boredom – disengagement – are on the near horizon.

I was not surprised when John later confided, after having spoken with his disenchanted employee, that high end stagnation was her complaint. It often is. Fortunately, in this case, it was not too late to intervene with a plan to help her move to a new challenge within the team.

Your organization needs to be envisioned as a collection of these S Curves. Every employee is on one, as are you. Ideally, about 60% of your team is operating in the highly engaged sweet spot, 20% is new to your business, or new to their role within it, and the final 20% is being prepared to jump to a new curve before stagnation undercuts performance. As a leader your job is to maximize the growth opportunity along each curve and proactively prepare for each employee's next role.

We recommend the following basic framework for this strategy:

Hire for high potential, rather than maximum proficiency

The goal, in most cases, is to hire or redeploy an employee at the launch point of a new curve. They will be challenged, learning, and growing from day one. At least some of high turnover and persistently high disengagement numbers result from the tandem practices of overinflating job requirements and then hiring the most overqualified applicant, ensuring that boredom is on the near horizon.

Hiring for potential lengthens the S Curve of Learning; it also requires that training and mentoring are well-developed functions within the organization. Helping new employees get up to speed is a responsibility that leaders can – and should – share with individuals who are in danger of running out of room on their own curve. Mentorship can be a new learning experience for them and a gratifying one.

Always consider the possibility of internal movement of personnel. Potential is nowhere better evaluated than on the job, over time. Provide your talented employees with new learning opportunities in-house whenever possible. Retaining engagement is as important as retaining the individual.

Manage employees as individuals on individual learning curves

Launch point: If you have hired, or redeployed, for potential rather than proficiency, an employee at the launch point level of their *S Curve of Learning* should experience considerable challenge. This phase of new learning should be demanding and, periodically, everyone should be in this stage again for ongoing growth. Appropriate metrics should emphasize progress in the role rather than arbitrary goals, and managers should monitor the early months to ascertain that the new employee and the role are a good fit. Value inexperience and encourage questioning; fresh eyes and new thinking are change-friendly and should be welcomed.

Sweet spot: After six months or so, depending on the complexity of a role, an employee should have developed a basic level of competence and be poised for an explosion of growth. This phase is characterized by rapid learning, creativity, innovation, high engagement, and productivity. Individuals on this stretch of their curve should be managed to extend the length of time they spend here. Provide stretch assignments to stimulate additional learning, shake up team configurations, and offer significant problems to solve.

Engage in frequent, regular discussions to ensure that employees know they are valued and prepare both them and you for the day when they will move to a new learning curve. Understand their ambitions for themselves and what they hope to achieve.

High End: It is hard to argue with the importance of those who have mastered their role, but although it may seem that your most valuable employees are those at the high end of the curve this is not necessarily true. The top end is a precarious position – the plateau can quickly become a precipice. Monitor enthusiasm levels as this phase approaches. Does the employee feel there is more to learn in their role, or is their perception and yours that they are exhausting their potential? Identify a timeframe and process for a changing role agreed upon. I estimate the average shelf-life of an employee on an *S Curve of Learning* to be three to four years. Then change is needed to stimulate additional growth. An organization full of stagnant employees will also be stagnant.

It is a challenge to accept this fact and act accordingly. There are impacts to near term productivity that occur when we move highly competent employees to new roles where they are not as adept.

Manage for change to master change

A changing business environment and world means evolving our management techniques as well. It cannot be business as usual if we want to be prepared and competitive in the face of change, much less if we want to lead change. Do not hire the same old way, do not expect people to want to stay unless you help them stay, and do not have a "we like you right where you are" attitude toward the organic, growing, learning machines that work for you.

Humans want to know how to do things. The opportunity to learn motivates beyond money, and even beyond praise. You can harness the power of human learning and growth to propel your organization into the future. An S Curve of Learning leadership strategy develops depth and breadth of capacity in people and promotes their engagement. They become nimble, adaptable, innovative, resourceful, and resilient in the face of change and adept at pivoting before it becomes absolutely necessary. As the individual workers go, so goes the organization. John was able to rescue this situation before it was too late and was better prepared to prevent its frequent recurrence.

Managing Change

30

Leading in Times of Change

Atchara Juicharern PhD

Change is not a stranger to humankind or business. In our history, we have gone from horse carriages to cars with engines, and to self-driving cars today. Digital technology has positively changed the way we live, communicate, and collaborate.

The "change" itself has also changed. While our world has constantly experienced change, the rate of change is speeding up. Markets and business models and technologies are transforming at an accelerated rate, unlike anything that past generations have witnessed.

Currently, the business environment needs to be redefined more often due to these unprecedented changes and a world of uncertainty and volatility – constant change has become our new normal. In particular, following the global health crisis, the business environment could be much more challenging. Virtual work settings present a growing challenge for rapid solutions and implementations.

This rate of change in the world is affecting leaders and organizations and, oftentimes, threatens their survival. Many of the leaders that I coached have revealed that although they breathe and experience change every day, employees in organizations still crave security and safety. In the best case, the leadership team is moving fast, but the rest of the organization continues its previous movement with inertia.

Take the case of Jack, vice president in a leading financial company. I have known Jack for years since he was a senior manager in a small department.

One Monday morning, Jack called me and shared his concern about team inertia and difficulties in moving people out of the comfort zone. His situation this year has also changed, as his boss has expanded his responsibility from leading one department to two departments. An important agenda was also to gradually make the two departments one in the near future. Most of the team members received information from Jack and his boss that this new combined department will become a key driver in successful digital transformation. They also made it clear that downsizing the workforce will not be included in the organization's agenda. Nevertheless, the team members were likely to direct their energy toward securing their current positions rather than firing their energy to develop the new team's capability.

Jack found himself drowning in handling the urgent, but not important, issues day to day and running around finding answers for people. He was fully aware that the organization counts on his leadership – but he did not know where to start or how to make it happen. He thought about providing his team with change management training; however, he and his team members could hardly find the time for it.

Atchara Juicharern (Cara), CEO of AcComm Group, was awarded #1 Coach in Asia by Dr. Marshall Goldsmith. She is a pioneer in developing a simplified coaching process that has helped executives successfully integrate coaching into their leading activities. Her innovative model has enabled the agility and transformation needed by modern organizations.

Coach Me! Your Personal Board of Directors: Leadership Advice from the World's Greatest Coaches, First Edition. Edited by Brian Underhill, Jonathan Passmore, and Marshall Goldsmith.
© 2022 John Wiley & Sons Ltd. Published 2022 by John Wiley & Sons Ltd.
DOI: 10.1002/9781119823803.ch30

As rapid change can create anxiety and confusion, organizations expect leaders to communicate a level of certainty about the path forward and to foster a sense of purpose for their teams. Leading in times of change today has become a critical leadership capability for this era.

In order to thrive proactively in a changing environment, we need a new type of leader that demonstrates open-mindedness, is able of facilitating team agility, fostering team members' continuous learning, and has the ability to become a coach. In other words, leaders need to engage in more communication and coaching rather than commanding and controlling.

Great coaches excel in genuine listening, unleashing people's talents, and aligning people's passion with the priorities of business. Today, leaders' and managers' coaching skills have become increasingly crucial for engaging their teams in continuous development, obtaining insights into markets quickly, and aligning strategic priorities.

A powerful one-to-one coaching conversation can help a person unblock his or her stagnation. However, like the situation of Jack, in order to lead people and teams through a volatile, uncertain, and complex environment at the speed of change in a proactive way, a stand-alone, one-to-one coaching conversation is not sufficient.

While one-to-one coaching is necessary for better engagement in change and for yielding greater speed in removing barriers, leaders need more advanced skills in order to navigate their teams through changes efficiently.

In 2018, I conducted a coaching study by surveying 480 Thai leaders from 28 organizations of different industries in order to better understand the context of how leaders and managers apply coaching within their teams. Sixty-six percent of the leaders used one-to-one coaching to help their subordinates adjust to changes, and 57% applied team coaching to drive changes. Yet, the majority of them sought ways to coach and facilitate the whole team productively and constructively (Juicharern, 2018).

My Suggestions

In order to help teams adapt and develop themselves in times of change, leaders need additional skills and tools that are practical and relevant to their strategic direction and execution. Learning at the speed of business today should be fast, yet deep and with strategic relevance. It begins with the self and then people and teams.

Leading Self

At a personal level, leaders also need to be able to renew themselves, develop resilience, and adapt to change quickly in order to succeed in an ambiguous and turbulent environment.

Every time we take a flight, we always hear this part of the safety announcement before the take-off: "In the event of a sudden decrease in cabin pressure, oxygen masks will drop from overhead – if you are traveling with small children, please put on your own mask before assisting them." This idea applies not only to flying, but also to living and leading. If we fail to save ourselves first, we are likely to fail in saving others.

Oftentimes, we overlook the fact that leaders also need help in shifting their frame of mind. Organizations need to provide deeper level of development for leaders, and it is necessary to equip them with the key skills and tools that enable them to motivate and lead themselves through times of change.

An inside-out approach also allows leaders to experience the skills and tools first. Having experienced them, leaders will understand their team members better and support them to adapt to changes at faster rate. **Jack experienced both the beauty and clarity of this process through our executive coaching sessions. He was energetic and more than ready to launch the next steps.**

Leading People

This is the set of skills that helps leaders exercise powerful one-to-one coaching conversations with each team member. Leaders at all levels normally need **a simple** structure rather than a complicate process to help them hold high-impact coaching conversations where development is needed. Done well, the team member is likely to feel motivated, empowered, and will voluntarily become a part of the change rather than "being changed."

Leading Teams

High-performance and agile teams are engaged in understanding the current customers' needs and wants, and they are quick in leveraging internal resources and strengths in responding to external triggers. Leaders need advanced skills for participative leadership and effective facilitation of team dynamics. Without this capacity, some teams may be detached from the senior leadership's change initiatives.

A best practice of developing leaders to master these skills is to use the real change issues in the practice sessions. In our team coaching sessions, Jack brought the real teams and issues into the practices, both Jack and team members acquired not only the new mindset and the skills, but also an inspiring change vision and a concrete plan to execute.

Conclusion

Toward the end of our coaching journey, Jack reflected that when he empowered the teams to create the answers and craft the united plan together, it was much more relevant to them, and they owned it. Jack became confident in navigating his teams in a participative way. Most importantly, he found himself much more productive and resilient in his new role.

Leadership development also requires certain changes – leaders at all levels need new capabilities to constantly navigate themselves and others, including teams, in times of change. The development process should integrate their real-life challenges, strategies, and executions into interventions so that they learn and lead at the same time. The strong connection of the self to the process will help to keep these capabilities in the organization for the long term, through changes that will imminently coming.

Homework and Exercise

The following questions can help you explore if leaders or the team leader of your organization need support for developing new leadership capability in order to be able to lead in times of change:

– *Is your team facing an unprecedented acceleration of change?*
– *How are you navigating yourself in this environment of constant change?*
– *How are you navigating your team?*
– *Do you need any new skills in leading your team at the speed of change?*
– *Is your team experiencing chaos or inertia?*
– *What processes or structures do you need in order to lead teams that are stable yet agile and flexible regarding change?*

Organizations with strong leaders who anticipate and harness the power of change will be the winners of tomorrow.

Reference

Juicharern, A. (2018). *Leader and manager as coach – An exploratory study of coaching within organizations.* Bangkok: AcComm Group. https://www.aclc-asia.com/post/leader-and-manager-as-coach-an-exploratory-study-of-coaching-within-organizations

31

Coaching the Team Leader

Peter Hawkins

When I first met Phillipe, he had just become CEO of a financial services firm that was growing fast. It was his first CEO role having previously been a COO elsewhere. Phillipe was a young very bright CEO who when I first met him was looking exhausted and haggard. Frustration and impatience poured out of him.

"So many of my direct reports just are not stepping up….I can't rely on them….I have to rewrite their reports before they go to the Board, ….they keep telling me what is wrong with their colleagues and blaming each other," he complained.

I listened deeply and could feel in my body both the frustration and the anxiety.

"How much longer can you last going on like this?" I asked.

"I will either be exhausted or crack before the end of the year unless something shifts." He replied, "Will you sort this team out for me – because I have heard that you are good at sorting teams out."

"I am certainly very open to supporting you and working with you and the team to discover the gap between where you are today and where you need to be in a year's time and then find out whether I can help you on that journey. I can't sort THEM out for you. It will require a shift in you, the team, and the relationships between you. Are you up for that?"

There was a long pause.

"I guess I know I have to change too – but currently I am spinning and cannot see a way out."

I shared how I deeply empathized with him, having been in a similar place myself when I was CEO of a consultancy business and it felt like it ALL rested on my shoulders. The more I delegated the more issues came bouncing back to me.

"Yes that is exactly what it feels like – spinning plates and making sure not only I, but none of my team let any of them fall."

This opened up a year's journey of partnering this CEO on his journey, which I have categorized as the journey from "Team Manager" to "Team Leader" to "Team Orchestrator" to "Team Coach" (Hawkins 2021, pp. 280–284).

Team Manager to Team Leader

Our second meeting focused on exploring the purpose of the team: "What could they uniquely do that their stakeholder world of tomorrow needed?" and "What could they only achieve by working collaboratively that they couldn't achieve by working in parallel?" He gradually realized he was not tapping into so much of the

Peter Hawkins has been coaching senior executives and their leadership teams for over 40 years across many sectors and in many different countries. He has been a global pioneer in Systemic Team Coaching. He is Emeritus Professor of Leadership at Henley Business School and Chairman of Renewal Associates, United Kingdom.

Coach Me! Your Personal Board of Directors: Leadership Advice from the World's Greatest Coaches, First Edition. Edited by Brian Underhill, Jonathan Passmore, and Marshall Goldsmith.
© 2022 John Wiley & Sons Ltd. Published 2022 by John Wiley & Sons Ltd.
DOI: 10.1002/9781119823803.ch31

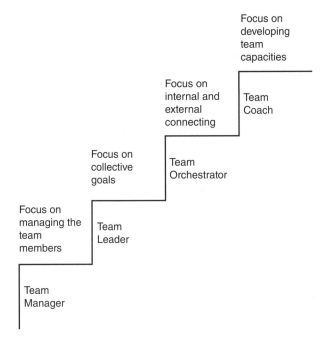

Figure 31.1 The journey from team manager to team coach: team leader's focus.

potential of the team. Having articulated the unique purpose of the team and what he termed "The collaboration dividend," we rehearsed how he was going to present that to the team. I asked him how he could ask the team for their help in developing this purpose and making it happen. Only on his third rehearsal in the session, did he find a place where he was asking from his head and heart and not indirectly telling them what to do.

At our next session, he was excited. He told me how the team had responded to his sharing the challenges and opportunities and asking for their help, by wanting to get involved in shaping the team's purpose and how they could achieve it together. He asked me to coach the day workshop they wanted to have to create this together.

Following what was a high-energy, participative workshop, I worked with Phillipe to explore how he could reshape their weekly team meetings. Now, they would be focused much less on each person reporting back to him on what they had done, and were going to do, and much more on joint team challenges and review of team performance. Once he had arrived at a new design with us both standing at a white board, brainstorming key issues, and moving them around, we explored how he could get the team to co-create the team meeting improvement together before he offered his suggestions. "If they are part of co-creating the way forward," I said, "they are much more likely to commit to and own making it happen."

After we had run a team workshop in which we explored the team at its best and at its worst; the team not only came up with a new team meeting deign, but also behaviors they would support each other in doing. These included: making offers of help; building on each other's suggestions; and challenging whether the agreements made were realistic. They also produced a list of team behaviors they would support each other in stopping, such as blaming others, either in the team or outside; interrupting each other mid-sentence; and talking about issues that only involved two team members and could be resolved in a one-to-one meetings.

I attended two of their weekly meetings following this workshop and offered three "time-outs" when I stopped the process in order to make an intervention. The first one was to invite each team member to comment on a helpful piece of behavior they had noticed from another team member that was helpful to the meeting. The second was about halfway through and was to ask each team member to complete the sentences, with no discussion afterwards:

"The most value creating thing we have done in the first half of this meeting is…."
"What would make the second half even more value creating is…."

Team Leader to Team Orchestrator

The next time we met one-to-one, he told me the meetings were much better, with much more flow across the table rather than everything directed at him. He was amazed at how creative some of them were at resolving each other's issues. There was a real feeling that he had moved from a frazzled team manager to a team leader. However, he went on to say that his time was still burdened by his direct reports coming to him complaining about other team members not keeping to their commitments or behaving badly. He resolved that, from that day, he would stop them in mid flow and ask them: "What did x say when you told them that?" and when they said they had not told them directly, he would say: "How can I help you have that conversation?"

Over the coming weeks, he gradually moved from being the conduit for communication to a "team orchestrator", not just internally redirecting conversations and getting out of being the go-between or referee. We worked together on how many of the meetings in which he was the spokesperson for the team and organization could be done by others. I had asked him pointedly, how many of the team members could step up and lead and represent the team if something happened to him? When after some thought, he had gestured a big fat zero, I asked him what would need to happen to get this to two or three, in the next 3 months. Having key team members go with him to important external meetings and then be the key representative, representing the whole team, accelerated this process.

Team Orchestrator to Team Coach

Nine months after we had first met, I asked Phillipe, "how can you take on more of my role in coaching the team?" In our sessions, we had already explored how individual sessions with team members could move from bringing problems for him to sort out, to a more of a coaching style, where he was developing their capability and capacity as leaders of the business. Now, we had to explore how he could coach the team collectively. He resolved that each month he would ask one of the team members to play a process facilitation role for a series of meetings and receive feedback from the team on what was helpful. He also said that he wanted to run the next team workshop himself but have me help him design it and then debrief how it went.

A year since we first met, I repeated the team 360° feedback process we had used at the start, getting feedback on the team's functioning, not only from all the team members, but also their key stakeholders (Board members, direct reports, two key suppliers, and three key customers). Following this, I coached my last workshop with the team, where we used the feedback to bank the collective changes as well as the learning and development of both the team and the team members, and work on how they would take the learning and development forward without my help in the coming year. They also gave me feedback on what they valued and what more and different I could have done in helping them.

I thought that was the end of the story but 2 years later I received a call from Phillipe, he was planning to move on, and asked if we could have a few sessions on managing his "last hundred days" and leaving well. But that is another story!

Having read this story, where do you think you are on the journey from team manager to team leader, to team orchestrator, to team coach? What two or three ideas from this story could you use in moving your leadership, your team, and the relationship between you, further along this continuum?

Reference

Hawkins, P. (2021). *Leadership Team Coaching: Developing collective transformational leadership* (4th ed). Kogan Page (translated into Spanish Chinese and Japanese).

32

Coaching and Culture Transformation for Sustainable Results

Dr. Peter Chee & Aaron Ngui

Lynn was visibly worried when she touched upon the subject of her work as the head of organization development of a large electronics manufacturer. "I was given a huge task by the Chief People Officer to create a coaching culture at work. Many of the leaders at the executive level are not supportive and are not convinced that coaching is the way forward." She continued, "They don't believe that coaching can have significant impact on business results and so do not want to spend the time and effort to learn the skill. I'm worried that I'm going to fail."

Lynn was given 18 months to enable culture change focused on a high-performance coaching culture to outperform competitors, win market share, and achieve bottom line results. This came after an economic downturn that negatively impacted profits and revenue. Some employees were let go through a voluntary separation package and various other cost cutting measures implemented.

Lynn's CPO had the conviction that a high-performance coaching culture would permeate the entire organization by empowering and unleashing vast human potential for high trust employee engagement to accelerate people development that enables effective strategies and execution for the attainment of bottom-line results, sustainable growth, and competitive advantage.

I told her that I appreciated the scale of the project entrusted on her shoulders. To me, the first thing was to find out if Lynn herself practiced coaching. "If there is no role-model to follow, there would be no one for others to emulate," I told her. She admitted with a rueful laugh that it was also difficult for her to coach her team too. "I would usually just tell them what to do quickly and expected them to follow my instructions," she laughed.

Intuitively, I knew that this was the moment for me to add more value by encompassing coaching techniques. I shared with her the Daily Active Question (DAQ) process, developed by Marshall Goldsmith. The DAQ is simple but profound. It starts with the person asking a question on something that is important to them, "Have I done my best today to ...?" For example, "Have I done my best to coach others to meet their goals?" if the answer is "Yes", then well done; if the answer is "No," then the individual immediately knows he or she has to step up to do their best the next day.

Dr. Peter Chee is the CEO of ITD World, a multinational corporation with the mission of transforming leaders to change the world for the better. He specializes in coaching, developing, and transforming, CEOs, CXOs, and senior global leaders from the world's leading organizations including Intel, United Nations, Siemens, PepsiCo, Coca-Cola, Micron, First Solar, and Western Digital. Peter ranks among the top global coaching gurus, with more than 33 years' experience in developing leaders from over 80 countries. He was awarded the #1 Strategic Innovation Coach by Dr Marshall Goldsmith.

Aaron Ngui is the Global Projects Head and Chief Editor for ITD World. He is involved in several initiatives including developing the Let's Coach app and ITD World eLearning programs. He is engaged in digital marketing and content creation for both online and offline marketing channels.

Coach Me! Your Personal Board of Directors: Leadership Advice from the World's Greatest Coaches, First Edition. Edited by Brian Underhill, Jonathan Passmore, and Marshall Goldsmith.
© 2022 John Wiley & Sons Ltd. Published 2022 by John Wiley & Sons Ltd.
DOI: 10.1002/9781119823803.ch32

I shared this technique with Lynn and her face lit up. She promised to use the DAQ as a constant reminder to coach her team instead of just bossing them around. She then shared with me her five-question DAQs. She got her assistant to be her accountability partner who used her phone to set a daily recurring reminder, so she never missed keeping Lynn accountable.

In our next session, she spoke brightly of her experience in coaching her team members with improved results. As we talked about next steps, she expressed interest in wanting to get better as a coach.

"I'd like to share with you the PIFR model, which means Prepare, Implement, Feedback and Reflect," I offered. "Putting the model in action means you would Prepare well before your coaching session. Perhaps you can think of questions to ask, and what the coachee wants to achieve during the session. Then comes the Implementation stage where you execute your plans as best as you can and stay flexible to fulfill the needs of the coachee."

"Next, you can obtain Feedback from your coachee. You can also obtain feedback from yourself by pinpointing what you can do better and note those down. When you Reflect, you would want to be very clear about what you would do to improve the next time around, and then repeat the PFIR process over again to continuously improve," I shared.

From the feedback received, Lynn realized that she needed to avoid advise oriented and judgmental questions and focus on empowering and buy-in questions. To ask better questions, she used trigger words such as "I am curious, please tell me more about this; I am fascinated, please share with me more about this." She prepared examples of powerful and buy-in questions to ask. Lynn also used a visual reminder at all her sessions to stay mindful in enabling people to set their own compelling goals instead of telling them what to do.

Over the next sessions, I also shared with her the Speed Coaching Tool (SCT) which she could use to quickly coach others for results. The SCT represents best practices and questions coaches can use to zoom in on issues and solutions within a short timeframe. She used this so effectively that other leaders in her organization started to take notice.

I then challenged her on how she could get buy-in from leaders and asked her what the concerns of those recalcitrant executives were. "Well, most of them say they do not have the time to coach," she answered. "What's one thing you can do with them so they can get results speedily?" I asked. With a twinkle in her eye, Lynn immediately caught on of my intuitive response and excitedly said she would share the SCT with her leaders.

"Peter, I am so glad I shared the SCT with my peers, the feedback from them was very encouraging." "How encouraging?" I asked. Lynn said many were skeptical, but she coached them on how to use the SCT effectively. Although they began tentatively, the results obtained lent credibility to Lynn's efforts and many more were brought on board as the coaching habit began to set in.

I continued to challenge her on what she could be doing better to get more buy-in from the wider organization, especially the key C-suite. This question struck her, and after a while, she told me she was going to start a coaching initiative modelled after coaching gurus in the world.

"I am going to coach 20 people personally and support them for the next six months in the pursuit of their breakthrough goals. As long as I am with them along the way and that they hit their targets, I think I should be able to convince more people of the power of coaching," she said.

With that challenge driving her on, Lynn ignited her "LS20" initiative and took on 20 persons the next week. She used her intuition, wisdom, and coaching skills to get the best out of them. Although some were just along the ride initially, her sincerity in wanting the best for them eventually won their hearts, with many obtaining the desired outcomes during the six months.

In a subsequent conversation, Lynn asked, "Peter, would you mind coaching my CEO?" I was elated. "No, I won't mind at all, but please tell me how this happened," I replied.

Lynn said the success of her team, coupled with the LS20 initiative and increasing interest in coaching among her peers and direct reports reached the ears of the CEO. "I was asked about the status of the project to create a high-performance coaching culture in the organization."

Realizing that this was a good chance to get the support of the entire C-suite, Lynn and the CPO strategized on how to make the best case to drive coaching within the organization. "I communicated the tremendous benefits derived from coaching, along with success stories and evidence of results. I showed my CEO the results, and he was delighted with the progress."

"That is interesting, how did you do it?" the CEO asked. Lynn shared two key factors which drove her onward. "I told him the first was my Self-Initiated Rewards (SIR) where I would reward myself with a recreational club membership when I succeeded." "The second is my Self-Initiated Consequence (SIC)," she continued, "In that I would have to donate $2,000 to a political party I detested and vote for it in the next election. I wanted to avoid giving them my money and support at all costs," she told her CEO as she tried hard to suppress a laugh.

Lynn said that she also applied the SIR and SIC to the people she coached which gave them the impetus to pursue their goals with full commitment. "I ensured the goals set followed the SMARTEST (Specific, Measurable, Achievable, Relevant, Time-bound, Engaging, Satisfying, and Team-based) principle." Lynn said having such compelling well-defined goals motivated people for results. The CEO seemed impressed but needed further nudging. "I then stepped up by asking him if he would want to be coached by you, so that is why I am asking you this today," she told me.

The results of my coaching the CEO, and Lynn driving the project, have borne fruit. The organization rapidly instituted a roadmap for the entire group to create a high-performance coaching culture. Lynn was placed in charge of the effort. Progress accelerated once the CEO was convinced by the power of coaching.

The CEO himself started coaching his team and direct reports. This positive practice and vibe cascaded down to the other management executives and support staff too. In 18 months, the organization overachieved on their bottom-line targets and won sizeable market share in a remarkable turnaround of fortunes, making this an unforgettable and fulfilling journey.

In this story, I mentioned about the Speed Coaching Tool (SCT) Lynn used to coach others. To utilize the tool effectively, I like to share with you the best practices to do so:

1. Listen fully and deeply, observe, and use your intuition
2. Ask great questions (And what else? Tell me more)
3. Appreciate and encourage
4. Provide feedback and suggestions with consent
5. Summarize, simplify-focus on what is most important
6. Move to action with timeline and commitment.

You can also apply these simple yet powerful questions in coaching for a duration of 15–20 minutes on a daily basis.

1. What's your most compelling goal?
2. How can you achieve it? (also consider your strengths and opportunities)
3. What stopping or blocking you? (also consider your weaknesses and threats)
4. What are your best game-changing solutions?
5. What support, resources, and systems do you need to win?
6. What are the different scenarios that you may face? (e.g., best case, worst case, and alternatives)
7. What do you need to do to be prepared for the different scenarios?
8. What are your action steps and timeline?

33

Agile Servant Leadership Is Not Fluffy

Jennifer Paylor

Jake Kirby was a key executive leading an agile team responsible for developing the next-generation cloud technology at a struggling enterprise. He was passionate about the technology and even more so about the mission of improving the work environment by shifting to an open and agile culture, from one of bureaucracy, control, and fear. Jake envisioned an agile workplace that was nimble, collaborative, open, and innovative where teams were self-empowered, taking risks, and learning from failure. After a long, hard fight, Jake realized that it would be nearly impossible to change a regime where bureaucrats are promoted to perpetuate a culture of fear.

During my executive coaching sessions with Jake, I was amazed at how much resilience he had to fight the many battles in order to serve the needs of the people. Every day, he would wake up to make work better for the hundreds of thousands of people in the company. Jake's peer leaders did not seem bothered about the employee disengagement, HR complaints, lack of innovation, red-tape, low customer NPS scores, and the employee-manager trust deficit. His peers were mostly concerned with getting their next promotion, and they used fear tactics to keep people oppressed. Jake saw how this way of leading was outdated and how it was killing the innovation the company so desperately needed to have a competitive edge in the market. It was extremely difficult to attract and retain top talent from the market. Despite the agile transformation and positive leadership campaigns, Jake's peer leaders were not willing to abandon their destructive leadership ways to bring about a better outcome.

Jake's agile team delivered a platform to the market in record timing. Something that would have taken 3 years took 9 months using the agile ways of working. Agile is more than daily standups, retrospectives, showcases, sprint planning, funnels, and velocity. At the core, it is about delivering more value to your stakeholders, quickly learning from failures through iterations, and celebrating success. Leading in an agile environment takes energy, resilience, motivation, growth mindset, courage, and vulnerability. An unhealthy ego should be the first to go!

One day, Jake informed me that he would not be on our virtual coaching session because he was not physically able to speak. He had been hospitalized and had lost his ability to speak due to a sudden illness. During his recovery period, Jake and I were able to stay in contact via email and text messages. Jake's manager did not check on him or his family, while he was in the hospital. Once Jake returned home and back to work, we continued our normal coaching sessions, and I could sense that he was emotionally hurt beyond repair. There was another time after this when Jake's daughter broke her leg at jockey practice in school and she had to have surgery. Jake told me that life-long dreams can easily be snatched away from anyone in the blink of an eye.

Jennifer Paylor is currently the Head of Learning & Development, Talent, and Culture for Capgemini in North America. She is an influential and provocative business thought-leader, and she holds a published patent for inventing a coaching system for guiding interactions. Jennifer is widely known for creating and operationalizing the largest internal corporate coaching practice in the world at IBM.

Coach Me! Your Personal Board of Directors: Leadership Advice from the World's Greatest Coaches, First Edition. Edited by Brian Underhill, Jonathan Passmore, and Marshall Goldsmith.
© 2022 John Wiley & Sons Ltd. Published 2022 by John Wiley & Sons Ltd.
DOI: 10.1002/9781119823803.ch33

During these moments with Jake, it was easy to make the connection between agile ways of working and servant leadership. If you read the Manifesto for Agile Software Development at agilemanifesto.org, you will see where the writers of the manifesto valued the following:

- Individuals and interactions over processes and tools
- Working software over comprehensive documentation
- Customer collaboration over contract negotiation
- Responding to change over following a plan
  (https://agilemanifesto.org)

Doesn't that sound a lot like Jake Kirby? The leader in an agile environment values individuals, interactions, working software, customer collaboration, and responding to change more than the usual bureaucratic practices that are common in machine companies. In order to bring about an agile culture where these values are prioritized, servant leadership is essential. In 1970, Robert K. Greenleaf published an essay entitled The Servant as Leader and wrote:

The servant-leader is servant first… It begins with the natural feeling that one wants to serve, to serve first. Then conscious choice brings one to aspire to lead. That person is sharply different from one who is leader first, perhaps because of the need to assuage an unusual power drive or to acquire material possessions…The leader-first and the servant-first are two extreme types. Between them there are shadings and blends that are part of the infinite variety of human nature.

The difference manifests itself in the care taken by the servant-first to make sure that other people's highest priority needs are being served. The best test, and difficult to administer, is: Do those served grow as persons? Do they, while being served, become healthier, wiser, freer, more autonomous, more likely themselves to become servants? And what is the effect on the least privileged in society? Will they benefit or at least not be further deprived?

According to Greenleaf.org, "Servant leadership is a philosophy and a set of practices that enriches the lives of individuals, builds better organizations, and ultimately creates a more just and caring world."

In this next section, we will see that servant leadership drives an agile culture, the growth of people, and the bottom line.

I have heard many executives dismiss using servant leadership to lead agile transformations as being "derogatory," "soft," "fluff," "religious," and/or "outdated." In reality, servant leadership positively impacts business results, customer satisfaction, time-to-market, innovation, value creation, and employee engagement by inspiring self-empowered teams, building community, risk-taking, learning from failures, helping people grow, and being in service to others.

In October 2018, Mckinsey published *Leading agile transformation: The new capabilities leaders need to build 21st century organizations*. From years of research, McKinsey found that "Agile organizations can develop products five times faster, make decisions three times faster, and reallocate resources adroitly and quickly" (De Smet et al., 2018).

Garry Ridge, CEO of WD-40, known for his servant leadership and agile culture said "Leadership is about learning and teaching. Why waste getting old if you can't get wise? We have no mistakes here, we have learning moments" (Skibola, 2011).

When asked about "transforming an ailing company into an industry darling," Cheryl Bachelder, past CEO of Popeyes Louisiana Kitchen answered, "adopt servant leadership" (Bachelder, 2018). Cheryl Bachelder is famously known for embedding servant leadership to grow the company's bottom line. For 9 years, she increased restaurant sales by 45% and doubled the profit. The stock price rose over $61 from $13. Bachelder wrote in her book, *Dare to Serve: How to Drive Superior Results by Serving Others* (Bachelder, 2018a), that "our belief was that serving people well would generate better business results."

There are company leaders who continue to ignore the incredible return-on-investment (ROI) from servant leadership as a part of their business strategy. They continue to pretend that machine companies can get away with going through the motions by adopting agile rituals and techniques into their bureaucracies only to find out that it will never ever succeed. Agility and bureaucracy are mutually incompatible. The nature of bureaucracies was not meant for agility, nimbleness, critical thinking, and, most importantly, servant leadership. It was just the opposite.

Max Weber, a German sociologist, political economist, and philosopher, is known for popularizing the construct of a bureaucracy. To him, a bureaucracy was the perfect way to manage large complex organizations. It was the lesser of two evils when compared to the feudalism. In Max Weber's *Economy and Society*, originally published in 1922, "the decisive reason for the advance of bureaucratic organization has always been its purely technical superiority over any other form of organization. The fully developed bureaucratic apparatus compares with other organizations exactly as does the machine with the non-mechanical modes of production. Precision, speed, unambiguity, knowledge of the files, continuity, discretion, unity, strict subordination, reduction of friction and of material and personal costs..." (Denham & Bratton, 2014, p. 264). Over a hundred years later, many companies still subscribe to this organizational design and management system and will go down in history as failures like Kodak, Blockbuster, and Polaroid.

We have been witnessing the crippling of the Frederick Winslow Taylor machine organizations based on scientific management due to the disruptive digital economy that has transformed entire industries and business models. Research from McKinsey shows "the agile organization is dawning as the new dominant organizational paradigm" (Aghina et al., 2018). At the core of these, nimble and agile organizations are servant leaders like Jake Kirby.

Jake Kirby is now a senior executive at a great cognitive and cloud company serving his team and customers while building the next-generation technology that is already saving lives. Last but not least, Jake's daughter is back on the saddle and on the path to becoming a great horse jockey one day in the future.

References

Aghina, W. et al. (2018). *The five trademarks of agile organizations*. McKinsey. https://www.mckinsey.com/business-functions/organization/our-insights/the-five-trademarks-of-agile-organizations

Bachelder, C. (2018a). *Dare to serve: How to drive superior results by serving others*. Berrett-Koehler Publishers.

Bachelder, C. (2018b). *Serving performs with Cheryl Bachelder*. CherylBachelder.com. https://cherylbachelder.com/books/dare-to-serve-by-cheryl-bachelder

De Smet, A., Lurie, M., & St. George, A. (2018). *Leading agile transformation: The new capabilities leaders need to build 21st-century organizations*. McKinsey. https://www.mckinsey.com/business-functions/organization/our-insights/leading-agile-transformation-the-new-capabilities-leaders-need-to-build-21st-century-organizations

Denham, D., & Bratton, J. (2014). *Capitalism and classical social theory* (2nd ed.). University of Toronto Press, Higher Education Division.

Skibola, N. (2011). *Leadership lessons from WD-40's CEO Garry Ridge*. Forbes. https://www.forbes.com/sites/csr/2011/06/27/leadership-lessons-from-wd-40s-ceo-garry-ridge/#42bd60391fae

https://www.agilemanifesto.org

https://www.greenleaf.org/what-is-servant-leadership

34

Leading Teams through Crisis

Karen Yanqun WU

In 2020, the Chinese people had a special Spring Festival. Coronavirus swept across China, not only endangering people's lives but also stopping all economic activities. In February, CEO Bruce called me and shared his depression. Bruce runs a business on marketing consultant services producing marketing videos and distributing various media for SME customers. Because of COVID, most of the clients paused their normal operations and Bruce's business was impacted heavily.

When the HR Head reported to Bruce the employee compensation plan, he was triggered. The company was in a very difficult time with no income, but the HR Head only focused on this administrative work – and the compensation plan caused even higher costs.

Bruce shouted at the lady, "You are not deserving to be in this executive position." The HR Head cried and told him that she was too tired and wanted to resign on the next day. In addition, Bruce also shared with me that his relationship with his other team members became tense under this big pressure. It was agreed to have a group coaching with his leadership team.

I developed the following 6C model, which provided a structure for this group coaching. It shows three phases the leaders need to pass through in turbulent times: Sensing the Crisis, Handling the Crisis, and Making Breakthrough. To bring the team to "Making Breakthrough" in a turbulent time, the leader needs to be compassionate, confident, and courageous in their inner core. In addition, leaders need to make a series of tangible actions, including proactively connecting people, candid communication, and co-creating solutions.

When an organization is in a turbulent period, it is very typical for people to feel insecure and unconsciously share their helplessness and anxiety, which leads to the rapid spread of negative emotions and systemic anxiety. Meanwhile, people have higher expectations on their leaders to find a way out. In this case, leaders have much higher pressure and tension than usual, which may cause them to make poor decisions with unclear thinking. So, the first step for the leaders is to be aware of their emotions and be compassionate with themselves and to the people around them.

Sensing the Crisis

Inner state: Compassion

Leaders with compassion can fully understand and accept everyone's negative emotions during the turbulent period and better support everyone to build a sense of security at the psychological level. This is the foundation in facing the crisis.

Karen is the founder and CEO of Co-wisdom Coaching (based in China), PCC from ICF, and co-founder of ICF Beijing Chapter. Karen has been named among the "Top 50 World Leaders in Coaching" by Thinkers50. She is the faculty of Global Team Coaching Institute and also a member of Marshall Goldsmith 100.

Coach Me! Your Personal Board of Directors: Leadership Advice from the World's Greatest Coaches, First Edition. Edited by Brian Underhill, Jonathan Passmore, and Marshall Goldsmith.
© 2022 John Wiley & Sons Ltd. Published 2022 by John Wiley & Sons Ltd.
DOI: 10.1002/9781119823803.ch34

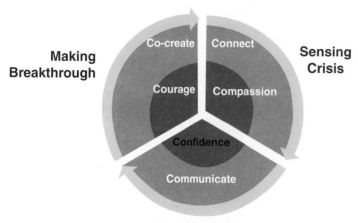

6C Model by Co-wisdom Coaching.

It cannot be ignored that leaders must first have empathy for themselves and be aware of their negative emotions faster than the normal person and avoid being stuck in this instinctive reaction.

In the group coaching session, I asked Bruce's leadership team to share their answer to the following two questions:

1. What is my current emotion? What is triggering my emotions?
2. What can I focus on now to help me calm down?

Everybody noticed that they were same – they were anxious, and their "bad behaviors" were triggered by anxiety. As examples, the Head of the Video Producing Team kept himself isolated and the VP of Sales resisted and complained when Bruce asked him to think about new business opportunities. The HR head was overwhelmed and felt lonely without any support from the team. Bruce noticed that his shouting added fuel to the fire. This conversation helped them to understand each other and calm down first.

When the leaders calmed down, they were able to empathize with others and focus on what they could do. It was time to expand their empathy and ability to all stakeholders so that they can take real action.

Outer action: Proactive connection to shorten social distance

In difficult times, leaders must put aside their privileges, take the initiative to connect with people, and show "I am same with you." It shortens the social distance with people and builds unprecedented trust. Only when you let people feel that you really care about them and stay with you, they are inspired and able to make a real change. Proactive connection can be just a short greeting from the heart such as "Are you okay now?" or remind everyone to take a break to prevent team burnout.

When I noticed Bruce and the leaders calm down and connect with each other, I asked them to empathize with their people and their customers and to think about what they can do to connect to those stakeholders. The questions below can help leaders create a heart-based connection.

1. What do I perceive the difficulties and challenges of stakeholders (such as the team, partners, and customers) to be during this period?
2. What can I do to make everyone feel cared for?

When I met with the leadership team, I divided them into three groups. Each group took different stakeholders into consideration.

The first group were asked to think about C-suite team's emotions, including those of the chairman. The leadership team started to understand that these leaders were depressed and worried that the company was going through a difficult and stressful time. They also realized that the CEO needs help from the whole leadership team.

Group 2 considered the employees, who were also under stress and looking for guidance from the leadership team. They were worried about their jobs and felt a lot of uncertainty and concerns about job security. The leadership team needed to show empathy and ensure that the employees were working together to find solutions in the workplace and helping them to be able to work on themselves to get through the tough time.

Group 3 focused on the clients' emotions. Because business had slowed down, the clients worried about their jobs and career development, while they had a lot of spare time in the home. The group was able to innovate in a new way and was able to develop an online video training program that was different than anything they had done before. The energy from creating this helped generate excitement and expand their business model from b2b to b2c.

Handling the Crisis

- Inner state: Confident
  To handle the crisis, the leaders must be full of confidence and hope, and then they can inspire the team and build collective confidence. Napoleon Bonaparte said that "A leader is a dealer in hope."
  Following the ideas from the "connect" step, I led the leaders to truly believe themselves and the organizations with the following questions:

  1. What are the strengths and qualities of your team that can help the company survive the crisis?
  2. What is your inner confidence, and what can you do to increase your confidence?

- Outer Action: Candid and consistent two-way communication
  When leaders feel strong and confident inside, it is the right time to start candid communication with stakeholders, telling people what is happening, what the leadership team is doing, why they are doing so, what the organization wants everyone to do, etc. Honest and consistent communication can effectively eliminate systemic anxiety.
  In addition to informing, the leadership team also needs to actively listen to the voices from the front line so that they can obtain comprehensive information and make the right decisions. The following questions help us to figure out a better communication plan.

  1. How do you want your communication to impact everyone?
  2. What methods would you use to make it two-way communication?

  In our group coaching, Bruce and the leadership team re-wrote the employee letter, not only showed their caring but also shared the activities they just planned and invited all employees to participate the co-creation.

Making Breakthrough

- Inner state: Courage
  Even though Bruce and the team were excited about the initial ideas, they still had fears because it required changes from the organization. Will the idea be successful? What's a new way of working when people are in quarantine?
  A coach's work is to support leaders to turn fear into courage. Any change needs courage, and fear is a signal to tell you where you need to do more. Remember, do not ignore small steps, success becomes true with continual, small progress. The following questions help leaders to design their early win and reinforce their courage:

  1. Think back to the difficulties you or your team have gone through. Where did the "courage" come from?
  2. What small achievements will make everyone more courageous?

- Visible actions: Co-create the solution and learn from practice
  Bruce and his team were full of confidence when they figured out some key milestones, but I knew they had more work. I asked them the below questions to build their resilience.

  1. What new attempts can we make to achieve short-term and long-term goals?
  2. How can we accept the "failure" in the attempt and learn from it?

One month later, Bruce told me that they completed the new product just 2 weeks after the group coaching sessions, and they successfully launched the online video training program.

In addition, this online training also generated more sales leads for their traditional products. Bruce said that they will continue this training product (even though COVID is still here) because it developed a completely new business model for them.

Although COVID is a special case, it is not uncommon for companies to suffer turbulence now more than before in this Volatility, Uncertainty, Complexity, Ambiguity (VUCA) era. We cannot change uncertainty. We can only change our own ability to face uncertainty. This is exactly why companies need coaching. With this 6C coaching model, this organization's leaders shared their positive feedback that coaching not only helped them solve their current challenges but also changed their cognitive model and developed organizational agility and resilience. The team and organization become stronger with a learning mindset.

35

Letting Go of Certainty

David Clutterbuck

This case is an amalgam of several.

One of the causes of the current global crisis in leadership is that in times of upheaval and uncertainty, people and organizations seek leaders, who offer certainty. But this comes at a price. If there is only one right way, then all other ways must by definition be wrong. The results include dictatorial behaviors, marginalization of those who dare to think differently, and polarization of opinion – often the easiest antidote to oppressive certainty is another equally uncompromising view of the "truth."

The leaders I coach – and who come to the coaches I supervise – are overwhelmingly people who recognize the dangers of too much certainty. Although they may be unfamiliar with the term "simplexity"[1] (the art of making complex issues simple but not simplistic), they instinctively recognize that simplistic perspectives and solutions do not work in a complex adaptive environment.

This was certainly the case with one CEO – let us call her Janice – of a medium-sized multinational business. The problem she faced, however, was that there was so much uncertainty, she was struggling to make decisions at all. What made things worse was that when she had overcome her "lack of knowing" to make two key appointments to her top team, she now had severe doubts whether these were the right people for the job. The assumptions she had made at the time – in consultation with the rest of her top team – were overtaken by changes in the company's operating environment. Instead of going for technical expertise and track record, she now thought she should have looked for flexibility and learning potential. Under pressure from within and without to demonstrate that she was in control, she felt increasingly less confident in her decision-making ability, to the extent that she was procrastinating about several big decisions that needed to be made to restore the sense of purpose and direction in the business. In our conversations, there were also hints of "imposter syndrome" – a sense that this once highly confident executive was now doubting her own fitness for her role.

It is at this point that coaching often becomes mentoring. Contrary to much of the unevidenced coaching literature, mentoring has never been a directive activity. It is best described as tapping into one's own wisdom to help the client discover their own wisdom. The mentor uses their knowledge of the wider context – in this case, the dynamics of complex, adaptive systems, to provide a different perspective that will enable different thinking in the client. He or she may also offer analogies that help the client find new perspectives. One analogy that raised a smile and helped Janice reconnect with her own creativity and belief in her own problem-solving capability was the legend of Atlas and Hercules. One of Hercules, 12 tasks was to relieve Atlas from holding up the world, while Atlas ran an errand. When Atlas returned, he refused to take over again. Hercules asked him to just hold the world briefly, while he put on a cap to reduce the discomfort. Of course, Hercules now had Atlas in the same bind, from which he had escaped.

David Clutterbuck is one of the earliest pioneers of coaching and mentoring and the co-founder of the European Mentoring & Coaching Council. Author of more than 70 books, including the first evidence-based titles on coaching culture and team coaching, he is a visiting professor at four business schools.

Coach Me! Your Personal Board of Directors: Leadership Advice from the World's Greatest Coaches, First Edition. Edited by Brian Underhill, Jonathan Passmore, and Marshall Goldsmith.
© 2022 John Wiley & Sons Ltd. Published 2022 by John Wiley & Sons Ltd.
DOI: 10.1002/9781119823803.ch35

How could Janice escape from bearing the weight of the world on her shoulders? She could walk away and let the world drop, but she quickly rejected that possibility. She could share the burden, but who with? The first possibility was her team. She realized that she had inherited and perpetuated a system that expected the CEO to take all the responsibility and have all the answers. Together, we explored her beliefs about this model of leadership and, to provide context, looked at what the evidence-based literature tells us about individual and collective leadership. It gradually became apparent that the leadership system she had allowed to grow around her was amplifying all her negative emotions and getting in the way of achieving the support she needed. Then, that fundamental coaching question: "What is the conversation you need to have with your team, both as individuals and together?"

A rapid realization for Janice was that, in seeking to be the leader the team expected her to be, she was simply making herself more vulnerable. And, paradoxically, that choosing to be more vulnerable toward them was a major part of the remedy. What the team needed from her was not a "right" answer, but a framework, with which they could pool their collective insights and ingenuity to face unpredictable change more confidently.

The late, great theoretical physicist Richard Feynman argued cogently that we should value doubt far more than being right. The question "How can you embrace uncertainty and make it a strength?" caused Janice to pause and reflect deeply. "I don't know," she replied. "What do you think would happen, if you asked that of your team?" "I don't know, but I'm going to try."

Of course, the system comprising Janice and her team was only one of many within this situation. Mapping as many of these systems as possible helped Janice to develop the framework she needed, on which to build the conversations that would enable her organization to become more nimble. Amongst these systems were that between the company and its customers, the company and its competitors, and various informal networks inside the company, who Janice knew did not feel listened to.

The conversation with her team had multiple positive impacts. First, they responded to her need to make the issues shared problems. When Janice shared how lonely she was feeling, every one of them responded that they felt the same. Second, one of the two "misfits" asked the question: "If this company is going through such turmoil and uncertainty, what is happening in our competitors? Doesn't it represent an opportunity to steal a march on them?"

Based on her own enhanced understanding of the systems, Janice was able to pose a number of other questions she had found stimulating during the coaching sessions and which she thought might help the team think collaboratively. Among them:

- "What would our customers say if we asked them: what should a company like ours do to support you in your turbulence?"
- "What's the last thing our competitors would expect of us right now?"
- "What are our key assumptions about all of the uncertainties we face? Suppose those assumptions are wrong…."

As she explained, it at a subsequent coaching session: "I suddenly realized that we really needed *more* uncertainty, not less. We had been putting stakes in the ground to give us some sense of being in control, but that couldn't work when the ground was constantly shifting. Giving up the need for these anchors, even temporarily, allowed us to ask ourselves and our stakeholders different questions and create different possibilities. I got a lot of initial pushback from that, but I asked them to trust me and they did. The result was we made a major shift towards defining our business more in terms of what our customers needed than of what we wanted to sell them."

In this session, we addressed the issue of how she could consolidate and build on these steps toward collective responsibility. I conducted an analysis few years ago of literature on the traits of great leaders in complex environments. I found four common qualities:

- Compassion – caring for both the business purpose and the people the business affects
- Curiosity – being genuinely interested in both the people and the systems
- Courage – being willing to challenge others and oneself
- Connectedness – seeing and valuing the links between the people and systems.

Janice was aware of these and how they relate to being an authentic leader. Looking at them again in the context of uncertainty provided insights into how she could modify her leadership style. One rule she created for herself was to have the courage to take tough decisions earlier. This was not just about overcoming procrastination; it was also about freeing resources (including mental and physical ones) to focus on other things that were more important. Another was to make sure that those tough decisions were taken with compassion for those people affected by them and to be more forgiving of herself and others when things did not work out. Around her, she needed a team who would share the behaviors and mindsets she was trying to role model – and give her honest feedback when she did not live up to her own standards.

And in her words: "I know you are going to ask me – what is the conversation I need to have with my team? I'm not going to tell them this is how things are going to be… but I am going to ask them to join me on the adventure to find out. Do we have the courage, curiosity, courage, and connectedness to embrace not just the uncertainty of what will happen in the business, but in ourselves? I don't know how many will come with me, but now I am comfortable about that!"

Learning from Janice's Experience

Consider the following questions:

- To what extent do people around you look to you to provide certainty?
- What is the impact of this on your leadership style?
- When is being certain beneficial and when does it hinder rapid change?
- What are the conversations you need to have – and who with – to encourage greater resilience in the face of uncertainty?

Note

1   Coined by Walter Goldsmith and me in a 1990s study of high performing companies.

Transition Management

36

Your First Hundred Days

Abdallah Aljurf

Mr. Wiley Jones (not his real name) was having a sip of his hot double-shot espresso (not his real drink) when he smiled at me and said, "I am leaving my job to follow my passion" (not exactly what he said). "I want to move on with my career and get a leading position with an international consulting firm. Do you know how I can succeed and prove myself after I join this firm?"

I smiled back and said, "Probably, all what you are looking for is within you" (I said it in Arabic). "My job will be assisting you in discovering the hidden treasures of knowledge and experience within you. I could help you to define your meaning of success, find your way to succeed, and go on a journey with you in your first 100 days until you fly on your own and shine like a star."

Two months later, I got a phone call from Wiley saying that he is going to join the firm next week and he does not know what to do. He was afraid to fail, send the wrong messages, or get dragged into operations from the first week.

I told him, "your 1st 100 days are the most important days in your new job, and I'll be more than happy to help you as a coach to find your way to succeed with this new firm. These priorities differ from a person to another. This will depend on your experience, goals, organization culture, complexity of your situation, your team, maturity level of your function, support of top management, and many other organizational factors."

We worked together on many of his priorities, including:

- Creating the right positive first impression
- Sending the right messages on day 1
- Developing and implementing an action plan for the first 3 months.

We were meeting every other week, and we exchanged WhatsApp messages whenever he needed more clarity about a certain issue. It was an exciting journey for both of us.

He faced so many challenges, including changing priorities for his top management, resignation of one of his mentors, merging his function with another department after one month of joining the organization, and cutting his budget, a top management decision of stopping recruitment although he was expecting three team members to be recruited to his team.

We broke each challenge to bite-size issues that could be resolved one after the other. We worked on building up his executive muscles, capitalizing on his strengths and expertise, while we were focusing on increasing learning and achieving results.

Abdallah Aljurf is the founder of ICF Saudi Arabia chapter, the author of the leadership development book *10 Lessons in 10 Years*, an experienced corporate consultant who is passionate about leadership development and coaching, and a professional coach, trainer, and speaker.

Coach Me! Your Personal Board of Directors: Leadership Advice from the World's Greatest Coaches, First Edition. Edited by Brian Underhill, Jonathan Passmore, and Marshall Goldsmith.
© 2022 John Wiley & Sons Ltd. Published 2022 by John Wiley & Sons Ltd.
DOI: 10.1002/9781119823803.ch36

Framing the Issue

The first 100 days in the life of an executive require special attention. This is the period where key people, including your stakeholders, are watching you, judging you, formulating their first impression about you, and validating their perceptions about you.

There are many books and references that show you what should be done in your first 100 days:

1. *Your First 100 Days in a New Executive Job* by Robert Hargrove
2. *The New Leader's 100-Day Action Plan* by George Bradt, Jayme A. Check, and Jorge E. Pedraza
3. *The First 90 Days* by Michael D. Watkins
4. *Your First 100 Days* by Niamh O'Keeffe
5. *Master Your Next Move* by Michael D. Watkins

This "100 days" period is where your make or break your record as a successful leader. Some executives look at this period as a honeymoon or a relaxation period where they just observe, try to understand the culture, see how the organization runs, or find some events to attend. Other executives might get pulled by daily operations and forget to balance between the daily issues and strategic view of the organization.

Other executives take it more seriously and come with a plan to learn, help, change, and make an impact. Those are the ones who thrive and shine in the organization. That is why hiring an executive coach is crucial at this period, so the executive could start, learning, producing results, and making things happen before the end of the 100th day.

Suggestions

1. Find a coach, a mentor, or a trusted friend: There are many executive coaches in the market. You could find them through your connections, your HR department, LinkedIn.com, www.coachfederation.org, or a quick search on Google. Once you find a coach with a good profile, feel free to ask for an introductory session to see if there is chemistry between you and your future coach. If you do not click, do not waste your time and money. Find another coach that you feel comfortable with. If you will not hire a coach for any reason, think of a mentor or a trusted friend. A good mentor would be someone who went through a similar experience at the same level and willing to share experiences with you. A trusted friend would help you to vent and bounce back ideas.
2. Get clarity: as soon as you can, using all resources and connections that you have to get clarity about the history, current situation, and the vision of your new organization.
3. Start with the end in mind: As Stephen Covey says in his book *The 7 Habits of Highly Effective People*. What is the end that you want to see at the end of your service period with this organization? What is the end result that you want to see on your 100th day with this organization? Can you visualize this result? Can you explain it to others? Can you inspire people to help you to get there?
4. Plan your 100 days: Plans are nothing, planning is everything. Have a plan to start with, keep modifying, adjusting, and enhancing your plan as you move on. Your plan could include many items including, but not limited to, your learning activities, your quick wins, communicating with key people, identifying your stakeholders, understanding their expectations, etc.
5. Assess your team: Decide on who will stay and who will have to leave. It is better to make this bold decision sooner than later. For those who will stay, decide how to capitalize on their strengths, motivate them, and keep them engaged. For those who will leave, decide on how to transfer them or give them options for leaving your team.
6. Execute your plan and review your progress on a daily and weekly basis.
7. On your 100th day, deliver a presentation to your top management, line manager, or stakeholders to show what you learned, what you achieved, and the way forward.

Conclusion of the Opening Story

Wiley Jones worked hard. He did 97% of the work. My 3% was just being a catalyst who helped him as an executive coach to think loudly, arrange his thoughts, challenge his assumptions, beat his limiting beliefs, and make better decisions that saved him time, effort, and money.

In the first month, he was able to focus on his priorities such as:

- Creating an elevator pitch
- Gathering the right data about the organization
- Designing a learning plan.

After that, he increased the market share of his company in the local market by 12%, he signed deals with three new government entities, and he utilized the local resources to prepare a mega-event that attracted more than 200 professionals from different parts of the world.

All of that and many other achievements happened in his first 100 days. At the end of our coaching program, I had a reflection session with him where he shared his key learning points, his achievements, and his plans of the coming year. I asked him about his major paradigm shift. He smiled and said, "Probably, all what you are looking for is within you."

Practical Activity (Takeaway)

Ask yourself as you move to your new executive or leadership role:

1. What was the purpose of hiring me? What encouraged me to take this role? And what are they (the board or my top management) expecting me to do or be?
2. How can I meet or exceed their expectations?
3. What's my plan?
4. What would be my biggest achievement in my first 100 days?
5. Who could support me in my first 100 days?

Source of help	Name(s)
Colleague(s)	
Boss	
Team member(s)	
Coach	
Mentor	

Once you write all the answers to these questions, keep a copy of the answers, and review them on a daily basis.

You might notice a change in your thinking after a week or two as a result of new knowledge, new connections, or fast business changes in your organization. That is totally fine, and you can feel free to modify your answers and change your plan accordingly.

Remember that plans are nothing. Planning is everything!

37

Managing Self-Doubt After a Promotion

Nihar Chhaya

As soon as I arrived at his office, I could tell something was wrong. My coaching client barely looked up at me from his desk as I took my seat across from him. Just a few weeks ago, in our last session, he was overcome with joy and optimism. But today, he looked like a completely different person, betraying fear through his blank stare and hopelessness in his slumped frame.

My client was the President of a business unit at a Fortune 50 company, promoted from his VP role just last month. And he was experiencing something quite bewildering and novel to him as a successful leader, but not at all surprising to me as an executive coach to leaders transitioning to the C-Suite.

This executive was undergoing a painful bout of self-doubt, suddenly unsure of his capacity to perform at the level others expected, despite wanting this position for so long. At certain moments, he ruminated with worry about his new job, and at others, he longed for the "easier" days of his last role.

As his coach, I knew that for him to avoid derailing in this high-profile role, we had to go beyond merely addressing the "outer" challenges, or the business and strategic aspects of his job. We also needed to navigate the "inner" problems that come with leading at a higher level, such as anxiety, doubt, and other self-sabotaging tendencies new executives struggle with, often out of plain sight.

I gently told my client, "You may be experiencing something uncomfortable, but rest assured other newly promoted executives do as well. We need to help you get out of your own way so you can bring your best to this job, no matter what obstacles lay ahead." He looked up with a slight glimmer of hope and asked me to share more.

The Many Triggers of Self-Doubt for Newly Promoted Leaders

After an executive promotion, self-doubt emerges in leaders for different reasons. You may worry about letting the company down if you do not perform the way they expected, or you may begin comparing your performance to your new peers at a higher level.

My client felt those doubts, but he was most worried about how to scale in such a sweeping role. He feared being held responsible for execution problems across such a broad spectrum of functions with no direct control over the work. He also doubted his ability to make the tough strategic and highly visible decisions expected of him.

Nihar Chhaya is an executive coach to the C-Suite and leaders at global companies, including American Airlines, Cigna, Coca-Cola, Draft Kings, 3M, Lockheed Martin, Raytheon Technologies, and others. A former Fortune 200 corporate head of talent development and a senior advisor to boards and CEOs on succession planning, he works with leaders on mastering interpersonal communication for superior business and strategic results.

Coach Me! Your Personal Board of Directors: Leadership Advice from the World's Greatest Coaches, First Edition. Edited by Brian Underhill, Jonathan Passmore, and Marshall Goldsmith.
© 2022 John Wiley & Sons Ltd. Published 2022 by John Wiley & Sons Ltd.
DOI: 10.1002/9781119823803.ch37

Finally, he felt a great deal of vulnerability in not having the subject matter expertise of many technical leaders on his team. He found it awkward to coach and develop the new people on his staff who were more technically knowledgeable than him.

To make things worse, he now had to hand off the things he was an expert in to empower his leadership team and optimize activity while spending time on nebulous, immeasurable issues, such as strategy and vision.

In our coaching, I suggested the following ideas to help him manage this mental burden:

Remember that your job is to lead your team, not outsmart them. To achieve large-scale goals at the executive level, you have to maximize team performance, not focus on your individual achievement. Recognize that you are not supposed to have the same expertise as team members, just enough knowledge to ask the right questions, and define how their work contributes to the vision and strategy of the department.

The more you try to compete with your team members' technical acumen, the more likely you are to detract from your role as a strategic leader and get stuck in the weeds of their work. In the process, you will disempower and demotivate them. Even worse, your involvement will create role ambiguity, hindering optimal team performance.

Look at your "expertise" as less related to specialized, technical aspects and more around the art of leading others. You can confidently coach those with more technical expertise than you because you are advising them not on the subject matter of their work, but on the necessary art of aligning their talent in practical ways to support the overall business vision.

Also, when you start engaging in more strategic activities, such as meeting customers, evaluating future scenarios, and influencing across the C-Suite, you will begin to see how the seemingly nebulous work of strategy requires operational discipline and measurement like any other job. So, delegating more of what you used to do will soon provide you relief, not regret, as you can now free up time to dedicate to your new strategic priorities.

Recognize doubt as a valuable part of your leadership narrative. Virtually every meaningful story you have heard follows a familiar tale: the hero is conflicted between being what the world expects of him and being true to himself. He experiences fear, doubt, anger, defensiveness, and many other emotions as characters on his journey test him until he takes complete ownership of his flaws and finds a sense of self *outside* himself.

In the same way, you are creating a narrative of your leadership journey, and this is a new step filled with hidden lessons that may not be apparent now. You may have the utmost confidence and sense of control until the day you find yourself overwhelmed by the job's complexities and spiral into self-doubt. To cope, you might push the doubt away, deflect it through defensiveness when given feedback, and dread taking on unfamiliar aspects of the role.

But if you can step outside of yourself and observe when these tendencies show up, you can keep them from limiting you and develop a meaningful leadership narrative for yourself. With that insight, you may then ask yourself, "what is this chapter teaching me?"

Shift from being fearful of what others will think of you in this role, to actively inviting what they see. Become the hero in your journey, seeing criticism or "tests" of performance not as the enemy but as lessons that help you lead yourself and others with intention and ownership, come what may.

Short-circuit doubt by adopting a ritual of saying "yes" to all sensations. Research has shown that when confronted with too many choices, we suffer from decision fatigue and a host of other painful feelings from regret to chronic inaction.

Leaders who experience self-doubt after promotions are consumed by *"what ifs,"* questioning the choices they make in their new role and even past life choices that led them to where they are. Because every potential item of doubt seems more critical than the rest, it is easy to fall into a never-ending spiral that will undeniably diminish the leader's effectiveness on the job.

Decide in your mind that all doubt is the same, regardless of issue or timing. By quickly "canceling" all triggers of doubt by accepting the sensations they bring, you keep moving and don't cherry-pick different emotions to let consume you. Say "yes" to *all of it*, and gently sit with the fear, worry, embarrassment, and frustration as they appear, just as you would effortlessly enjoy feelings of relief, joy, pride, and excitement at other times.

Saying "yes" to whatever sensations arrive with doubt is not about suffering just for the sake of it. It is about training yourself to understand that the key to leadership success at any role is about being *adaptable*, not perfect. The more you can comfortably adapt to the unpredictability of both the people you lead and your reactive mind, the more effective and resilient you will be.

My client experimented with these suggestions by keeping a list of them on his desk as a reminder. While there were days when he struggled to turn off his worry, he did report that these perspectives helped him feel more hopeful when he was down.

He resonated most with the idea of being adaptable rather than perfect. He called adaptability the "executive superpower" and something he would keep practicing as he crafted his leadership story.

My client also recognized that time was his friend. Every day that passed was another day that he had proved a prior doubt wrong. I reminded him of the saying, "Wherever you go, there you are." If he could take time every day to shift his mind from regrets of the past or worries about the future, he might notice that he is already doing the thing that he doubted was possible just a few days ago.

When you experience self-doubt, try this exercise:

Shift your mind from the future to the present. Describe the situation you are experiencing as if you were writing a chapter for someone to read.

Then ask yourself, "if this situation was supposed to teach me something useful, what could that be?"

Write down your answer and then return to imagining the future: this time uniquely armed with this useful lesson in your toolkit to bring you confidence.

Remember that it is not just success but failure as well that develops your superpowers of adaptability and continuous learning. With continuous practice in these skills, you will always be successful in leading yourself and others.

38

Self as Leader

Pamela McLean

Leaders Have Blind Spots

John was not sure coaching was necessary given his experience and his track record, yet his new boss asked him to "give it a try," and he somewhat reluctantly signed on. John had recently received a promotion to a new role and while he felt all was going mostly well, his boss, without offering specificity, hinted that he needed to make some adjustments to be a success in this larger role.

John and I started our coaching on this note, and in our early conversations, he was a bit guarded, describing himself as someone dedicated to work, focused on results, at ease directing others to and disinclined to develop personal relationships with his team members. He reflected that his past role of several years was quite tactical and that his team worked within a highly defined structure – this new role was just slightly out of his comfort zone.

As we approached our work, John agreed to seeking stakeholder input to provide us with a view into how he was experienced by others and potentially discover where he might make pivots to create more comfort for himself in this new role and hit the mark for his boss. Upon completion of interviews, two themes emerged: John was described by everyone as smart and competent, while experienced as aloof, arrogant, and inaccessible – making it hard for others to connect, feel respected, and have a sense that John was interested in their perspectives.

When we met to review the findings, John was surprised by how his colleagues experienced him. He was heartened that they acknowledged his skill, but he did want to be viewed as arrogant or aloof. Given there was significant agreement by the team, he took the feedback seriously and became more invested in our work together. He wanted to dig in and figure out how to shift this perception. We started in small tactical ways to help gain momentum, while simultaneously going deeper to gain an understanding of this "arrogance factor" that others perceived – examining the roots and the blind spots.

The Human Side of Leading Others

As we delved deeper, we explored his relationships with team members, what he demanded of them, how he interacted, and how he demonstrated his interest and care. As our trust built, John revealed that he had never given the human side of his work much attention. Problem is people do not follow a leader because they are

Pamela McLean, PhD, CEO, Hudson Institute of Coaching, is a psychologist, master coach, and coach supervisor. She has authored several books, including *LifeForward*, a book on transitions in aduladthood; *The Handbook of Coaching*, examining the essential ingredients in leadership coaching; and *Self as Coach, Self as Leader*.

Coach Me! Your Personal Board of Directors: Leadership Advice from the World's Greatest Coaches, First Edition. Edited by Brian Underhill, Jonathan Passmore, and Marshall Goldsmith.
© 2022 John Wiley & Sons Ltd. Published 2022 by John Wiley & Sons Ltd.
DOI: 10.1002/9781119823803.ch38

hardworking and strategic – people follow a leader because they have a human connection and they feel seen, known, and respected by their leader.

In the end, the theme of John's story resembles stories of other dedicated leaders I have worked with. Great smarts, hardworking – yet often giving inadequate attention to the human side of leading others. In today's complex and interrelated world, the old command and control rules are simply outdated and insufficient. Leaders able to thrive today are committed to their own continual development and attuned to the power of cultivating human skills in all of their interactions.

"Know thyself" is one part of the equation in great leadership, and the other equally important part is knowing one's impact on others. John knew how to use his smarts to deliver, but he was hindered by his lack of self-awareness and his blindness to how those around him experienced him. The direct impact on John's team was evidenced in the stakeholder comments – his behavior was demotivating and uninspiring, and his lack of self-awareness and human skills were actually impeding his goal of getting results. His role as a leader required stronger collaboration, connection, and a willingness to create opportunities for others to grow, develop, and take their own initiative.

Leaders need to start at home to "know thyself" in order to inspire others to follow them. John had invested little time in this part of his development. The early stakeholder input served as a wake-up call for him, and, not long after, we arrived at an important tipping point when John began to experience the value of our coaching work – a space where he felt respected and challenged to candidly examine how he was showing up. He was able to make a connection between his "command and control" style – and his growing up years. He laughed a bit remembering a message he absorbed from his father – "just the facts, no feelings necessary." When someone is able to make this connection with their past, it creates an understanding and compassion for how one's style came to be. This can create a powerful turning point in the work that facilitates a lasting shift.

Practicing to Build New Habits

Once John began to make the connections between his old story and its impact on his current ways of showing up, he was ready to start practicing new behaviors. Where to start when building behaviors is always an important consideration. In my recent book, *Self as coach, Self as leader* (McLean, Pamela [2019]), I outline several dimensions of the inner landscape of a leader and examine practices for cultivating one's capacity in the dimensions that are most relevant. The paradigms for great leadership in today's VUCA world are more demanding than ever before, and knowing one's inner landscape and committing to continual cultivation is paramount in order to inspire others to follow and to reach the results that matter the most. Figure 38.1 shows a model exploring six dimensions of one's inner landscape that are particularly relevant for a leader and leader as a coach.

Figure 38.1 Six dimensions of one's inner landscape.
Source: The Hudson Institute of Santa Barbara.

Examining John's leadership challenges through the lenses of this model provides a useful perspective on where he can begin to make small changes that allow him to be experienced as accessible, interested, and caring.

The inner landscape of any leader is naturally shaped by the experiences of one's early years in a family system and broader culture. These experiences create scripts and stories we bring into our adult lives. John uncovered early influences that were important links in our work – "just the facts, no feelings necessary!" Left to his well-honed habits, these early scripts drove his outer behavior and John was starting to understand the important connection between his old script and his current approach to his interactions.

Two dimensions of self as leader were most relevant in our work, and we developed practices to strengthen his human connectedness. Here is a brief look at the dimensions that provided guidance for us.

Presence, the way a leader shows up in every conversation, is a testament to who the leader is. John self-described as directive and disinclined to engage in conversations that could have created a trusting connection with others. His people portrayed him as aloof and arrogant. His presence had been sending a message that he was not interested or available. A simple practice John implemented early in our work was to consciously begin to extend himself by slowing his pace, practicing more presence in each moment, and asking questions to learn more about his people.

Empathy, the way a leader demonstrates care and relates to what others describe and experience, builds the foundation for trust and psychological safety in a team. Great leaders genuinely care about those they work with, and this creates the conditions required for real conversations and great work. John wanted his team to succeed, but he had not developed his capacity to connect empathically. He was missing opportunities because he had not seen the necessity, had not believed it might be important. His old story – "just the facts, no feelings necessary" – had been driving how he showed up in his interactions. His first step in growing his empathy began with noticing the small opportunities to show he cared. The small act of asking how a project is going and how he might be of support was an early practice.

Inasmuch as John took his work very seriously, albeit at the expense of human relationships and morale, those attributes ultimately served him in his willingness to invest in our coaching in order to cultivate the human skills he needed in order to be at his best in his new role. His willingness to seek input and examine the roots of his old style took courage and set the stage for us to go deeper. Over the course of our engagement, we could both track the shift in his early reticence to a trusting partnership that allowed us to explore blind spots and build goals and practices that allowed him to show up in ways that put relationships first, invited connection, and created a stronger sense of trust and respect.

Reflections for the Reader

Cultivating the human skills required to be a great leader is a journey, not a destination. Each of us brings our earliest experiences to our way of relating to others, and the work of reshaping our human interactions to meet the needs of life today is rewarding and demanding work for all of us.

Here are a few reflections for your consideration connected to each of the dimensions of self as leader.

- What old stories and scripts might be driving some of your human interactions today?
- How might you consciously practice more presence with your team? How would it positively impact all of you?
- In what ways, do you exhibit you care to those on your team and fellow colleagues? Are there ways you might do this more often?

Reference

McLean, P. (2019). *Self as coach, self as leader: Developing the best in you to develop the best in others.* Wiley Press.

39

Executive Transition

Cathleen Wu

What got you here won't get you there

– Source: *Marshall* Goldsmith (2010)

Arthur's Challenge

Arthur, the China COO of this world's leading software and technology solutions provider, has been suffering for 9 months, almost immediately from the day he was put in this newly created position. This is his most difficult season since his joining 12 years ago. His first role here was a senior pre-sales engineer and the last was Head of China Pre-sales Technology Supporting Department. The Pre-sales department won the Global Pre-sales Reward the year before.

His bosses, the Asia Regional COO and China GM, were also dissatisfied and shocked by his recent performance. "I'm disappointed, as he didn't function as the COO as we expected. In order to avoid conflict and please everybody, he never made tough decisions. There are increased complaints from sales VPs, and we are losing senior directors and managers under Arthur as they were not convinced by his leadership. I initiate this coaching program as the last try. We have to move him away if no improvement in 3 months," the regional COO complained such to me in the initial sponsor interview.

The company's fast-moving, aggressive, and results-driven atmosphere can be clearly smelled in the air at their office. At the same time, they are rewarded as Best Employer because of their outstanding investment on caring and developing people.

This is a typical internal executive transition case. Both Arthur and I have captured the sense of urgency and severity. Although the roles and responsibilities of the COO have not been thoroughly defined yet, he has to deliver results to the average level and prove that the bosses' decision to promote and develop him was right.

The Issue and Our Plan

Most people have roller coaster experiences in the first few months of a transition. At times, the excitement of learning new things comes to the surface, and you can be on top of the world. At other times, the frustrations and uncertainties come to the fore and you can easily start to doubt yourself. The more senior the role, the more you are in the spotlight, and the more important it can be to get it "right" from the start. It has become

---

Cathleen Wu is an experienced executive coach and team coach. She brings to her coaching a vast wealth of experience collected over 30 working years and is motivated by her passion for individual, team, and organization development and her deep belief that people are creative, resourceful, and full of potential.

Coach Me! Your Personal Board of Directors: Leadership Advice from the World's Greatest Coaches, First Edition. Edited by Brian Underhill, Jonathan Passmore, and Marshall Goldsmith.
© 2022 John Wiley & Sons Ltd. Published 2022 by John Wiley & Sons Ltd.
DOI: 10.1002/9781119823803.ch39

commonplace for politicians to be measured on their "first 90 days" in performance and personal brand. In many ways, this rings true as a business leader takes on a new role.

Obviously, Arthur has lost the ideal time window. He adopted the old way of thinking, working, and relating while failing to identify and work on the necessity to make changes. His old personal brand and image of being accountable, diligent, and sticking to rules worked well in the previous pre-sales role, which was technical solutions focused. The COO role, which takes charge of all the non-sales functions (pre-sales, after sales, sales compliance, etc.), urges him to reach a deliberate balance between supporting the sales function on one hand and restricting sales on the other hand and to demonstrate his strategic thinking and whole picture vision going much beyond technical perspective. In this sense, the famous quote from Marshall Goldsmith – "What got you here won't get you there" – is highly efficacious.

For mixed reasons, Arthur is eager to turn around the situation. He does not want to "lose face." More attractively, we envision together his next 10 years of professional and life aspirations. He therefore would like to leverage this chance to steadily move toward the desired future.

My philosophy is "it's never too late," so the next 90 days and 180 days are still worth expecting. We decide to phase the 6-month coaching journey in three stages: (1) to gain quick wins on key stakeholder relationships, (2) to shift the focus from a senior technical leader to a senior executive, and (3) to advance his mental and thinking capacity that will grow his ability to think and act in more complex, systemic, strategic, and interdependent ways.

The Journey and Outcomes

In China (and this might be true under many cultural contexts), people relationships go before work tasks. The higher the position, the higher the level of complexity and dynamics of stakeholder networks. The dissatisfaction from line managers, complaints from peers, and loss of subordinates imply that Arthur underestimated the importance of trust level networking in the new landscape and failed to prioritize key relationships.

We start from drawing the Stakeholder Map where key groups of people and clusters of people under each group are identified and rated in terms of the strength of mutual trust levels. We then deepen the thinking by asking reflective questions: "Who is missing in current radar? Who are the key players you need to influence? Who has the "low-hanging fruit" potential? Who are most challenging to network with? Who is a "connector" that can be leveraged?" By these steps, Arthur prioritizes five people he will put conscious efforts in networking and make this as his quick-win endeavor.

The second stage is about mastering the big shifts of focus where surprisingly few leaders, including Arthur, pay attention to. Connor and Jerry published their insights in *Developing the Talent Pool Through Learning Agility* in 2012 that the focus shift from senior leaders to senior executives falls in four categories:

1. from "facilitating performance of others" to "building other leaders to take their own lead,"
2. from "delivering excellence of day-to-day practices" to "leaving a legacy and making distinct differences,"
3. from "leading teams" to "leading stakeholders," and
4. from "growing the weak spots in leadership competence" to "making the most of latent strengths to spark leadership spike."

By assessing the importance of each category required by the current role and his level of mastery, Arthur works out his two leadership focus shifts in 6 months and corresponding action plans for the next 90 days. Inspired by the shift of "leading stakeholders," he also takes an extra step to seek feedforward (future-focused feedback) from his team and other key stakeholders on his desired shifts. Not surprisingly, this step is well perceived by stakeholders as his declaration and commitment to make real change.

Our third coaching stage goes to the master competency that integrates the traditional outside-in method of leadership development (which identifies a leader's external challenges and determines the competencies required to meet these challenges) and a newly emerged inside-out approach (focusing on the mental and thinking capabilities). According to the original research of Jane Loevinger in 1976 and later study and applications by Bill Torbert in 2004 and Bill Joiner in 2007, leaders evolve through a series of recognizable vertical development stages: Opportunist, Diplomat, Expert, Achiever, Redefining, Transforming, and Alchemical (listed from earlier to later stages).

The implication of this set of development stages is that the later the stage, the wider perspectives we see the world, and therefore, we can influence and integrate more. This opens Arthur's eyes and sheds light on his longer-term development direction. He is at the Expert stage, which used to work well in his previous capacity, while the current COO role and the fast-changing technology and business competition context urge him to upgrade to an Achiever.

Based on the this, we gradually work out his development plan by applying three kinds of developmental methods: high-pressure experiences, collision of different points of view, and construction of new meaning. Furthermore, he develops a habit of making deep self-reflections on the progress, the occasional fall back, the learning, and the impact on stakeholders.

The step-by-step outcomes of this coaching journey are quite encouraging: the regional COO made positive comments in the mid-term check-in meeting of this coaching assignment ("Arthur's improvement was impressive..."), Arthur is rated "average" at the year-end performance appraisal (which could have been as bad as "below expectation"), and the China region is rewarded by the global organization because of its outstanding collective collaboration. As a bonus to me, Arthur requests to extend our coaching partnership for another 6 months to continue his efforts on becoming a good stand Achiever.

The Insights and Conclusion

Not all executive coaching cases turn out to be effective and successful. To summarize the top three successful factors from Arthur's case:

1. The executive's strong commitment to make changes, driven by both push (outside in) and pull (inside out) motivators
2. The coach's use of relevant theories and well-designed approaches (in this case, Stakeholder Map, Focus Shift of Senior Executive, and Vertical Development Stages)
3. The executive's discipline and courage to take real actions, demonstrate vulnerability, and do constant and deep reflections.

The Suggested Reflective Questions to You

✓ How successful were my previous transitions as a leader and executive?
✓ What do I learn from Arthur's transition case?
✓ What kind of leader and people I aspire to become in next 5–10 years, and why?
✓ What are required to shift and transform to achieve my aspiration?
✓ How can I set up my supporting system?
✓ How do I expect an executive coach to play a critical role in my transition?

References

Connor and Jerry. (December 2012). Developing the talent pool through learning agility. *Human Resource Management International Digest, 2012* <ISSN: 1358-6297 Reference: 41AC295>

Goldsmith, Marshall. (2010). *What Got You Here Won't Get You There: How Successful People Become Even More Successful*. United Kingdom, Profile.

Joiner, B., & Josephs, S. (2007). *Leadership agility*. Jossey-Bass A Wiley Imprint, San Francisco, CA.

Loevinger, J. (1976). *Ego development*, Jossey-Bass A Wiley Imprint, San Francisco, CA.

Torbert, B., & Associates (2004). *Action inquiry*., Berrett-Koehler Publisher, Inc. San Francisco, CA.

Execution

40

Objectives and Key Results

Patti P. Phillips PhD

Andy Grove was a no-nonsense executive who changed the world. As one of the founders of Intel, along with Gordon Moore and Bob Noyce, Andy helped build this successful computer chip manufacturing company. He also did something that no other top executive of a major corporation had accomplished. He delivered over 40% annual stockholders' return for 11 years in a row. In 1997, almost three decades after Intel was founded, Andy Grove was named *Time* magazine's Manager of the Year. According to *Time*, "Andy was the person most responsible for the amazing growth in the power and innovative potential of microchips."

OKR Definition

The secret to Andy's success is a system he developed called objectives and key results (OKRs). Building on the work of Peter Drucker, who had developed and coined the term "Management by Objectives," Andy made goal setting powerful, systematic, and transparent in Intel. He explained that OKRs have two parts. The first part is a direction (something that you want to do or achieve). The second part is the key result, the measure that shows if the objective has been achieved or shows the progress you have made toward achieving this objective. This system permeated the culture.

John Doerr, who worked under Andy at Intel before joining the venture capital firm Kleiner Perkins, spread the use of the OKR system. This firm funded many startups in Silicon Valley, including Google. Many of the Silicon Valley organizations adopted OKRs. Writing in the foreword to John's book, Larry Page, Google's co-founder, credits much of Google's success to the OKRs that were developed early in the process with Doerr's help (2018).

This OKR system creates a powerful opportunity for any leader who wants to drive performance and have an impact on the organization. Figure 40.1 shows one-sentence OKRs, whereas Figure 40.2 shows objectives with multiple key results.

Patti P. Phillips, PhD, is CEO of ROI Institute, Inc., the leading source of ROI competency building, implementation support, networking, and research. She helps organizations implement the ROI Methodology, provides consulting services, and facilitates workshops for major conferences worldwide. Patti is the author, coauthor, or editor of more than 75 books.

Coach Me! Your Personal Board of Directors: Leadership Advice from the World's Greatest Coaches, First Edition. Edited by Brian Underhill, Jonathan Passmore, and Marshall Goldsmith.
© 2022 John Wiley & Sons Ltd. Published 2022 by John Wiley & Sons Ltd.
DOI: 10.1002/9781119823803.ch40

After program completion, the following conditions should be met:

- Improve the health status index by 5% during the next calendar year.
- Reduce the student debt load by 30% in 3 years.
- Increase the average number of new accounts from 300 to 350 per month in 6 months.
- A 20% reduction in overtime should be realized for staff in the third quarter of this year.
- Reduce citizen complaints from an average of three per day to an average of one per day.
- Reduce operating expenses by 10% in the fourth quarter.
- Reduce product returns per month by 15% in 6 months.

Figure 40.1 Typical Objectives with One Key Result.

Objective: Improve market share of our CRM.

Key Results: 1. Secure 20% monthly increase in new accounts by June.
    2. Improve brand awareness by 15% in one year.
    3. Increase net promoter score (NPS) by 25%.

Objective: Improve retention of critical talent.

Key Results: 1. Implement management development program for store managers.
    2. Adjust salaries of critical talent to market data.
    3. Improve engagement scores.

Objective: Improve the image of the police force.

Key Results: 1. Decrease citizen complaints about excessive force by 60% in 6 months.
    2. Train police officers to develop an outward-bound mindset.
    3. Review process.

Objective: Increase female entrepreneurs in Zimbabwe.

Key Results: 1. A female entrepreneur program will be implemented by February 1st.
    2. At least 50 microfinance loans will be approved for females each quarter.
    3. At least 40 female-owned businesses will be registered each month.

Figure 40.2 Objectives with Multiple Key Results.

The Power of Objectives

Since the 1960s, there has been much research on the power of objectives. This research has been documented in many books, including Doug Gray (2019), Phillips and Phillips (2008), and Niven and Lamorte (2016).

Figure 40.3 shows the relative performance given the specificity and reach of the objectives. While performance can be achieved without objectives, the more specific the objective, the better the performance. Specific objectives that require performers to exert extra effort result in the highest level of performance.

For example, a sales manager leading a sales team would expect the team to sell to current clients and obtain new clients. That is the sales team's role. Even without objectives, you will have sales and clients. But that is not enough. You need objectives. Vague objectives will drive more performance than no objectives. Reminding the team that we have an objective to increase sales with existing customers, secure new accounts, decrease product returns, and decrease customer complaints will increase sales and performance. Mentioning these terms without precision will drive more performance because the sales team understands the direction you want to go.

Objectives set with very specific results (OKRs) are more powerful because they drive increased performance. For example, you may want to increase sales with existing customers by 20% in 9 months or secure five more new accounts per month per sales associate in 4 months. This precision motivates the team to improve, they see where the goal is going, and there is no doubt of when that should happen. It is something that can be measured. This is not a perception, belief, or an opinion. It is a fact.

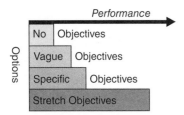

Figure 40.3 The Power of Objectives.

Still, even greater performance can be achieved if specific objectives require performers to stretch their efforts. Andy Grove believed in setting stretch objectives and getting the team to do more. It is important not to use these stretch objectives as weapons for performance review. Allowing people to stretch beyond what is minimally required in the objective is a great motivator, but only if there are no serious repercussions if they do not meet their stretch goals. Team members like to stretch, excel, and achieve.

Rules for Objectives

Several important rules are necessary to make setting objectives workable, consistent, understandable, and effective. Here are the 10 rules:

1. **Ensure objectives are measurable and represent the minimum acceptable performance.** The KR portion of the OKR is often in the records or data system, representing data that is already tracked and reported.
2. **Consider fewer objectives rather than many.** Too many objectives create confusion and could be a recipe for failure.
3. **Involve experts to help set the OKR.** The individuals responsible for the metrics need to set the objectives, but often with input from experts.
4. **Keep objectives relevant to the situation.** It is important for everyone involved on the team to understand how they are connected to the objective and can relate to it quickly.
5. **Create stretch objectives, but make sure they are achievable.** Stretch objectives can drive extraordinary performance. Individuals are willing to stretch, but the objective must be possible to achieve.
6. **Allow for the flexibility to change as conditions change.** An objective is set based on what is feasible for the team. You must have the flexibility to make adjustments along the way when conditions change or when some unknowns enter into the process.
7. **Accept failure as a process improvement opportunity.** A missed objective is a great opportunity to learn. We learn from every failure and mistake.
8. **Use objectives as tools for progress and not weapons for performance review.** They should motivate the team to achieve performance and not necessarily be part of the performance review process.
9. **Set time limits for achieving objectives.** Key results almost always have a time factor.
10. **Use the objectives to provide the focus for the entire team to reach that success.** If the leader sets the objective, the team should be determined to do whatever they can to make it achievable.

OKR Bonus: Consider Objectives for the Team at Different Levels

The objectives described here are often for business performance, the impact data, normally in the area of output, quality, cost, and time. The question quickly becomes, "How do we reach that objective?" This means that the leader will influence the team to take specific actions or use specific behaviors. Objectives are needed for those actions or behaviors. If these actions or behaviors are new to the team, there may be a need to learn something new to reach that objective. This might translate into learning objectives for the team, learning new

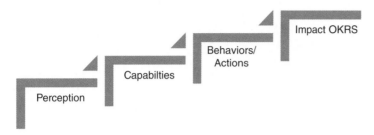

Figure 40.4 Ascending Objectives Lead to the Ultimate OKRs.

behaviors to accomplish the original OKR. Finally, the team must see this effort as relevant, important, and something they will explore. Objectives could be set at this level, perception.

These are ascending objectives that lead to the ultimate OKR. Objectives set at lower levels are aimed at achieving higher-level OKRs, as shown in Figure 40.4.

Together, these objectives provide a road map for developing a high-performance team. They are powerful, proven, and make a big difference in leader success. Just ask Larry Page, co-founder of Google.

References

Doerr, J. (2018). *Measure what matters: How Google, Bono, and the Gates Foundation rocked the world with OKRs.* New York, NY: Portfolio/Penguin Random House Publishing.

Gray, D. (2019). *Objectives and Key Results (OKR) leadership.* Franklin, TN: Gray Publications.

Niven, P. R., & Lamorte, B. (2016). *Objectives and key results: Driving focus, alignment, and engagement with OKRs.* Hoboken, NJ: Wiley.

Phillips, J. J., & Phillips, P. P. (2008). *Beyond learning objectives: Develop measurable objectives that link to the bottom line.* Alexandria, VA: ASTD Press.

41

Identifying and Approaching Different Types of Problems

Nankhonde Kasonde-van den Broek

Introduction

Every business is built on the premise of solving problems, but successful businesses have a deliberate strategy on how to deal effectively with different types of problems.

I have been coaching management teams across Africa in both the private and public sector over the last 10 years. Through these experiences, I have had the opportunity to unpack a number of challenges that come with effectively executing C-Suite roles. One of the challenges I have come across repeatedly is the ability to make decisions timely. This starts with an appreciation of the problem to be solved so that the correct course of action can be taken. However, the definition of the situation is affected by the perspectives of the stakeholders involved. Each of us has a different perception of the same situation (or the context of the problem), based on the mental models we use to make judgements on reality.

Understanding Types of Problems

Recognizing that there is a problem is the first step in problem resolution, but knowing the type of problem should be your second. The understanding of an organizational problem can positively or negatively affect the design of solutions and, subsequently, the results. According to Rittel and Weber (1973), there are two types of problems. A Tame problem is a situation problem that one can manage. It has known steps or actions that one can take to resolve it, and often requires following tried and tested procedures. A Wicked problem has no precedence and is more complicated to resolve. It requires leadership because it has some inbuilt complexities in the context of the problem, which reveal themselves at each attempt to solve the problem. In the next section, I will illustrate these problem typologies through two client coaching experiences. As we go through these experiences, I invite you to reflect on some questions:

1. Who were the stakeholders in the problem?
2. How did the stakeholders see the problem (Tame or Wicked)?
3. Were they able to differentiate their approach based on the type of problem?
4. What did the stakeholders do well?
5. What do you think the stakeholders could do better?

Nankhonde Kasonde-van den Broek is an executive coach, organizational change architect, and entrepreneur. She has over 20 years of experience supporting multi-nationals, international organizations, and governments. She is an accomplished professional with a wealth of African, international, and multi-cultural experience in designing and leading large-scale change across multiple sectors.

Coach Me! Your Personal Board of Directors: Leadership Advice from the World's Greatest Coaches, First Edition. Edited by Brian Underhill, Jonathan Passmore, and Marshall Goldsmith.
© 2022 John Wiley & Sons Ltd. Published 2022 by John Wiley & Sons Ltd.
DOI: 10.1002/9781119823803.ch41

Problem Identification in Action

An example of this challenge came through coaching an executive in a leading construction company. The CEO, Charles, was struggling with a situation triggered by a fatality. The fatality came, despite a key performance indicator of zero deaths. Since the company was an industry leader in health & safety, Charles saw the problem as one of leadership and instructed the executive management team to improve leadership capabilities focusing on health and safety across middle management. My company developed and implemented a leadership development program. During the implementation of the program, it however became clear that the problem was actually Wicked and the solution became less certain.

Information from coaching sessions with middle managers revealed that there was no trust amongst middle and senior management and across peers. It was clear that health and safety were, in principle, understood as a priority by the employees, but measures to increase health and safety were not properly implemented out of fear. This fear was partly driven by a national and organizational culture where hierarchy was important, and this stood in the way of open and honest communication. This prevented warning signs, even when critical, from being raised.

When we understood its true nature, we were able to reframe (Bolman & Deal, 2013) the problem. With this information, the way forward required a new approach. The executive team had been focusing on the situation and not the overarching context.

In another example, a leading financial institution engaged our company to run a program to help develop and embed the group's values. After 5 successful years since entering the market, Ralph, the CEO, and other Executive Team members thought that there was a need to shift the focus from financial targets to people and processes. They had to come up with the best approach to achieve this shift. More specifically, as the business was transitioning from being a start-up to a mature business, it was felt that increased ownership of and accountability for results by employees was needed to continue growing the business.

The bank's Human Resources team considered this to be a Wicked problem because it was defined as a problem of organizational culture. They wanted our company to work with stakeholders across the organization to discuss a set of pre-defined questions on the values of the staff and come up with a local interpretation relevant to the country context.

John, the Head of Risk management, however, defined the problem differently. He thought it was a Tame problem, and he proposed that it required the development of specific leadership capabilities. With the reframing of the problem came the need for a new approach.

Factors Influencing the Understanding of the Problem

In both these cases, the decision-makers responded to what they thought the problem was. In the case of Charles, the fatality was perceived as a lack of effective application of health & safety procedures by individuals. Charles eventually realized that the casualty was more of a reflection of the condition of the company's relationships and would, therefore, have been better served by a Wicked definition.

For the bank, the decision-makers argued about the formulation of the problem: human resources versus risk management. In this case, the cultural context affected the interpretation of the values. Ralph, the CEO, was able to identify the complexity in the problem and went with the problem definition and approach proposed by human resources. He saw that the problem was Wicked and would need to be reviewed over time based on progress made.

How to Identify Whether You Have a Tame or Wicked Problem

Tame problems are usually technical or transactional in nature and arise to highlight a breakdown or gap in a business process. Therefore, indicating that a solution for Tame problems is available in the form of re-engineering a business process or developing a new standard operating procedure. These changes often result in an increase in efficiency, quality, or effectiveness that can be measured. As a leader, you are in a position to encourage innovations from the team members as they resolve the problem.

Wicked problems tend to highlight a breakdown at several different levels at the same time. One of the key signs of a Wicked problem is whether or not a behavioral or relational issue exists. This reflects more deeply the context and/or culture behind the problem. At the heart of Wicked problems lie opportunities for the behavioral change of a transformational nature.

For Wicked problems, it is important for the leader to give the problem back to the people with the problem and work with them to resolve it. It requires continuous consultations and trying different suggestions to make progress (Heifetz et al., 2009). It does not have a clear finite point in time when it will be resolved. This is because in most cases it includes behavioral change, which takes time.

Generally, Tame problems can be managed, while Wicked problems require leadership. The leadership challenge in both cases is not a lack of competence but rather an open mind and a level of courage to ask the stakeholders involved more questions about the problem.

Final Thoughts

This chapter examined the importance of framing a problem correctly and the consequences of not choosing the right approach. I agree with Grint (2005) that a leader chooses a method based on the persuasiveness of the presentation of the problem. In organizational cultures that are by nature hierarchical, this can be misleading and costly for organizations because there is no one willing to challenge the framing.

Taking into account the context of any situation is important in framing a problem correctly. Sometimes C-Suite roles do not have the luxury of being as tuned to the ground as they would like or need to be. While I do not go into the personality of the decision-maker and the choice of approach, I do not dispute the linkage. In this chapter, I wanted to bring your attention to the ability to understand different types of problems objectively to be more effective as leaders. Choosing the wrong approach to respond to a problem creates stress for all involved. Some leaders' ego leads them to continue down the wrong path, rather than admitting failure and responding appropriately to a problem (Bolman & Deal, 2013). We can all identify examples of what that can lead to.

References

Bolman, L. G., & Deal, T. E. (2008). *Reframing organizations: Artistry, choice, and leadership* (4th ed.). Jossey-Bass.

Grint, K (2005) Problems, problems, problems: The social construction of 'leadership'. *Human Relations* 58(11): 1467–1494. https://doi.org/10.1177/0018726705061314

Heifetz, R. A., Linsky, M., & Grashow, A. (2009). *The practice of adaptive leadership: Tools and tactics for changing your organization and the world.* Harvard Business Press.

Rittel, H. W. J., & Webber, M. M. (1973). Dilemmas in a general theory of planning. *Policy Sciences*, 4, 155–169. Elsevier scientific publishing company. https://doi.org/10.1007/BF01405730

42

A Leader's Courage for a Team's Success

Oleg Konovalov

I was almost a half-way through a training program on leadership and corporate culture with the executives of a medium-sized software company, when I realized something felt wrong. That feeling became stronger with every team coaching session.

It felt like a well-sponsored football team that is afraid to win. Such a team is afraid of itself more than that, anything could change the status quo.

"The big guys shouldn't be paying much attention to us", "We have a great product, but nothing to celebrate yet", "It is out of our 'league'", or similar thoughts were prevalent. "We are not ready for big goals yet" – was the striking statement from a Senior Vice President.

I went for a chat with a CEO, who appeared to be the main source of that fear, who said, "we should not take a risk and grow as it goes." As a result, the company was not performing to its full capacity. They were even afraid to think about the creation of a strong vision that would drive their company to success. Their growth was limited by a lack of courage.

Courage to Change the Game

Ideas that change the world come from bold and brave thinkers. Those visionaries who think outside the comfort zone disrupt the world with creative solutions to problems. Think for a moment, how would you deal with the next brave idea coming from an employee or colleague that may change the status quo and better serve your customers?

Business involves discovery, and leaders must be explorers of new and effective business solutions. This requires them to be bolder than their conservative and cautious predecessors. They face new and difficult to predicaments daily. These new problems will require new solutions that will have to come from adaptable and decisive thinkers.

Courageous thinking is essential for the creation of a strong and vivid vision. Every long, tough, and unknown journey begins with a courageous decision. Vision demands courage as any exploration does. In simple words, courage is a necessary attribute for those striving to create and execute a great vision.

Courage is contagious. The more courage we display in advancing our vision, the more we will inspire others to join us. A leader's courage encourages engagement from others in the organization.

Fear is also contagious. Fearful leaders cast fear and doubts on their people creating a company that is fearful, rigid, and outdated.

Dr. Oleg Konovalov is a global thought leader, author, business educator, consultant, and C-suite coach. He is named among the top eight global experts in leadership and shortlisted for the Distinguished Award in Leadership by Thinkers50 2021. He is on Global Gurus Top 30 in Leadership, has been recognized as #1 Global Thought Leader on Culture by Thinkers 360, and is #1 Global Leading Coach (Marshall Goldsmith Thinkers50).

Coach Me! Your Personal Board of Directors: Leadership Advice from the World's Greatest Coaches, First Edition. Edited by Brian Underhill, Jonathan Passmore, and Marshall Goldsmith.
© 2022 John Wiley & Sons Ltd. Published 2022 by John Wiley & Sons Ltd.
DOI: 10.1002/9781119823803.ch42

Courage leads to engagement and mutual encouragement. A leader's personal courage is important, but the team's courage is even more important in securing success. A leader cannot move further than the team. The inspired team does not need pushing or pulling but only a nudge in the right direction. The ability to inspire is worth a fortune. A great part of engagement is about challenging people's inner doubts and helping them out of their mental bubbles. All great leaders exhibit this behavior.

Courage Is a Skill That Can Be Developed

The truth is that everyone feels fear. Fear gets in the way of making critical decisions by fostering one's own capacities. This is a normal human reaction.

Winston Churchill once said, "Fear is a reaction. Courage is a decision." Courage is a skill that helps to overcome fear and can be developed. It depends on how we live every day and get ready to respond to something unusual or seemingly beyond our control. As soon as you turn your fear into courage, your knowledge and experience would offer solutions to even the most difficult tasks. It is you who decides whether or not fear controls you.

Going back to the above-mentioned training program, I see an opportunity to help my client's top executives develop courageous thinking as a leadership skill.

Ruining a comfortable cocoon of comfort zone thinking is never easy. This cocoon lives on a reflective habit of hiding weaknesses and fears behind any number of excuses – local context and habits, possible negative public opinion, never-done-it-before, and so on. Not to mention a myriad of "ifs," "buts," and "howevers."

It was critical to guide them out of the debris of self-doubt by demonstrating that courage is a skill that can be developed using my own experience. Courage cannot be taught by books but only through real experience and boldly questioning one's own limits. Here, I learned that sharing my own experience is critical for encouraging others.

Leaders need real and transferable experience to be shared with them in order to grow. My personal experience of courageous thinking and acting is something I found critically valuable for coaching leaders by example. People need a coach's real experience to gain confidence that everything is possible.

I know about courage from my experience fishing in rough seas and facing massive gales on a small trawler. At first, you feel sick during a moderate storm and scared of not having any control over the situation. Then, gradually you adapt and learn how to manage yourself and what best to do in such rough conditions. At a certain point, you enjoy and even look forward to the storm.

Courage is a skill that can be developed. In order to develop it, I do not recommend you jump into cold water every day or do something risky. Instead, I would ask you to look at it differently. Courage is acting and thinking boldly in the face of something unexplored, huge, and complicated. In such cases, one competes not against somebody else but against one's own fears.

In practical terms, I asked my client to answer three simple questions as often as possible:

- What disrupted your thinking and progress with your vision?
- What was your response to this disruption?
- What fear have you managed to fight or seriously reduce over the last 2 weeks?

Courage Offers a High Return

Three months later, I met with the client and asked him three questions – How has courageous thinking changed you as a leader? How difficult was it to break out of comfort zone thinking? How did it influence your people?

The client admitted that the result was unexpectedly great – "Breaking my own boundaries allowed me to make myself much bigger and capable of leading people and myself to success. My team trusts me in projects. They express the highest degree of trust in the sense that together we can achieve anything without doubt."

He continued, "The feeling of being a strong team is growing. We receive new ideas almost daily now that have resulted in new valuable features in our software. We recently signed a contract which we could only dream about before. We grow from inside. As the leader of this business, I feel positivity, confidence, and people's craving to explore more. What is most important, we have a vision for ourselves and work on creating our long-term vision now."

Courageous thinking helps leaders to develop their employees and their business. This is critical for their teams helping people rise and be explorers themselves.

Here are four practical suggestions to consider:

- One can develop courage by asking oneself bold questions and finding answers which lie beyond one's own fears and usual habits of thinking. Only by challenging yourself can you become a catalyst for change and thrive as a ground-breaking visionary. Lack of courage will eventually lead to a professional and personal crisis.
- We always have time to correct mistakes if we are courageous enough to admit them and have a strong will to change for better.
- There is always a good mentor or coach behind every leader of success who helps to develop his/her capacity. A good mentor or coach helps to attune a courageous thinking, which will result in outstanding personal and professional development.
- The desire for mental comfort prevents change and personal and professional growth. Comfort is a swamp that destroys a person's will. This is a force that is difficult to defeat. It always presents new excuses and reasons why you should not act on your vision. In practice, many leaders think, "I do well enough and don't need to do better" without even trying to leave their comfort zone. This leads to short-term thinking and the eventual destruction of whatever they might have accomplished before.

43

The Pause for Progress

Bill Carrier

"Have you ever played golf?" I asked my client. "Or watched it?"

He nodded, "Sure." The leader of a billion-dollar division within a Fortune 100 company, he and I were having coffee during our coaching session. Though a star performer, like so many executives, he was maxed out. The stress and work were taking their toll – there was, in his mind, simply too much to get done. Now, on top of everything else, a major strategy change had just been announced.

"What happens on the tee box?" I continued.

"Well…you put the ball on the tee, take a moment, and then swing," he replied, eyeing me a little uncertainly.

I nodded, "Does anyone ever put the ball on the tee, step back about twenty feet, sprint to the tee, swing as hard as possible while on the run, then chase after the ball while it's flying?"

My client looked at me like I was a little crazy.

"Then, when they catch up to the ball, do they try to hit it while on a dead sprint, and basically play that way the entire round?"

"Of course not!" my client chuckled. We both smiled.

"Why not?" I asked.

"Well, you'd have no control, so your score would be terrible. You'd be exhausted before you finished the first hole – if you even did finish it! And you'd probably have a heart attack by the time you got to the first green."

I nodded and we both laughed.

"So why do you work that way?" I asked.

He flinched and then froze, cheeks coloring a little, eyes full of the realization that this conversation was about something more than golf.

"Are you really playing your game in the way you're most likely to win?" I continued. "Are you enjoying it?"

He paused for a moment, "No. I'm not. But what's the alternative?"

I smiled and said, "You already know. So let's talk about it."

Many leaders in today's world – CEOs especially – run from meeting to meeting like a golfer sprinting from tee to tee. The speed can feel exhilarating at times, especially when profit and impact numbers are good. But there are consequences.

Because they hurtle through their days, they focus almost exclusively on operational issues at the expense of strategic thinking and decision-making. This has longer-term negative consequences. Because they move so quickly through meetings, they often create and carry frustrations from one meeting to the next, which leads to cloudier judgments and diminished effectiveness.

Bill Carrier, president of Carrier Leadership Coaching, Inc., is an executive coach for high-impact CEOs and senior executives. He is the executive director of the Marshall Goldsmith *100 Coaches* program for the top leadership professionals in the world, co-founder of *The Future of Coaching* magazine, a former Rotary International Ambassadorial Scholar to Brazil, and a graduate of the United States Military Academy at West Point.

Coach Me! Your Personal Board of Directors: Leadership Advice from the World's Greatest Coaches, First Edition. Edited by Brian Underhill, Jonathan Passmore, and Marshall Goldsmith.
© 2022 John Wiley & Sons Ltd. Published 2022 by John Wiley & Sons Ltd.
DOI: 10.1002/9781119823803.ch43

For many CEOs, it feels like there's not only not enough time, but survival seems to be at stake. They see no way to stop. The solution is actually simple. Don't *stop*… instead, *pause*.

Think about the golf example again. What do the most successful professional golfers do? Before a drive, an iron shot, and especially before a putt, they pause. If they are frustrated with the previous shot, they take a moment to let go of that negative energy. When they are preparing for a new shot, they take a moment to think about their strategy, about the terrain and how it will impact their results, and about their own presence and whether they are on point. They notice the tension in their grip and take the time to adjust to fix anything that is off. The pause is a critical part of their path to winning.

There is a growing body of research on the value of pausing in learning and performance. In fact, one recently published paper noted that the mere option to pause increased performance – very likely through increased self-regulation – and that pausing during high-stress situations clearly decreased cognitive load. Military commanders have long used a "tactical pause," a momentary interruption in action, to clarify the operational situation.

I have helped corporate CEOs and senior leaders implement a similar technique I call the Pause for Progress. It is a brief and purposeful break in the action that allows them to decompress and reorient on their purpose, the business environment, and their personal executive presence.

The Pause for Progress may feel counterintuitive, but it contributes to better leadership and business outcomes because it reduces ineffective stress and increases the power and effectiveness of action. It gives leaders a moment to shape their future with more of the intent that best serves them and the teams they lead.

The pause is not a stop. It is not trading action for endless strategizing or shifting from making things happen to waiting for other people to do them.

Stopping would require having to build momentum again, which uses your finite energy. With a pause, your momentum is conserved. When it is over, you continue with the same or even more force – and with a much better mindset.

In every coaching session with my CEO and senior leader clients, we begin with a short Pause for Progress conversation. In this, we are helping the leader check out of the operational mindset and into a strategic mindset.

Often, irritating issues evaporate because the Pause for Progress helps them see that a particular issue does not really matter. Other times, issues will gain traction because they are more readily recognized as genuinely important to the big picture.

This short powerful Pause for Progress enables the leader to decompress and reorient. We are then able to pay better attention to the most important issues and opportunities the company and the leader have in front of them.

Here are some examples of what I have seen clients accomplish with the simple addition of the Pause for Progress:

- The very dynamic, often directive CEO of a SaaS (software-as-a-service) firm decided to invest deeply in delegating and growing his direct reports. Among other things, we agreed he would use the pause to ask questions instead of offering advice. The increased feeling of trust and autonomy contributed to double-digit growth and a remarkable nine-figure acquisition of the firm.
- A senior leader had been working late every night to the point of burnout before we started our coaching engagement. By the time we completed our work together a year later, he was working fewer hours, with less stress, and having more impact than ever before. He had grown the company's results, tripled the size of his team, and taken on eight times as much responsibility in the organization.
- A senior leader of a large organization started taking a Pause for Progress to create a weekly list of what matters. The resulting focus on priorities helped drive an increase of more than $70 M in revenue in just 18 months.

My client and I were out for a coffee again, several months later. "Bill, I've got to tell you, it's been a great couple of months. I've had more time to think strategically. The CEO publicly congratulated me for our division's performance. Our other divisions are adopting some of the leadership development practices I created with you." He shook his head and grinned. "I'd have never thought it possible – but you really can get more done by doing less! That Pause for Progress really works."

I smiled. "Let's pause there and get another coffee."

What can you do to make sure you use the Pause for Progress to guide your work more effectively? Here are two suggestions:

Step 1: Pause your plan: Decompress.

When would a Pause for Progress benefit you best? Remember, this is a short break in activity to decompress and reorient on what matters. For many leaders, a great time is the first minutes of a meeting to get a team to gel. Also, for many leaders, a repetitive reflection on what matters for the day, the week, the month, and the year creates lasting value.

Step 2: Plan your pause: Re-orient.

What do you do when you make a Pause for Progress? Depending on the pause and its purpose, the technique may be so simple it is understood (small talk at the beginning of a meeting to let everyone decompress, for example) or so complex it requires a written reminder and checklist (like scheduling a set time each week for planning).

In almost all pauses, it pays to attend to the items I mentioned in the golf analogy:

- *What's the point of your game?* In other words, what's the purpose of the event, meeting, or action you're engaging in? When you remember with clarity your purpose, you are more likely to achieve it.
- *What's the lay of the land?* In other words, what's the current environment actually like versus what you expected or what you just experienced somewhere else? When you notice the reality in front of you, you are better prepared to take advantage of opportunities and adjust to challenges.
- *How are you playing?* In other words, how much is your head and your heart in the action in which you're currently engaging? What's your personal executive presence? When you're fully able to engage – not rehashing earlier meetings or future anxieties – you can get more done, more quickly, more powerfully, and with less need to rework.

44

There Is No Such Thing as Work/Life Balance

Brian O. Underhill PhD, PCC

As reports of COVID-19 spread began increasing in frequency throughout the world, I sat down with my new client, the VP Engineering of a Silicon Valley tech firm, at a local coffeehouse. Our goal today was to review the feedback I had collected after interviewing his boss, peers, and direct reports.

"Well, Arun," I said, "It looks like your towering strength may also be your largest area for development. Everyone working with you says: 'he volunteers for everything, takes anything on, gets the job done, great at execution, makes it happen, gets the trains to run on time.'" I continued "And..."

"BUT!?..." he interjected.

"AND..." I jokingly retorted, "Arun takes too much on, it gets to the point where he never sleeps. Any time you write him, he answers 24/7, works 16–18-hour days, doesn't delegate, does it himself. It is just not sustainable. We worry about his health." I went on, "Your boss even joked that if you left the organization, he'd have to hire 2–3 people just to replace you!"

As we wrapped up and walked toward our cars, he talked about how his family was his #1 priority. And he asked me if I saw any "fatal flaws" in his feedback. I very softly pointed out the irony that if family truly was his #1 priority, he was not currently living it. And that his feedback had no real fatal flaws – except THIS.

As executive coaches, we routinely work with leaders who are high-performing, high-achieving individuals. They regularly work harder than nearly anyone, often putting in more hours than one could believe. That is not atypical for an executive. It is partially the reason why they have gotten to where they have, through dedication and hard work. Yet, Arun took that to an entirely new level – putting in more hours (cheerfully, I might add) than any of the hundreds of leaders I had coached in 25 years.

As lockdown kicked in, we pivoted next to a videocall. "It's just the way I've been since middle school," he explained. "My [late] father is my role model. He was a hard worker and selfless, he got tremendous satisfaction taking care of everyone. I wish I could be at least half as selfless as he was."

Yet, we were entering a "perfect storm season" of challenges that would soon work against him: (1) This new pandemic work-from-home lifestyle meant he could work even more hours than in the past. (2) His family had a pre-planned move back to India, while keeping the same job, meaning his temptation to stay up and work USA hours would be real. (3) While his boss was incredibly worried about his workload, an upcoming restructure would put another division under his management.

Coaching an over-achieving leader requires multiple levels of intervention in order to drive improvement. There are plenty of practical day-to-day behavioral adjustments to be made, but we must also explore the deeper drivers. Without looking at the these, old habits will creep back in when things get tough.

Brian O. Underhill, PhD, PCC, is the founder and CEO of CoachSource, the world's largest pure play executive-coaching provider. He is an industry-recognized thought leader, international keynote speaker, and published author. Brian's executive coaching work has successfully focused on helping leaders achieve positive, measurable, long-term change in leadership behavior.

Coach Me! Your Personal Board of Directors: Leadership Advice from the World's Greatest Coaches, First Edition. Edited by Brian Underhill, Jonathan Passmore, and Marshall Goldsmith.
© 2022 John Wiley & Sons Ltd. Published 2022 by John Wiley & Sons Ltd.
DOI: 10.1002/9781119823803.ch44

Behavioral Adjustments

We worked together to create a variety of (often daily) action steps:

- He first analyzed his calendar in great detail, categorizing every item and learning how he was spending his time – and contrasting that with how he SHOULD be spending his time. A variety of adjustments were made on which meetings he would stop attending, send a surrogate, or even shorten/defer (his calendar naturally had 55 hours of meetings every week, before doing any actual work!!) We realized how many meetings were "relics" from the past that continued indefinitely, without anyone questioning "do we still really need this meeting?"
- Starting first with "baby steps," he committed to holding sacred a late afternoon/early evening break (approx. 5–9 pm) to walk with his wife, play with his son, and enjoy dinner together. He measured this daily and shared results with me in each call. This quickly became a non-negotiable, and if he did not stop on time, he "penalized" himself by having to prepare the dinner or buy his son a toy. He eventually hit 62 days in a row of protecting this time.
- He defined more aspects of his work that could be delegated to his team, and since they were not complaining of being overloaded in my interviews, I knew there was room to work with here. More and more was offloaded to the team.
- He let everyone around him know of this development objective. Everyone was supportive and pledged to help, to be more understanding when he says "no," delegates more, or does not raise his hand when volunteers are sought. (In one staff meeting, his boss was looking for someone to head up a project – the boss said, "Anyone can volunteer for this except Arun!" drawing sympathetic laughs from all.)

Deeper Mindset Drivers

- My feedback gathering indicated Arun to be an incredibly pleasant, amicable individual – who (as can be the case) wanted to please, help others, and never say "no." "I like making things easier for my team. I don't leave a problem until I have it solved for them." We had dig in deeper – would it be possible to say no, without feeling like he was disappointing people?
- Along these lines, I convened Arun and his boss in a joint Zoom to clarify that it was NOT his boss nor the organization that was pressuring him to work this hard. His boss worked perhaps 50–55 hrs/week, and a typical VP at this firm might average around the same. (Arun was 80–90 hrs initially.) Perhaps, this would help him be comfortable with fewer hours.
- Arun originally told me, "Everything must be 100% to perfection", which helped explain why he did so much himself. We then explored when something could be 80% instead and defined areas around him less mission critical where a lower quality standard would be "good enough." We discussed when it might even be OK for the team to fail at something – very valuable for their learning. Reinforcing this point, his boss actually said, "With all the innovation we are doing, there should be more failure than there is." Arun decided to "lead from the back, not from the front."

After a few months of regular meetings and good progress, I unexpectedly lost touch with Arun. He had moved to India as planned, but oddly was not responding to my meeting requests. Once we reconnected, he apologized deeply and let me know he'd actually been out on medical leave…an odd medical condition arose putting him out of commission, which the doctor related to stress – perhaps from moving during the pandemic, while attempting to keep US work hours, while living in India (exactly what I was concerned about earlier!), he had not worked in several weeks.

As his coach, I felt a great sense of failure – had we not done enough, fast enough, to prevent this health scare? Should I have pushed for deeper, more immediate change? This felt like a major setback in our work together.

BUT… the blessings of having to be completely offline? He couldn't work, and he had to get used to "letting go." He HAD to delegate and empower his people, and they did so with flying colors. He realized life eventually goes on at work, whether he's there or not. "I learned that no one is indispensable." He gained a new perspective of what was really important in life: his health, his family. The next health scare might be much more serious, he realized there is no reason to flirt with the limits of one's body.

After 6 months of coaching, I formally surveyed everyone around him. Had he become a more effective leader since coaching began? 100% of all 12 raters said he had improved. Had he gotten more effective at delegating? Again, 100% agreement (with 7 of 12 selecting the highest improvement level). Said one, "I've seen Arun make great strides to delegate more." We celebrated success.

BUT, had he got better at "managing his workload to a more reasonable quantity?" He scored a 4.6 on the 7.0 improvement scale, averaging just between "no change" (4) and "slight positive change" (5). Three raters felt he had gotten worse. There was much work still to be done. "Do I have the same rigor to improve that I did when coaching began?" he reflected. "Do I have the danger of stepping back into bad habits?"

He realized that old habits may have returned, and thankfully the survey warned us. As of this writing, he has recommitted to making change, we'll be exploring further methods to break bad habits, and he has asked for coaching to continue another year to help reinforce it.

Work/life "balance" is a misnomer. It is not a balance. It is a choice. We each make conscious and unconscious choices that affect this balance. Here are some questions to ask yourself, if you are struggling in this area:

Why – truly why – do you work as hard as you do? What are you hoping to GAIN or REPLACE or ESCAPE by working this hard?

Examine your values in life – rank order them. Are you prioritizing your time according to these values?

Are you really delegating as you could be? Only do what only you can do.

Imagine life circumstances force you to work at half your usual capacity, with no exceptions – how would you manage your workload?

45

The Leadership Success Definition Should Include Impact (and Maybe ROI)

Jack J. Phillips PhD

Good Company grew from a small operation to a thriving business of more than $100M in revenue. This respected family company makes high quality personal care products.

The executives wanted continued success and thought coaching could help achieve this goal. The CEO engaged our coaching services for leadership development. When we asked, "What is the goal of the coaching?" the focus was primarily on behavior. They wanted to improve teamwork, communication, information sharing, delegation to team members, and performance issues. These responses focused on behavior change for their leaders.

Then we asked several questions, "If you do this, how does this help the business?" The executives were reluctant to talk about the business because they were still thinking "how can coaching really help the business?" With encouragement from the CFO, we persisted and got them to pinpoint key performance measures that would improve if they became better leaders through the coaching process. In essence, our coaching was focused on improving specific business impacts, including sales growth, product development, profitability, quality, and social responsibility.

These executives realized that leaders are not successful unless they drive business measures, expressed as key performance indicators. The success of leadership is a value chain. Is it how others see the leader (reaction)? Is it what is learned from the leader (learning)? Is it the actions taken because of the learning (application)? Or, is it the business measure influenced because of their actions (impact)? And is this worthwhile for the leader, for those the leader is influencing, or for the organization (ROI)? The answer is *yes* to each question.

The Dilemma

In a 2018 Sunday board meeting in London, John Flint, CEO of HSBC, was fired. The move came after months of concern over Mr. Flint's leadership style and ability to take decisive action. Mr. Flint had a long career with HSBC. When faced with a problem, he liked to spend time considering it and would map out potential actions and outcomes. He sought to make HSBC a more inclusive and pleasant place to work, developing a plan he called "Healthiest Human System" to encourage a better work-life balance for employees. His messages resonated with the bank's staff, and his results were disappointing. Six months before he was fired, HSBC's full-year earnings were worse than expected, in part because costs were outweighing revenue growth. He did not deliver the business impact (Patrick, 2019).

Jack J. Phillips, PhD, chairman of ROI Institute, is a world-renowned expert on measurement and evaluation. A former bank president, Phillips is author or editor of more than 100 books, including *Measuring the Success of Coaching* (ASTD Press, 2012), and has provided coaching and consulting services in 70 countries. His work has been featured in the *Wall Street Journal*, *Bloomberg Businessweek*, *Fortune*, and on *CNN*.

Coach Me! Your Personal Board of Directors: Leadership Advice from the World's Greatest Coaches, First Edition. Edited by Brian Underhill, Jonathan Passmore, and Marshall Goldsmith.
© 2022 John Wiley & Sons Ltd. Published 2022 by John Wiley & Sons Ltd.
DOI: 10.1002/9781119823803.ch45

"Good business leaders create a vision, articulate the vision, and relentlessly drive it to completion."

Jack Welch
CEO April 1981 to Sept. 2001
GE market cap $402B

"Every job or decision looks easy until you are the one on the line."

Jeff Immelt
CEO, Sept. 2001 to July 2017
GE market cap $222B

- These are the market caps at the departures.
- Welch is known for his focus on key impact measures.
- Under Immelt's tenure, GE lost almost half its value.

Figure 45.1 General Electric Leadership Impact Comparison.

Impact Measures are Everywhere

Fortunately, impact measures are everywhere at all levels in an organization. At the top of an organization, the success of a leader is clear. For a publicly traded business, the ultimate impact measure is perhaps market value (the stock price times the outstanding shares – market cap). The top leader makes a big difference, as illustrated in Figure 45.1.

For Gail McGovern, President and CEO of The American Red Cross, her number one measure is the amount of received donations and operating revenue. The number two measure is the percent of money spent that goes to humanitarian services and programs.

Lorraine Martin, President and CEO of the National Safety Council, a nonprofit organization, has a top priority to prevent deaths at home, in the communities, and on the road.

While these impacts are obvious for top leaders, similar impacts for lower-level leaders are also obvious. They are rolled up into and support the top leaders' "business" measures.

The Basics of Accountability

In many situations, a fresh look starts with a look into the past with some advice from well-known leaders. Here's what two US presidents said about leadership success. John Quincy Adams said, "Successful leaders inspire others to learn more, do more, and become more." Ronald Reagan said, "The greatest leader is not necessarily the one who does the greatest things. He is the one that gets the people to do the greatest things." Let us break this down into steps or levels.

Level 1: Inspiring others means that others are reacting to the leader based on their perception of that leader and the leader's behavior. **Reaction** is critical, and without a positive reaction, the leader may not have success.

Level 2: **Learning** more means that we learn from our leaders. These important takeaways may be information, ideas, behavior, or skills.

Level 3: Doing more means a leader must drive action. Leaders must influence others to take action. Without action, the leader has little influence. Let us label that **application** as the followers apply what they learned from the leader.

Level 4: Becoming more is the consequence of doing more. This is the **impact** of the leader, the consequences of action. To become more must be important to the individual, the leader, and the organization. Often, this information is fully reflected in the performance data for the individual and organization.

Level 5: Finally, there is one piece that John Quincy Adams did not mention, but it is worth adding. Is this a worthwhile journey for the leader? Is the effort worth it for the followers? The best way to measure the worth of the journey is with the concept of return on investment (**ROI**), a financial term for comparing benefits to cost.

This concept is simple, yet powerful. Success does not occur until impact is achieved. It suggests that the evaluation of leadership should not stop at the learning level or at the leader behavior level. Leadership should be

Success level	Leadership qualities	Leadership challenge	Leader label	Value chain label
1	Admirable	Make it exciting	Charismatic	Reaction
2	Intelligence	Make it matter	Teacher	Learning
3	Bias for action	Make it stick	Influencer	Application (action)
4	Results focus	Make it credible	Impactful	Impact
5	Value add	Make it worthwhile	Valuable	ROI

Figure 45.2 Success Profile.

evaluated at the impact level. What impact are the leaders having with their team through their actions, activities, and behaviors? Impacts are typically output, quality, time, and costs, for tangible measures, and teamwork, collaboration, and engagement, for intangible measures.

Most organizations fail to define the success of leadership at the impact level. We see this routinely in organizations with significant investments in leadership. Years ago, we evaluated leaders on how we reacted to them. Then, we began to evaluate them on what they know. About two decades ago, the focus shifted to an evaluation based on behaviors, their actions. Now, the focus is on impact and maybe ROI.

A Complete Success Profile

Leadership descriptions come in all shapes and sizes. Figure 45.2 explains the success levels of leadership, which represent a chain of value that must exist for leaders to be successful.

Each level of success is needed for the next level to be successful. If the leader is not interesting and respected, there will be little or no learning. Without learning, there is no application. Without application, there is no impact. Without impact, the ROI is negative (–100%).

A leader must obtain results on five levels. John Flint of HSBC failed to provide results at the impact level, and although he was well liked by the employees (reaction), it cost him his job. A leader's success is connected to results and the journey must be worth it for those involved. A leader does not have the option of focusing on one level of success but must operate on all levels of outcomes.

Conclusion

The coaching at Good Company ultimately proved successful and convinced the top executives that great leaders deliver great results on five levels of outcomes, including impact and ROI. Survey feedback revealed that the leaders perceived the coaching to be valuable and important to their success (reaction). Surveys also revealed that they were learning more about their teams and how to make them more successful (learning). Action plans revealed how they were working with the teams in a different way (application). These action plans also documented important improvements in key performance measures such as new product development, sales growth, efficiencies, and retention (impact). When these measures were converted to money and compared to the cost of coaching, the result was a positive ROI.

Without impact, leaders are ineffective. The great leader can deliver on all levels of outcomes in the face of many challenges. For more details on this concept, see our new book, *Proving the Value of Soft Skills* (Phillips et al., 2020).

References

Patrick, M. (2019). Lack of action led to CEO's ousting. *The Wall Street Journal*, August 6.

Phillips, J. J., Ray, R., & Phillips, P. P. (2020). *Proving the value of soft skills*. Alexandria, Virginia: ATD Press.

Career Development

46

From C-Suite to CEO

How to Get Promoted & Survive the Leap

Mark C. Thompson

The race to the C-Suite has become one of the most rewarding and risky undertakings you can consider in your career. While compensation is at record highs, the average tenure of C-level executives is the shortest in history. After 70 board and C-Suite executive coaching engagements, I have seen a pattern emerge about how to prepare yourself for the challenge.

A Case History for Success and Failure of C-Suite Executives*

When one of the world's largest banks named Dr. Geneva Bezos among several internal candidates for the future CEO role, a dramatic race to the corner office ensued among her peers on the leadership team. If that was not competitive enough, the board asked recruiters to offer outside contenders as a comparison set. It is not unusual for boards of both public and private organizations to launch a high-stakes internal and external championship for the top job. For Bezos, she knew that there were many issues that would impact who would be selected as CEO, including many that appeared out of her control. While her overall credentials and technical qualifications were critical, there were five other key questions she had to address. Each of these factors are critical to your success in seizing any C-Suite opportunity:

1. **Board Dynamics:** Each director on your board can make or break your chances for promotion. As a CEO or a candidate for that role, you must be sensitive to the needs of each board member as if they each were your supervisor because, ultimately, they have that power. Most people do not realize that no one else in an organization has as many bosses as a CEO. Bezos had more than 80 directors at the bank! She needed to learn about and address the political climate with each director, each of whom served on board committees around the world with differing charters, from audit to compensation to strategy. Fortunately, her board welcomed hearing from her and promptly agreed to one-on-one meetings. Succession planning is a major preoccupation for most boards (Lorsch & Khurana, 1999) as regulations increase each director's fiduciary responsibility, requiring much higher independence and greater scrutiny of management.

Mark Thompson is a *NYTimes* bestselling author and the world's #1 CEO Coach ranked by the American Management Association and Global Leading Coaches/Thinkers50. Forbes described him as having the "Midas Touch," with clients including World Bank CEO Jim Yong Kim, Pinterest cofounder Evan Sharp, and Virgin founder Richard Branson.

* This is a real story, but with name substituted to protect privacy.

Coach Me! Your Personal Board of Directors: Leadership Advice from the World's Greatest Coaches, First Edition. Edited by Brian Underhill, Jonathan Passmore, and Marshall Goldsmith.
© 2022 John Wiley & Sons Ltd. Published 2022 by John Wiley & Sons Ltd.
DOI: 10.1002/9781119823803.ch46

Most directors are former CEOs, former audit partners with professional services firms, or professors with strong expectations for the candidates' development. Interestingly, there are always critical measures that board members will tell me as a coach in private that they are not willing to share directly with my candidate.

- As a C-Suite candidate, how will you build the necessary relationships and coalitions with individual board members? Do you have an advisor to help capture how each director is measuring each candidate's viability?

2. **Peer Dynamics:** Are you the type of person that your peers would be willing to work for? Dr. Geneva Bezos realized that the final selection for the CEO's job often comes down to realizing that your peers will play a part in evaluating whether you are worthy of being their boss. Your peers do not have the biggest vote, but it is difficult for a CEO, CHRO, and the board to gain confidence for your candidacy if your colleagues think you are an arrogant jerk jockeying for position. Bezos knew her peers would be asked by the committee charged with finding a successor. "You're taking a serious shift in your role," she observed. "You're moving from peer and possible competitor to 'likeable' boss."

- What criteria are your peers using to judge you? How are your current CEO and CHRO evaluating who they wish to recommend as successor?

3. **Bench Dynamics:** You cannot grow or scale your business quickly if you are making all the decisions. For Bezos, she realized that the leader must resolve differences between team members, but most of the time a leader's job is putting together the right team, and putting the right questions in front of them to change their inherent internal built-in biases.

- Have you built the capable, trusted bench needed to replace you? Have you invested in your leadership team and what cultural changes are required for the company's next phase and your promotion?

4. **Strategic Dynamics:** When I met Steve Jobs, I was selling to him the idea of including my company's audio technology, known as MP3. He showed great counterintuitive courage with the iPhone at a price point back when "smart phones" were a relatively new idea and critics thought it would be disastrous with no keyboard. Jobs added useful apps that no other competitor dared to integrate, like music and video. Most companies instead wanted to follow the market leaders, BlackBerry and Nokia, who at the time had 80% market share. What would have happened if Apple followed the market leaders? It is risky to just stick with what's worked in the past.

- What's your strategy to respond to shifting market dynamics and disruptions in your industry?

5. **Personal Dynamics:** "When you sit down Sunday night to look at your week, what percentage of your calendar is focused on being proactive?" Steve Covey prodded me during an interview at his home. "Are you just responding to one meeting request after another, or an emergency here or there? Crises must be managed, but the difference between being proactive rather than reactive is making the time to really decide where you want to lead and grow your organization without fear or anger."

- In Greek mythology, the difference between the quests of those leaders who were successful and those who failed was not whether they were flawed as individuals, but rather whether the hero had the courage to admit weakness and mistakes and ultimately become vulnerable to change. How will you learn to be resilient to setbacks and frustration and remain focused on what matters?

As Dr. Geneva Bezos planned her ascent, she realized she would face her own behavioral challenges. Every leader has coping mechanisms that hide beneath the waterline that undermine your chances for selection when you are under the added pressure of "running for office" as CEO. C-Suite candidates have impressive track records of achievements, but when they are just about to make the leap to the pinnacle of their career trajectory, why do so many of these talented corporate stars make fatal judgment calls, miss crucial market cues and developments, alienate key people, and falter in their delivery of results?

Psychologists Robert Kaiser et al. (2015) created an inventory of eleven "dark side" traits or derailers. When under stress, leaders reflexively respond with a pattern that they may not even be aware of or have found ways to dismiss or excuse as they climbed the ladder. These include being too easily annoyed, hard to please, taking excessive credit, and giving excessive blame. Under pressure, leaders can become disturbingly distrustful, cynical, sensitive to criticism, focused on the negative, slow to make decisions, and indifferent to others' feelings. Even Bezos felt that she, like most high achievers, had too many of these traits. As her coach, I emphasized that it was important to recognize that some derailers are simply over-used strengths, or at least were identified as strengths in a previous role.

Dr. Geneva Bezos embraced her faults. As a result, her insecurities vanished, and the board saw she grew faster than her competitors for the job. "Nobody expects you to be perfect," she observed, "but they do expect you to be responsive to the profound changes needed to succeed." Bezos also believed that recognizing her own derailers made her much more empathetic toward others and a vastly better coach in developing her team.

In *Built to Last* and *Good to Great*, Prof. Jim Collins insisted that leaders like Bezos share a paradoxical combination of "hubris and humility." They exhibit the *hubris* to believe and convince the team they can lead a huge organization through uncharted territory – even though that vision can border on irrational exuberance. But the best leaders also exhibit the *humility* to realize that no one ever does anything sustainable or scalable alone, nor does the success of a leader occur without humiliating and existential setbacks along the way. Those realizations are what sets successful C-Suite candidates apart.

In *Success Built to Last: Creating a Life That Matters* (Thompson et al., 2005), the sequel to *Built to Last*, I interviewed 200 leaders, many of whom related stories of their climb up the organizational ladder. Most were challenged by feeling they must suffer observation in a glass house and over-analyzed and yet also ironically faced with an acute sense of isolation. The network of trust they believed they built is complicated by the politics and power dynamics as colleagues compete for a position. These leaders longed for a safe, private sounding board to bounce ideas around. Many found the support of an executive coach essential during the marathon. As a C-Suite candidate, your race to the top of an organization is fraught with peril and error, but what you are doing is creating an opportunity to have a great positive impact on the lives of thousands of employees and customers that is built to last and ultimately to become a better version of yourself as a leader.

# # #

References

Thompson, M., Porras, J., & Emery, S. (2005). *Success built to last: Creating a life that matters.* Prentice Hall.

Kaiser, R., LeBreton, J., & Hogan, J. (2015, January 1). The dark side of personality and extreme leader behavior. *Applied Psychology*, 64, 55–92. https://doi.org/10.1111/apps.12024

47

Personal Leadership Brand: How to Take Control of How You "Show Up"

Mongezi C. Makhalima PhD

About 2 years ago, I was invited to coach a number of executives at one of the national government agencies in South Africa. One of the executives I coached in this group raised the issue of her personal reputation. While she performed well and had delivered excellently on her goals under very difficult circumstances, her main challenge was that she was struggling to earn the respect of her peers and recognition as a key contributor within the organization. She especially wanted to reverse the perception of her by the CEO that she was still junior to the rest of the executive team. She was struggling with credibility. And this is a common challenge for many leaders.

After over 30 years of doing this work, one of the key issues I find I deal with a lot in the last 3–5 years in the boardrooms of the world is how leaders "Show up." A word used often by many coaches that many leaders however seem to struggle to translate into practice.

I define *credibility* as the ability to create trustworthiness. But this is just one element in the overall personal branding matrix. The personal branding matrix outlines the four elements of the leader's personal brand (see Figure 47.1).

Personhood (Who am I really?)	Personal value perceptions (What's my value to me and to others?)
Personal brand promotion (How do I push my brand?)	Personal brand locale (Where can/should my brand be found?)

Figure 47.1 Personal Branding Matrix.

Dr Mongezi C. Makhalima is an organization development specialist and chartered executive coach with over 30 years of experience in working with organizations and leaders. He is a chairperson of the Africa Board for Coaching, Consulting and Coaching Psychology (ABCCCP) and Thinkers 50 Top 50 Global coach. Mongezi is passionate about inspiring leaders using his knowledge of coaching and psychology.

Coach Me! Your Personal Board of Directors: Leadership Advice from the World's Greatest Coaches, First Edition. Edited by Brian Underhill, Jonathan Passmore, and Marshall Goldsmith.
© 2022 John Wiley & Sons Ltd. Published 2022 by John Wiley & Sons Ltd.
DOI: 10.1002/9781119823803.ch47

First it is important to define what branding is, before discussing these four elements. Pryce-Jones (2007) defines branding as what you stand for internally and externally. I define personal branding as what people say about you in your absence, the collective and individual perceptions and impressions of you as a leader. These perceptions and impressions are influenced by:

1. **Personhood** – This is the leader's personal credibility, values, beliefs, assumptions, and behaviors. This is possibly the most important element of the four and when it is well defined; it forms the crux of the personal branding matrix. In my research on credibility and what makes a professional credible, eight elements emerged that I have reduced to an acronym SKARP. This means you should do an inventory of your:

   - **Skills** – What are those things you are really good at doing (better than 80% of the people you know). Most times many of us are distracted because we do not know our strengths – and as a result, our energies are scattered all over – distracted even by our attempts to find an answer to this – in an unstructured, unfocused way.

   - **Knowledge** – What do you know for sure – what is the TRUTH that you have that can be supported by evidence? This could be what you learned in your years of experience, what you studied for years, or really just learned on your grandfather's knees. We tend to compete externally when we should be focusing on how what we know can add value to others. If we do not know what we do not know, it is difficult to be still by choice.

   - **Attributes** – Here, you need to look at your *values, your attitudes, your motives,* and *your personality*. I have realized that many of us are not aware of how strong the influence of our *values* is – but we are also not aware of the value clashes that we experience. We therefore spend a lot of time blaming the external elements for our "strange" behavior and our pain/discomfort when we should be looking inside. The same applies to our *attitude*. When we do not like something, we do not do it to the best of our ability. Yet, it is strange how many people show up at my offices looking for coaching that are doing things they do not like because they are trying to please the external world. Many of us work and live in a social context: teams, partners, social clubs, while shopping, etc. Our *personality* presents the mask we wear in our interactions with others. Do you know your own mask? Do you know for sure what others see when they see you? Finally, our *motives* and drives influence our behavior every day. And as a leader, it is important to not just react to the primitive drives within you, but to be able to name them and manage them actively because this is the foundation of all behaviors. As you can see, the attributes are the lion's share of your brand proposition.

   - **Results** – What have you achieved so far in your life? (And the answer to this cannot be "NOTHING", especially if you are reading this.) What value have you added to others that can be measured in a real and tangible way? We spend a lot of time attracted by the outside world because we are seeking the validation that says we are doing good – we are "passing" – in relationships, at work, etc., but most of the time because we hold an external standard of achievement, we do not realize what greatness already lies in us – we become the slaves to that noise.

   - **Purpose** – It is said that each of us has a unique fingerprint; different from anyone in the world, and that we each have a purpose. I believe this. What I have found interesting though with many people I encounter is that many have no clue what THAT purpose is. What I have found fascinating though is how when I take people through the process of discovering this purpose, they realize they knew it all along – and become animated and energized.

2. **The Personal Value Perceptions (Personal Brand Equity)** speaks to how much in value, be it in impact or financial value the leader is worth. One leader I have worked with shared an example of how he has seen his personal value increase through the years in the eyes of the employers, from the time he was a junior staff member in the team to where he was negotiating for a salary for an executive role he currently holds. His reflection though, which is the experience of many leaders, is how he tends to undervalue himself.

3. **Personal Brand Locale.** Location has a strong impact on personal brand perception. For example, I have very limited experience in working with West African countries and East Asian countries and therefore my brand perception to that clientele in terms of utility and value may be lower. And any of the personhood elements in the 1st quadrant could have an impact on the leader's brand perception and impression. It is important for the leader to pay attention to how where they are, and where they are from, can have an impact on their brand value.

4. **Personal Brand Promotion**. This element is self-explanatory and touches on the activities the brand takes on to drive brand perception and impression. Imagine if one of the best-known brands in the world, Coca-Cola, did not have the kind of prominent and exciting adverts that it has across the world? How would people know that it exists? The same applies to our personal leadership brand. We are constantly communicating. Does it not then make sense that we take control of this communication process? With personal branding, it is obviously not necessary to do the massive big ad campaigns (indeed, for some personality types, these can have a negative impact on leader's credibility).

So as a brand, are you able to put names to all the brand artifacts or elements that constitute your personal brand? Or do you just show up and hope "You have showed up?"

By being clearer about each of the elements in the Personal Brand Matrix, the leader is able to create more trust and be more in control of how they "Show up." Allowing people to treat them as THEY are, rather than who people think they are.

And this was the work we did with this leader. In the reflections after two meetings, she realized that she THOUGHT her credibility only lay in her results. This is a common challenge for high performers, especially those who have been promoted from lower ranks to senior and executive positions. She also realized that she did not know enough about herself or did not have the language to speak about herself in a way that positioned her in the eyes of her stakeholders.

Six months down the line, her reputation had increased with her instituting some communication strategies to share the successes with her team in as far as they affected her stakeholders. In short, she took a marketing approach to her work, and started thinking, not like a specialist in her field, but as a marketer who is a specialist in IT, audit, or whatever other skills.

Which of the personal credibility elements do you feel you should focus on to increase your personal leadership brand both within and outside the organization?

Reference

Pryce-Jones, J. (2010). *Happiness at work, maximizing your psychological capital for success.* London: Wiley-Blackwell.

48

Decision-Making – Cutting Through the Fog of Shoulds and Fears

Marcia Reynolds PsyD

Anna had been offered a new position in another department that was higher paying and would give her greater visibility with the leadership team. She had been a successful team leader and agreed to take on a struggling team to prove she could turn them around. She was on the path to meeting her goal when the offer came in. She told me she was not ready to take the new job and asked how she could turn it down without closing doors on future promotions.

I asked for her permission to explore her decision before she determined how best to turn down the job offer. When she agreed, I asked, "Put yourself in both positions successfully a year from now. From that point of view, which one leaves you feeling more regret for not choosing the other?"

She told me about the good work she was doing with her team. They trusted her, their engagement was increasing, and the results were indicating that they were on their way to exceeding their quarterly goals. She was proud of her team, but then said, "The salary in the new position would give me money for a new house. I would have a new team to lead and new challenges. I'm just not sure the timing is right."

I asked her, "What makes for right timing?"

She told me about how leaving her current team could cause a setback in their progress, but she would learn so much if she took on the new position. I said, "It sounds like both options are good timing for you. So which would leave you with the greatest regret?"

After a thoughtful pause, she said, "I want the new job. I'm just afraid people will say I gave up on my team. That I'm selling out."

The coaching shifted to Anna answering questions that helped her define what selling out meant to her and if this definition actually applied to her current scenario. She conceded that she was not really selling out. She then explored what doors would open for her and her family if she took the new job.

Within a few minutes, Anna declared that she would have more regrets if she did not take the new position. She sighed and said, "My team is strong now. They probably can go on without me."

The coaching session shifted to what it would take for Anna to feel comfortable with accepting the new job offer. She explored what the new position would look and feel like, which led her to defining what she felt she needed to learn in order to be successful in her new role. She realized she also had some fears of failure that added to her hesitation. Once she declared her choice, she could determine where she needed some mentoring and skill building.

Dr. Marcia Reynolds is a world-renowned expert on inspiring change through conversations. She has delivered programs and coached leaders in 43 countries and reached many more people online. She has authored four award-winning books, including *The Discomfort Zone, Wander Woman, Outsmart Your Brain*, and her latest international bestseller, *Coach the Person, Not the Problem*.

Coach Me! Your Personal Board of Directors: Leadership Advice from the World's Greatest Coaches, First Edition. Edited by Brian Underhill, Jonathan Passmore, and Marshall Goldsmith.
© 2022 John Wiley & Sons Ltd. Published 2022 by John Wiley & Sons Ltd.
DOI: 10.1002/9781119823803.ch48

When Shoulds Drown Out Desires

Making decisions is difficult when there are conflicting voices in one's head that on the surface, appear to be a conflict of values. My coaching is often focused on helping my clients clear away the fog of *shoulds* and *what ifs* to identify what they really want to achieve. Sometimes, the shoulds are valid circumstances that need to be considered in the decision. Other times, the shoulds are old and inherited beliefs that are holding them back.

I do not advocate for making "pros and cons" lists until the shroud of limiting beliefs and conflicting values is removed. With the help of a coach or on your own, define your desired outcome and why the outcome is important to you now. Then honestly explore *who* is defining what is important in this situation, you or other people.

You need to discern whether you are deciding for yourself or choosing based on what you assume others might think about your decision. You also need to consider if you are looking at the situation with clear eyes or with eyes blurred by past missteps. Whose voice is stronger – other people and your past self or the wiser person you are today? When you talk about what you *really* want to do, listen for the words *but, should,* and *I'm worried about* to discover what is behind your hesitation with moving forward.

Whether you are facing a decision that will impact your career or one that changes direction for your team, exploring what *you really want* with a coach before moving forward will help you clarify both your desired outcome and the reality behind your options.

Have a Conversation With the Voices in Your Head

When you hesitate in deciding on an important issue, write down all the reasons that make you doubt yourself. The answers often include how other people might judge you, how you are judging your own ability to succeed, what you are afraid you will lose when you move forward, and how you might happen if your decision hits roadblocks you did not consider.

Some people spend their lives living out other people's expectations of them without giving their dreams a chance. Their *shoulds* get in the way of their dreams. I often help my clients articulate the real criteria they have been using to make decisions. Then, we look at what criteria would be more useful and fulfilling to use for making decisions today.

Identify and claim who and what is affecting your decisions. You can then better weigh your options, bearing in mind your personal desires while considering the needs of others.

3 Tips for Clarifying Factors in Your Decision-Making

Listen to the story you are telling about what is making your decision difficult, then answer these questions:

1. **What do want to do even if you are uncomfortable saying it?** State what *you* want to do before you list out the reasons why this might not be the best choice. Do not censure yourself while you are describing what actions you want to take and what you think you can achieve if you take these steps. Consider what you will regret a year from now if you choose to do something else.
2. **What is causing you to hesitate making a decision or to change the way you always do something?** Describe your fears and what you might feel guilty about if you move in the direction you most want. How important are other people's needs and judgments? Do you know if these needs and assessments are real or are you making assumptions without asking? Summarize the voices in your head so you can clearly determine what is valid and what is based in fear.
3. **What do you feel is most important?** Once you describe what is making you hesitate or choose something you do not want, ask yourself, "What *I really want* to do…" Answer this question, and then ask it again two more times. Stating your desired action with conviction will help you build the courage you need to move forward as well as give you the words to use when explaining your decision to coworkers and family members.

Final Thoughts

Once Anna differentiated her desires from her *shoulds*, she realized that the leadership in her company saw her as an asset with potential. She did not need to stay in one position for a specific amount of time before she could take on new challenges. And she did not have to worry that others would fail if she was not standing by their side. She could always work with the new team leader to ensure a smooth transition.

Remember that the roadblocks in decision-making are usually the voices swirling in your head. These voices need to be spoken and considered so you are clear about the choice you really want to take.

49

Future-Proof Yourself for Complex, Disruptive Times: Learning Faster Than the Pace of Change

David B. Peterson PhD

"When successful leaders fail, what is the #1 reason?"

Of course, there are many possible factors, but the primary reason *successful* leaders go off the rails? It is not micromanaging, arrogance, complacency, or even failing to listen, although those are certainly not rare. The #1 reason successful leaders fail is they do not adapt when things change. Decades of research on derailed leaders drives this point home (Hogan et al., 2011). Rising star leaders can get blinded by their success and fail to adapt as they advance, as they deal with new stakeholders, as economic factors shift, and as the competitive landscape evolves.

Let us consider a classic scenario: Arjun, brilliant and beloved by his team, was the CEO of his third startup when his company was acquired by a large tech firm. He believed that joining a larger organization would help them scale faster, with fewer distractions. He wanted to focus on technology and product issues rather than dealing with HR, legal, finance, supply chain, and other aspects of running the business.

By joining a large corporation, Arjun knew that he would no longer be calling all the shots. But he was shocked at how slow things moved at the new company; every significant decision required review by multiple teams, and he was not their top priority.

I started working with him to help him and his team navigate this new organization. He was an extremely quick learner and readily built allies within the broader company. Two years later, the acquisition was viewed as a huge success and Arjun was sought out by other leaders to share the secrets of his journey.

Slowly, however, the company's strategy and product mix started to shift as the marketplace, competitors, and customer expectations evolved. He started to sense more tensions in his conversations with senior leadership, and he was spending more and more time with other functions, especially legal and marketing, where he felt like his product was not getting the attention they needed. This was exactly what he had hoped to avoid by joining a larger company. As the going got tougher internally, key members of his leadership and product teams found other jobs in new, growing parts of the broader business. He had a harder time recruiting the top talent he needed. Still, Arjun held tight to his original vision and strategy and the loyal followers who remained praised his commitment and clarity.

At this point, he reached out to me again for additional coaching and strategic guidance. As he painted the picture of his current challenge, it was clear he was exhausted and at his wit's end. We explored a number of options, ranging from simply leaving to start another company, to spinning off the business, as well as different ways he could adapt to the changing company direction. After years of fighting for what he believed in, he was

David B. Peterson, PhD, Chief Transformation Officer at 7 Paths Forward, LLC and CEO of Peterson Leadership, LLC has been recognized as a world-class executive coach and thought leader for over 25 years. From 2011 to 2020, he was head of Google's Executive Coaching & Leadership team, where he built one of the world's most innovative and high-impact coaching programs, and was selected as the #1 Corporate Coach in the world.

Coach Me! Your Personal Board of Directors: Leadership Advice from the World's Greatest Coaches, First Edition. Edited by Brian Underhill, Jonathan Passmore, and Marshall Goldsmith.
© 2022 John Wiley & Sons Ltd. Published 2022 by John Wiley & Sons Ltd.
DOI: 10.1002/9781119823803.ch49

reluctant to make significant changes in his approach or his vision. After hours of discussion over several months, he decided to take some time off for reflection and personal renewal.

He came back 2 months later refreshed and reinvigorated. However, he was determined to double down on his previous strategy and approach. He wrote strategy documents to convince people that he was on the right path. He started to alienate some of his strongest allies across the organization. Although we spent a lot of time on packaging his message and influencing key stakeholders, my fundamental view was that he would be better served by adapting to the new context and pivoting his strategy as well. He would not budge. Almost a year later, frustrated and worn out yet again, he decided to leave. The passion, drive, vision, charisma, and brilliance that enabled him to succeed early in his career failed to get him through this new challenge because he simply refused to adapt as the market and context changed around him. As a footnote, the new leader who replaced him quickly pivoted the strategy, built new partnerships, and revived the customer loyalty that had started to erode. Today, it is still viewed as a successful venture, and Arjun as a brilliant entrepreneur who was simply unable to scale the business.

What are the lessons?

No matter how brilliant your idea or how talented you are, things inevitably change, and you have to adapt. As captured in the title of Marshall Goldsmith's (2007) book, *What Got You Here Won't Get You There*, Arjun's stubbornness, passion, and charisma, essential for his early success, were not enough for the challenges of leading a large business in a big corporation where he refused to compromise.

And there is a larger lesson to extract, once we come to terms with the fact that the pace of change is accelerating, and the world is becoming faster and more complex every day (Diamandis & Kotler, 2020). Even more importantly, different kinds of things are changing in different ways. We are entering an age of continual change and disruption.

Therefore, leaders need to learn and adapt faster than the pace of change. Yet, precious few are prepared.

Learning Faster Than the Pace of Change

Learning faster than the pace of change has quickly become an *essential* skill for surviving and thriving in this ever-changing landscape. Such learning requires time to reflect, explore new areas, and experiment with new ideas.

Yet, virtually every leader feels like they are too busy and overwhelmed to make time to proactively invest in their own development. By default, they focus on the most urgent issues and struggle to find time for the longer-term issues that are key to future success. Even when they recognize this dilemma, they feel powerless to change.

So, what can they do? What can *you* do to make sure you don't get blindsided by change and disruption?

The good news is that you can start making small changes right now to increase your agility and resilience. Taking small steps every day will help you build the capabilities you need without making dramatic changes to your life.

Here are four practical tips to help you future-proof yourself for whatever lies ahead.

1. **Cultivate a new learning mindset**
   Building agility for the future starts with the right mindset, which can be illustrated by analogy to your financial investments. Consider why you bother to save money; for most people, it is an investment in the future. Rather than spending all your money today, you delay immediate gratification so you can have a better future: a better home, travel, comfortable retirement, or whatever is important to you. Part of the mindset then is weighing what matters to you in the long run and getting clear on why you want to invest in your future. Clarity on what is truly important to you is the motivational fuel that will propel you through the uncertainty and stress of turbulent times.

2. **Seek diverse experiences**
   In a world that is becoming ever more challenging and disruptive, the best way to prepare is to gradually increase one's exposure to diverse, novel, and adverse experiences in order to learn to cope and overcome challenges one has not previously encountered (Peterson, 2021). Research shows that such experiences, especially early in one's career, prepare leaders to handle the intense demands and disruptive challenges they will face later (Dotlich et al., 2004; Van Katwyk et al., 2014).

Just as elite athletes push themselves to their limits to increase strength and performance capacity, leaders can increase their capabilities by working at the edge of their comfort zone. They learn to handle unanticipated challenges by repeated experiences outside their comfort zone. Simply put, there is no comfort in the learning zone and no learning in the comfort zone.

3. **Reflect with curiosity**

    However, merely having a series of diverse, novel, and adverse (DNA) experiences will not get you far unless you take time to reflect on those experiences, so you can make sense of what happened and figure out what you want to do differently as you go.

    One way to ease into reflection is to take one minute every day to ask yourself what you have learned that day and what new behaviors or experiments you want to try tomorrow. Over time, you can expand from one minute a day to weekly, monthly, quarterly reflection, and beyond: What do you want to learn in the next week, month, quarter, etc.? Where do you want to be in 1 year, 5 years, and 10 years, and what do you need to do differently to get there? The Reflection Calendar (Peterson, 2021) is a useful framework to structure your reflection and accelerate your development by investing just a few minutes a day.

4. **Engage your network**

    Sustaining your investment in personal development is difficult to do alone, especially when you are working at the edge of your comfort zone. Engaging with trusted colleagues or a supportive community enables you to garner emotional support and encouragement, make better sense of what you're going through, and gain new perspectives and ideas. Find a few partners – ideally people who are also interested in fostering their own learning agility – where you can share what you are doing and learning.

Start Now

When I was younger, I would tell myself, "I'll start investing in my development in 2–3 months when I have more time." Well, I never had more time, no matter how long I waited. This dawning insight was solidified by the wisdom in Karen Lamb's (n.d.) comment, "A year from now you may wish you had started today."

There is never a convenient time to begin, so you might as well start now. What will you do, today, to make sure you are growing faster than the pace of change?

References

Diamandis, P. H., & Kotler, S. (2020). *The future is faster than you think: How converging technologies are transforming business, industries, and our lives.* Simon & Schuster.

Dotlich, D. L., Noel, J. L., & Walker, N. (2004). *Leadership passages: The personal and professional transitions that make or break a leader.* Jossey Bass.

Goldsmith, M. (2007). *What got you here won't get you there.* Hyperion.

Hogan, J., Hogan, R., & Kaiser, R. B. (2011). Management derailment. In S. Zedeck (Ed.), *APA handbook of industrial and organizational psychology* (Vol. III, pp. 555–575). American Psychological Association.

Lamb, K. (n.d.). Karen Lamb quotes. Quotes.net. Retrieved March 21, 2020, from https://www.quotes.net/quote/14998.

Peterson, D. B. (2021). The DNA of VUCA: A framework for building learning agility in an accelerating world. In V. S. Harvey, & K. P. De Meuse (Eds.), *The age of agility: Building learning agile leaders and organizations* (pp. 327–364). Oxford University Press.

Van Katwyk, P., Hazucha, J., & Goff, M. (2014). A leadership experience framework. In C. D. McCauley, D. S. DeRue, P. R. Yost, & S. Taylor (Eds.), *Experience-driven leader development* (pp. 15–20). Wiley.

50

How to Select a Coach

CB Bowman-Ottomanelli

CB opened the Courage Consultant to support inspires others to go for the gold by finding courage in simple solutions to complex problems. To re-envision how we think about courage in terms of profitability and a willingness to see failure as a success.

Prior to this she opened an association for corporate executive coaches as a result of a colleague who was head of talent management for a Fortune 500 company Calling her because he was going to become certified as an executive coach. Given he was already a lawyer in the employment space and was globally certified as a human resource professional, she asked him why.

He said, "I've been trying to find business savvy executive coaches for my senior leadership team. I interviewed over 25 master certified coaches, and not one of them knew what a Return on Investment (ROI) was, or what a share of market (SOM) meant. He asked me, "how can those coaches effectively coach on the issues that my C-suite and senior executive employees are facing when they don't speak the same language as my leaders?" As a result, I decided to get trained as a certified coach, since I understand the business side and its complex issues."

At the end of his coach training, he called upset. "I now have to be shadowed by a certified coach during my coaching sessions to complete my certification!"

I asked him what the problem was, and he said, "These certified coaches don't understand business."

I laughed and asked, "So are you saying if you could find certified coaches who understood basic business models you would have not needed to go through this certification?"

His response was a resounding, "yes."

The problem he was having in hiring executive coaches for his high-level employees was not unique. Executive Coaches were requesting these assignments but they were clukless about business triggers[1] affecting executive behavior. Additionally, many were trying to coach leadership development without understanding the issues that may be encouraging non-productive behavior and poor leadership in these environments; it was just not working!

Out of this conversation, the Association of Corporate Executive Coaches (ACEC) was created, with the purpose to identify master-level corporate executive coaches as members. The first challenge was to define what we mean by a "corporate executive coach." Our second challenge was to define "mastery."

From the perspective of the decision-maker, the term "Executive Coach" implies that the coach has experience as an executive and experience in coaching executives. If we then add the label "Master-level," the requirements should be exponentially higher.

Perhaps, we can start with the following fundamentals to identify this level of corporate executive coaches:

1. They must have an understanding of various business components affecting executive behavior.
2. They have in their coaching portfolio several tools and methodologies, not just one to address various issues and growth opportunities. And they must know when to use which tools.

CB Bowman-Ottomanelli is the CEO of the Association of Corporate Executive Coaches (ACEC) and the MEECO Leadership Institute, a non-profit research institute for organizations who use executive coaches. ACEC supports master-level corporate executive coaches who coach the top tier of Fortune 1000 companies.

Coach Me! Your Personal Board of Directors: Leadership Advice from the World's Greatest Coaches, First Edition. Edited by Brian Underhill, Jonathan Passmore, and Marshall Goldsmith.
© 2022 John Wiley & Sons Ltd. Published 2022 by John Wiley & Sons Ltd.
DOI: 10.1002/9781119823803.ch50

3. They have a basic understanding of psychology as related to their clients and the stakeholders involved in the process. *Stakeholders should represent at least 90% of the people that the coachee has contact with in their work. For example, board of directors, employees at all levels, customers, competitors, peers, etc.*
4. They have experience in both coaching and consulting and have an awareness of the difference between them.
5. They have served time as an executive at the top of the house, preferably other than in their own business.
6. They have served as a coach with at least 5 years coaching at the executive level.
7. They have contributed to educating the public about executive coaching and leadership.
8. They have shared knowledge in the field with their colleagues and are considered "thought leaders."
9. They have a sustainable and diverse practice/business.
10. They must know business terms, influencers, and dynamics.

The following criteria are commonly – and often unsuccessfully – used in isolation of the above to predict the success of a coaching engagement:

1. Relying on a friend or colleague's **references** (Behavior and causation, along with experience, will be different for each coachee).
2. Relying on **certifications.** The value that each coach received from their certification training will be different. Most certifications are focused on the number of clock hours a coach has accumulated with clients versus business results.
   Mastery cannot be determined by clock hours in the field. This has little if anything to do with the success of the coaching engagement; there are too many variables; for example,
   - What were the coaches' learning experiences?
   - What was included in the training? For example, was it only coaching tools and methodologies?
   The impact on the client's business would be a stronger measurement of coaching success.
3. What is the coaches' professional background in terms of types of client experience?

4. Relying on the **fees** as a value indicator. **Coaches use various algorithms** to determine costs. These include:
   - The level of the client in the organization
   - If the company is a for-profit or a non-profit
   - The coaches' years of experience
   - The complexities of the assignment
   - The length of the engagement
   - The coaches' standing and reputation in the field
   - The client's level in the organization
5. Relying on chemistry with a coach may be an error. The coach that you feel connected with might be the person who is only saying what you want to hear and not what you *need* to hear.
6. You cannot rely on the company's **ROI** as a result of using a particular coach. Coaching is not yet an isolated measurement; there are too many variables/ influencers to measure successful outcomes. For example, can you say that ROI improved by 4% due to coaching? No! Because there were influencers like advertising campaigns, there might have been a change in product or service cost or a difference in the organization's competitive frame, and more. You cannot measure coaching effectiveness using the same measures typically used to measure business success. Using ROI in isolation of understanding the impact of influencers is dangerous. What you can do is to consider your specific goals in relationship to outcomes directly as a result of improved relationships with others and a change in your behavior as a result of the coaching engagement. Ask yourself what the coaching engagement triggered that resulted in the requested or needed change.
7. Can you rely on a coach being a **member of a specific association**? Not necessarily! Many professional associations focus on the research and the scientific part of coaching, which can wind up blurring the lines between tools, therapy, and coaching, or they primarily focus on hours coaching clients.

If you cannot rely on these common measurements for selecting a coach, what can you use to gauge the capabilities of a corporate executive coach?

What if we cross-reference the coaching levels with the capabilities to increase the chances for selection success?

Here is a framework, which can enable clients to understand the capabilities, and the potential impact a coach can deliver at each level of expertise. By better aligning the executive coach capabilities with client and business needs, we can significantly increase the chances for success.

Coach level	References	Certifications/assessments/Tools	Experience Business	Fees	Chemistry	Client ROI	High-level Association Membership	Education/Professional /academic	Thought Leader	Experience coaching at senior levels	Publications/Research
Coach	✔	✔						✔			
Executive Coach	✔	✔	✔	✔				✔			
Master Corporate Executive coach	✔	✔	✔	✔	✔	✔	✔	✔	✔		
Enterprise-wide Business Coach™	✔	✔	✔	✔	✔	✔	✔	✔	✔	✔	✔

Some may say that the above criteria blur the lines among business consultants, management consultants, and coaches. I would counter with the argument that few organizations understand how to hire executive coaches who have the capabilities and capacity to understand their clients and the dynamics or triggers* that drive business results which is critical to the success of the engagement.

There is no blurring of the lines in taking a holistic approach to being an enterprise-wide business coach™ with a focus on total client results. You cannot take a one-dimensional approach to leadership development or to solving issues. Do not make this mistake with your executive coaching selection criteria.

> In choosing the right corporate executive coach, organizations will realize the significant Return on Investment and performance with executive coaches with the right skills and knowledge can deliver.
> Starting at the Master Corporate Executive Coach (MCEC) level, there is an understanding of business challenges /opportunities and human dynamics that together propel organizations to achieve exceptional performance.
>
> *Dan Darcy former VP Strategy & Manufacturing Integration, Hershey Chocolates*

Another important element in selecting a coach is to determine your readiness in working with an executive coach. Consider this exercise: Ask yourself if you can answer "yes" to all of these components and give examples of your preparedness:[2]

1. *Cognitive*: Do you have the ability to accept new knowledge and process it? Give three examples of how you have done this recently.
2. *Motivational*: Do you have the general desire or willingness to do something? How will this be demonstrated? Give three examples.
3. *Emotional*: Do you have positive feelings about growth and change? Can you voice three examples.
4. *Behavioral*: Are you ready to display/demonstrate change? What are three examples?

The bottom line is, are you and your employees, colleagues ready, willing, and able to accept and demonstrate change? Without readiness all of the information in the world about how to identify a great executive coach will not be useful nor will the hiring of a corporate executive coach be helpful.

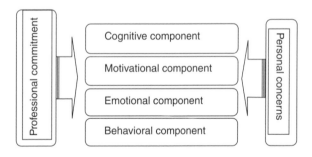

Notes

1 "A trigger is any stimulus that reshapes our thoughts and actions. In every waking hour people, events, and circumstances that have the potential to change us are triggering us. These triggers can appear suddenly and unexpectedly"... Marshall, M. (2015). Introduction. In M. Goldsmith and M. Reiter, *Triggers* (p. XV). New York: Crown Business.
2 Semenova, G. (2019). Psychological readiness to use distance learning among teachers involved in digitalization. 753–763. 10.15405/epsbs.2019.12.80.

Further Resources

Any of the contributors of this book would welcome hearing from you. Each is generally easy to find with a Google or LinkedIn search. Please reach out!

Professional coaching associations
Association for Coaching
EMCC
International Coaching Federation Credentialed

Coaching Providers
CoachSource - www.coachsource.com
CoachHub - www.coachhub.com

Stakeholder Centered Coaching: https://get.mgscc.net

Additional online directories:
African Executive Coaching Council https://aeccouncil.com/find-a-coach
Association of Corporate Executive Coaches https://acec-association.org/directory

Coach Me! Your Personal Board of Directors: Leadership Advice from the World's Greatest Coaches, First Edition. Edited by Brian Underhill, Jonathan Passmore, and Marshall Goldsmith.
© 2022 John Wiley & Sons Ltd. Published 2022 by John Wiley & Sons Ltd.
DOI: 10.1002/9781119823803.both01

Your Personal Board of Directors: Contributor Biographies

Abdallah Aljurf is a leadership development consultant who has developed more than 2,000 corporate leaders in the past 15 years. Abdallah is the founder of ICF Saudi Arabia Chapter. He established that chapter in 2015 with the help of group of enthusiastic Saudi ICF coaches. Abdallah was the president of that chapter in 2015 and 2016. In addition, Abdallah is a dynamic public speaker who speaks about leadership, coaching, and values in our digital age. He is the Champion of Toastmasters International Speech Contest for the years 2014 and 2015 on the level of Saudi Arabia. He inspired and motivated hundreds of leaders in the United States, Malaysia, Sri Lanka, Egypt, Kuwait, UAE, the United Kingdom, Switzerland, and other countries. Abdallah is a Systems Engineering graduate from KFUPM (King Fahd University of Petroleum and Minerals). He held management and leadership positions in seven different national and international companies. Abdallah has worked on several projects to develop leaders in the past 15 years as a manager, talent management consultant, executive coach, leadership trainer, workshops facilitator, and an inspirational speaker. His next challenge is developing 100,000 young CEOs to make them ready to lead and deliver business results in any international environment in the corporate world. Abdallah was nominated for the "Thinkers50 Marshall Goldsmith Coaching award" in 2019 among 50 Leading Global Coaches.

Brenda Bence Internationally recognized coach Brenda Bence works with C-Suite executives and senior leaders to help them achieve positive career- and life-enhancing change. A Harvard Business School graduate, Brenda spent the first 20 years of her career building mega brands for Fortune 100 companies, where she was responsible for billion-dollar businesses across four continents and 50 countries. After Brenda left the corporate world, she founded her own company which now has offices in both the United States and Asia. She is highly sought after across six continents for both her leadership coaching and keynote addresses. Through working with many of the world's most recognized companies – 95% of which engage her services repeatedly – Brenda has inspired hundreds of thousands of leaders across the globe. The author of 11 books that have won more than 40 book awards, Brenda has lived and worked internationally for the past 25 years. She has visited almost 100 countries and has fuddled her way through trying to learn six languages.

CB Bowman-Ottomanelli, MCEC, MBA, BCC, CMC *Founder and CEO, Association of Corporate Executive Coaches (ACEC) and Workplace Equity & Equality (WEE); Founder of the MEECO Leadership Institute* CB Bowman-Ottomanelli is best known for bringing clarity and accountability to the world of executive coaching. She founded three change-making organizations, the Association of Corporate Executive Coaches (ACEC), dedicated to mastery level coaches who are working with the top tier of organizations; and the MEECO Leadership Institute, which is a certifying body for Master Corporate Executive Coaches (MCEC) and its focus is on master corporate executive coaches who are "enterprise-wide business partners™." CB's work with ACEC has introduced rigorous credentialing to the corporate executive coaching ranks and has introduced metrics to underscore accountability. She is certified to serve on corporate boards, and her emphasis on pro bono work

Coach Me! Your Personal Board of Directors: Leadership Advice from the World's Greatest Coaches, First Edition. Edited by Brian Underhill, Jonathan Passmore, and Marshall Goldsmith.
© 2022 John Wiley & Sons Ltd. Published 2022 by John Wiley & Sons Ltd.
DOI: 10.1002/9781119823803.both02

and continuing education shows that her heart and her brain are aligned. CB is a graduate of New School for Social Research. She received her MBA from Pace University where she served on the advisory board for Lubin School of Business and as an adjunct professor in the marketing department. She served as an instructor at Rutgers University Center for Management Development and as an adjunct professor at Mercy College teaching organizational behavior, and Human Resource Management. CB is a contributing author in the book *Complex Situations in Coaching: A Critical Case-Based Approach* and has published several articles on Coaching. CB is a member of MG100, was selected as one of the world's top brand professionals in 2021 by Global Gurus, and was ranked by Marshall Goldsmith Top Global Coaches as the #1 coach for increasing the quality of coaching for her work as the CEO of the Association of Corporate Executive Coaches (ACEC) and the MEECO Leadership Institute. CB served as Chairperson for the North Plainfield, New Jersey's Historic Commission for 6 years.

Richard E. Boyatzis is Distinguished University Professor of Case Western Reserve University, Professor in the Departments of Organizational Behavior, Psychology, and Cognitive Science, HR Horvitz Professor of Family Business, and Adjunct Professor in People/Organizations at ESADE. He has a BS in Aeronautics and Astronautics from MIT, and a MS and PhD in Social Psychology from Harvard University. Using his Intentional Change Theory (ICT), he studies sustained, desired change at all levels of human endeavor from individuals, teams, organizations, communities, and countries; specifically, he has been researching helping and coaching since 1967. He was ranked #9 Most Influential International Thinker by HR Magazine in 2012 and 2014. He is the author of more than 200 articles on leadership, competencies, emotional intelligence, competency development, coaching, neuroscience, and management education. His Coursera MOOCs, including Inspiring Leadership Through Emotional Intelligence has over a million and a half enrolled from 215 countries. His nine books include: *The Competent Manager*; the international bestseller, *Primal Leadership*, with Daniel Goleman and Annie McKee; *Resonant Leadership*, with Annie McKee; and *Helping People Change: Coaching with Compassion or Lifelong Learning and Growth*, with Melvin Smith and Ellen Van Oosten. He is Fellow of the Association of Psychological Science, the Society of Industrial and Organizational Psychology, and the American Psychological Association.

Peter Bregman helps successful people become exceptional leaders and stellar human beings. He blends his deep expertise in business, leadership, and people to deliver quantifiable results such as *Turnarounds* (e.g. turning a $30M loss into a $140M gain), *Revenue/Stock Growth* (e.g. growing revenue from $400M to over $1 billion), *Executive Team Development* (e.g. shifting from silos to a unified leadership team resulting in stock price growth from $19.38 to $107.50), and *Personal Development* (promotion to C-level, 10× stock price growth, and sleeping well through the night). Peter is recognized as the #1 executive coach in the world by Leading Global Coaches. He coaches C-level executives in many of the world's premier organizations, including Allianz, Twilio, Electronic Arts, CBS, Mars, Pearson, Citi, Charity Navigator, United Media, FEI, and many others. Peter is ranked as a Top 30 thought leader by Thinkers 50 Radar and has been selected as one of the Top 8 thought leaders in leadership. He is ranked by Global Gurus as one of the Top 30 best coaches in the world and one of the Top 30 best leadership speakers/trainers in the world. He is the award-winning, bestselling author and contributor of 18 books, including, most recently, You CAN Change Other People: The Four Steps to Help Your Colleagues, Employees—Even Family—Up Their Game. He also wrote Leading with Emotional Courage: How to Have Hard Conversations, Create Accountability, and Inspire Action on Your Most Important Work. His book, 18 Minutes: Find Your Focus, Master Distraction, and Get the Right Things Done, was a *Wall Street Journal* bestseller, winner of the Gold medal from the Axiom Business Book awards, named the best business book of the year by NPR, and selected by *Publisher's Weekly* and the *New York Post* as a Top 10 business book. He is also the author of Four Seconds: All the Time You Need to Replace Counter-Productive Habits with Ones That Really Work, a *New York Post* "Top Pick for Your Career" in 2015, and Point B: A Short Guide to Leading a Big Change. Peter created and leads the #1 Leadership Development Program in the world, a four-day program that transforms the way people lead by increasing their confidence in themselves, their ability to connect with others, their commitment to what's most important, and their emotional courage. Peter designed the proven, proprietary Big Arrow process to align people to work together to accomplish an organization's most important work, leveraging the Big Arrow Measurement tool to quantify the leadership and organizational gaps that block successful execution. Peter is the host of the Top 10 Business

Podcast, Bregman Leadership Podcast, with over 1.5M downloads. He is also a regular contributor to *Harvard Business Review*, and his articles and commentary appear frequently in *BusinessWeek*, *Fast Company*, *Psychology Today*, *Forbes*, *PBS*, *ABC*, *CNN*, *NPR*, and *FOX Business News*. Peter earned his BA from Princeton University and his MBA from Columbia University. He can be reached at pbregman@bregmanpartners.com.

Bill Carrier president of Carrier Leadership Coaching Inc., specializes in coaching senior executives in leadership, executive presence, and organizational impact. He is the executive director of the Marshall Goldsmith 100 Coaches for the top leadership professionals in the world. A graduate of the United States Military Academy at West Point, former Army officer, and Rotary International Ambassadorial Scholar, Bill anchors his coaching work in extensive practical leadership experience and the firm belief that we are all part of something bigger than ourselves. As a coach and thought partner to CEOs and senior leaders, Bill leverages best-practice from neuroscience, ontology, movement psychology/somatics, and West Point leadership development. Executive coaching clients include CEOs, CTOs, and SVPs of corporations from $100 million to $70 billion in annual revenue; a winner of the Navy's Zumwalt Award (annually given to the best captain of a ship in the US Navy); TED Fellows; and senior executives at the Board of Governors of the Federal Reserve. Bill contributes to the coaching profession in many ways. He is a co-founder and co-editor of *The Future of Coaching* magazine, a Founding Fellow of the Institute of Coaching at Harvard Medical School, and a founding member of the Coaching Excellence in Organizations (CEO) community of practice. Bill has been a member of the Board of Directors of the International Consortium for Coaching in Organizations (ICCO) and is on the accreditation committee of the Association of Corporate Executive Coaches (ACEC).

Ron Carucci is a co-founder and managing partner at Navalent, working with CEOs and executives pursuing transformational change for their organizations, leaders, and industries. He has a 30-year track record helping executives tackle challenges of strategy, organization, and leadership. From startups to Fortune 10 organizations, non-profits to heads-of-state, turn-arounds to new markets and strategies, overhauling leadership and culture to re-designing for growth, he has helped organizations articulate strategies that lead to accelerated growth, and design organizations that can execute those strategies. He has worked in more than 25 countries in four continents. He is the author of nine books, including the Amazon #1 *Rising to Power* and, his most recent release, *To Be Honest: Lead with the Power of Truth, Justice and Purpose*. He is a popular contributor to the *Harvard Business Review*, where Navalent's work on leadership was named one of 2016's management ideas that mattered most. He is also a regular contributor to *Forbes*, and a two-time TEDx speaker, and a proud member of the MG100 Coaches community. His work has been featured in *Fortune*, *CEO Magazine*, *Inc.*, *BusinessInsider*, *MSNBC*, *Business Week*, *Inc.*, *Fast Company*, *Smart Business*, and *ThoughtLeaders*.

Dr. Peter Chee Chee is the CEO of ITD World, a multinational corporation with the mission of transforming leaders to change the world for the better. He specializes in coaching, developing, and transforming CEOs, CXsOs, and senior global leaders from world leading organizations including the United Nations, Intel, Siemens, PepsiCo, Coca-Cola, Micron, First Solar, and Western Digital. Peter ranks among the top global coaching gurus, with more than 33 years' experience in developing leaders from over 80 countries. He was awarded the #1 Strategic Innovation Coach by Dr Marshall Goldsmith. He is the co-author of *Coaching for Breakthrough Success* with Jack Canfield; *12 Disciplines of Leadership Excellence* with Brian Tracy; and *Becoming an Effective Mentoring Leader* and *The Leader's Daily Role in Talent Management* with Dr. William J. Rothwell. He also co-authored *5 Levels of Mastery* with Goldsmith, the world's #1 executive coach. Peter is the developer of the Certified Chief Master Coach (CCMC) and Certified Coaching and Mentoring Professional (CCMP) programs. Both are accredited and recognized by the ICF (International Coach Federation). He created the Coaching Mastery Model (CMM), Coaching for Breakthrough Success (CBS) Metta Model, The Coaching Principles (TCP), Situational Coaching Model (SCM), and Achievers Coaching Techniques (ACT).

Nihar Chhaya is a Wharton, Columbia, and Georgetown–educated executive coach to the C-Suite and leaders at global companies, including American Airlines, Cigna, Coca-Cola, Draft Kings, 3M, GE, Lockheed Martin,

Raytheon Technologies, and many others. He is the president of PartnerExec, helping executives master inter-personal communication for superior business and strategic outcomes. Formerly a Fortune 200 corporate head of executive development and a senior advisor to the boards and CEOs on behavioral assessment and succession planning, Nihar's coaching practice helps companies thrive in an uncertain and competitive world by developing better leadership at the top. Nihar is a recognized thought leader in the field of management and executive coaching and is a regular contributor to *Harvard Business Review*, *Fast Company*, and *Forbes*. He is also a frequent keynote speaker at the World Business and Executive Coaches Summit (WBECS), selected to develop thousands of aspiring coaches in the industry. Nihar teaches the highly rated seminar, "Maximize Your Leadership Potential" for Executive MBAs at the Cox Business School at Southern Methodist University, and has received consecutive Teacher Excellence Awards as evaluated by the students. Nihar also presents on executive development to the Georgetown University alumni community. Nihar is a designated Master Corporate Executive Coach (MCEC) with the Association of Corporate Executive Coaches and holds the Professional Certified Coach (PCC) credential with the International Coach Federation. He was selected by Marshall Goldsmith as part of the 100 Coaches (MG100) community of the world's top executive coaches. Nihar received his MBA at the Wharton School of the University of Pennsylvania. He also received an MA in International Economics at Columbia University and a BS in International Economics at Georgetown University with course-work at the London School of Economics.

David Clutterbuck is one of the earliest international pioneers of coaching and mentoring. He works with individuals, teams, and organizations to help them have the conversations they need, to bring about significant, positive change. He is a co-founder of the European Mentoring & Coaching Council, for which he is now a Lifetime Ambassador. Of his 70+ books to date, around half are in the field of coaching and mentoring. He wrote the first English-language evidence-based books on team coaching, on coaching culture, and on developmental mentoring. David has supported thousands of organizations around the world, in all major sectors, in the creation and implementation of internal training programs in coaching and mentoring over the past 40 years. He continues to research and publish on good practice in coaching, with an emphasis on creating a credible evidence-base. David's clients range from entrepreneurs to managers at all levels in organizations and from individuals to teams. He often works with CEOs coaching them one-to-one in developing their coaching skills. His co-authored books on coaching and mentoring tools and techniques are used widely across the world in developing coach competence. David is currently piloting a program that aims to create 5 million school age coaches and mentors.

Alisa Cohn Named the "Top Startup Coach in the World" at the Thinkers50/Marshall Goldsmith Global Coaches Awards in London, Alisa Cohn has been coaching startup founders to grow into world-class CEOs for nearly 20 years. A one-time startup CFO, strategy consultant, and current angel investor and advisor, she was named the number one Global Guru of Startups in 2021, and has worked with startup companies such as Venmo, Etsy, DraftKings, Wirecutter, Mack Weldon, and Tory Burch. She has coached CEOs and C-Suite executives at enterprise clients such as Dell, Hitachi, Sony, IBM, Google, Microsoft, Bloomberg, The New York Times, and Calvin Klein. Marshall Goldsmith selected Alisa as one of his Marshall Goldsmith 100 Coaches – a gathering of the top coaches in the world – and Inc. named Alisa one of the Top 100 Leadership Speakers, and she has also been named one of the top voices of thought leadership by PeopleHum for 2021. Her articles have appeared in *HBR*, *Forbes*, and *Inc.*, and she has been featured as an expert on *Bloomberg TV*, *BBC World News*, and in *The New York Times* and *The Wall Street Journal*. A recovering CPA, she is also a Broadway investor in productions that have won two Tony Awards, and is prone to burst into song at the slightest provocation. An amateur rap artist, she wrote and performed a rap called "The Work is in You."

Ben Croft is a multi-award-winning entrepreneur who specializes in the Business and Executive Coaching profession. He is the CEO of the World Business & Executive Coach Summit, co-founder of Conversational Intelligence for Coaches and six other active companies, and the founder of his Non-Profit EthicalCoach. Last year Ben's company WBECS Group was named the fastest growing education company in the United Kingdom in the INC 5000, and he has now embarked on his most ambitious project to date – Ethicalcoach.org. An organization that helps charities/NGOs build organizational capacity through coaching. EthicalCoach delivered its inaugural project at the United Nations in Ethiopia. The 2-day EthicalCoach NGO Leadership Summit saw 400

NGO leaders come together for a series of talks and high-level workshops with an international and local team of coaches. Between them, they support more than 9 million Ethiopians and a number of the leaders and teams have been awarded coaching grants as part of the 2-year program. Ben is well known in the coaching profession for his annual summit that has grown to become the world's leading event for the industry with 46,000 professional coaches attending in this its ninth year. Aside from this summit, Ben's companies also publish many of the world's top thought leaders for the profession including David Peterson, head of leadership at Google. This year, in partnership with Professors David Clutterbuck and Peter Hawkins, he also launched the Global Team Coaching Institute.

Scott Eblin Named as one of the Top 30 coaches in the world by Global Gurus, Scott Eblin is the president of The Eblin Group, a leadership development firm committed to helping clients lead at their best and live at their best in a constantly changing world. As an executive coach, global speaker, and bestselling author, Scott works with leaders in some of the best-known companies and organizations in the world. He advocates simple, practical, and immediately applicable steps that help leaders consistently be at their best — not just in their professional lives, but also at home and in their communities. Scott is the author of two books, *The Next Level: What Insiders Know About Executive Success*, now in its third edition, and *Overworked and Overwhelmed: The Mindfulness Alternative*. He is an honors graduate of Davidson College and holds a master's degree in public administration from Harvard University. Scott also has a certificate in leadership coaching from Georgetown University and was a 10-year faculty member of that program. He also holds the designation of Registered Yoga Teacher from the Yoga Alliance.

Lisa Ann Edwards creator of MyExcelia.com and leading expert in the field of coaching, possesses a unique skillset — cultivating excellence in others while delivering tangible results. Her specialized ability to provide measurable return on investment for clients has demonstrated upward of 251% ROI, and lifted employee engagement nearly 20%. Lisa is the globally acknowledged pioneer and thought leader on Coaching with ROI, a methodology she developed specifically for coaches to deliver measurable and tangible results in a traditionally unmeasured space, elevating the perception, impact, and importance of coaching worldwide. A featured speaker at 150+ universities and professional associations around the world, she has trained more coaches how to measure, evaluate, and demonstrate the monetary impact of coaching than any other and has authored, co-authored, or contributed to over 15 publications and translated into more than four languages. As a globally respected collaborator, author, speaker, and educator of more than 10,000 coaches globally, Lisa has developed MyExcelia.com, an automated platform to measure and communicate the ROI of coaching. Lisa's current pro bono work includes evaluating the impact of the International Coaching Federation Foundation's coaching work in collaboration with the United Nations.

Priscilla Gill, EdD is a challenger and transformer. She is passionate about helping leaders flourish and transform organizations to unleash the greatness of others and maximize diversity. Her positively powerful approach facilitates creative disruption and supports leaders to achieve innovative goals in a hyper-connected, ever-changing world. As Director of Workforce Learning and an Executive Coach at Mayo Clinic, Priscilla directs the enterprise learning function to assist physicians, scientists, and administrative staff in adapting to the rapidly changing healthcare environment. Priscilla previously led Mayo Clinic's Coaching and Mentoring Center of Excellence and served as Administrator of Diversity and Inclusion for Mayo Clinic in Arizona. She has over 20 years of similar executive-level leadership experience with other organizations where she established new practices in Leadership and Organizational Development, Diversity and Inclusion, and Coaching. She has served as a community leader to develop and support women of African descent, a member of the board of International Coach Federation Phoenix, and an executive committee member of The Conference Board's Enterprise Coaching and Development Council. Priscilla earned her Doctor of Education degree in Organizational Leadership and Human Services Administration from Nova Southeastern University. She received her Master's in Business Administration from Nova Southeastern University, and her bachelor's degree in Organizational Communication from Rollins College. Priscilla Gill is an Assistant Professor at the Mayo Clinic College of Medicine, a faculty member of the Mayo Clinic School of Continuous Professional Development CME Programs and a recognized Organizational Development Innovator.

Philippe Grall helps successful executives become inspiring role models to everyone in their sphere of influence. His mission is not only to create better leaders, but happier people. In short, to shine in business and in life. He calls this integrated approach "Your Inner Diamond." Based in Tokyo, Philippe and his équilibre team apply his unique methodology through one-on-one coaching, group training, dynamic speeches, proprietary mobile apps, and inspirational events throughout Asia and internationally. His clients include a diverse group of C-level executives from major global brands Godiva, Chanel, L'Oreal, Van Cleef & Arpels, and Amgen Biopharma. Philippe is a member of Marshall Goldsmith's 100 Coaches, a select group of professionals hand-picked from over 18,000 applicants worldwide. He has a master's degree specializing in marketing, communication, and retail management from ISTEC. Combined with his business acumen, Philippe applies over 35 years of experience in personal development from the world's top authorities in their field: from Neuro-Linguistic Programming to Tibetan Lojon Meditation. "I've always wanted to make the world a better place by sharing what I've learned with as many people as possible," says Philippe. "That's my basic coaching philosophy: Learn, practice, and share. I believe that everything we learn can be applied to unlimited positive growth."

Professor Peter Hawkins, PhD has been coaching senior executives and their leadership teams for over 40 years across many sectors and in many different countries. He has been the leading global pioneer and thought leader in Systemic Team Coaching, having carried out extensive research, written a number of the bestselling books, and provided trainings to people from over 100 different countries. He previously played a similar role in coaching supervision. He is chairman of Renewal Associates, United Kingdom; Emeritus Professor of Leadership at Henley Business School; and joint founder and co-dean, with Professor David Clutterbuck, of the Global Team Coaching Institute. He is Honorary President of Association of Professional Executive Coaching and Supervision and also the Academy of Executive Coaching, and is present on the advisory board of Ace-Up. He has also delivered over 100 keynote speeches, including for all the major coaching bodies around the world. In 2019, he was given the Marshall Goldsmith award of being one of the World's Top 100 Coaches. He is currently researching and developing the greater role that coaching can play in addressing the climate and ecological crisis. He is also the author of over a hundred publications, including many bestselling and internationally translated books, such as:

1. *Leadership Team Coaching* (Kogan Page, 2011; 4th ed, 2021) (translated into Chinese, Japanese, Spanish, and Hungarian);
2. *Leadership Team Coaching in Practice* (Kogan Page, 2014; 3rd ed, 2022) (translated in Chinese);
3. *Systemic Coaching: Delivering Value Beyond the Individual*, with Eve Turner (Routledge 2020);
4. *Creating a Coaching Culture* (McGraw-Hill, 2012) (translated into Dutch);
5. *Coaching, Mentoring and Organizational Consultancy: Supervision, Skills and Development* (with Nick Smith), McGraw-Hill/Open University Press, 2nd ed, 2013).

Nicole Heimann is the founder and co-CEO of Heimann Cvetkovic & Partners AG, an award-winning Boutique Executive Advisory Firm of world's leading experts in leadership alliances. The company has won the Global Excellence Award as the Best Executive Coaching & Advisory Firm in Switzerland. Nicole is co-founder and board member of the Bullens Heimann & Friends Foundation, Global Chair in the Global Excellence Council of the International Federation of Learning and Development (IFLD), and Advisory Council Member to the Organizational Leadership & Development Network (OLDN). Nicole is a multi-award-winning executive coach and executive team coach; author of the book *How to Develop the Authentic Leader in You: Integrating the Seven Dimensions of Leadership Intelligence* (BoD – Books on Demand 2018); and a keynote speaker on authentic leadership and leadership alliances. Nicole has been coaching boards, CEOs, senior executives, and their leadership teams for the last 20 years, and has been working for some of the world's biggest and most successful companies. In 2021, Nicole was honored with the prestigious CEO Today Europe Award in the category "outstanding leadership, vision and entrepreneurship"; chosen as one of the 15 World Class Mentors 2021 by IFLD (International Federation of Learning & Development); became part of the IFLD Hall of Fame; and has been honored by people Hum's list of Top 200 Global Thought Leaders. In 2020, she was nominated as one of the Top20 Learning Professionals by the IFLD and as one of the Top50 Global Thought Leaders and Influencers by Thinkers360. In 2019, Nicole was recognized with the Thinkers50 Marshall Goldsmith Leading Global Coach Award. Nicole is a member of the prestigious "100 Coaches," best leaders and coaches globally selected by Dr. Marshall Goldsmith, and she is the biographer in the full-feature movie documentary *The Earned Life*. As an expert in authentic leadership, Nicole is a topic partner for leadership trends and has contributed to leading publications such as *Leader to Leader*, the award-winning quarterly report on management, leadership, and strategy. Nicole is Belgian; she is married with a family of seven children and has been living in Switzerland for more than 20 years. She is fluent in English, German, Dutch, and French.

Sally Helgesen cited in Forbes as the world's premier expert on women's leadership, is an internationally bestselling author, speaker, and leadership coach. She has been ranked number 6 among the world's Top 30 leadership thinkers by Global Gurus, honored by the coaching consortium MEECO for her transformational influence on organizational cultures and chosen as the Thinkers50/100 Coaches world's top coach for women leaders. Sally's most recent book, *How Women Rise*, co-authored with legendary executive coach Marshall Goldsmith, examines the behaviors most likely to get in the way of successful women. It became the top seller in its field within a week of publication, and rights have been sold in 17 languages. Previous books include *The Female Advantage: Women's Ways of Leadership*, hailed as the classic in its field and continuously in print since 1990, and *The Female Vision: Women's Real Power at Work*, which explores how women's strategic insights can strengthen their careers. *The Web of Inclusion: A New Architecture for Building Great Organizations* was cited in *The Wall Street Journal* as one of the best books on leadership of all time and is credited with bringing the language of inclusion into business. Sally delivers leadership workshops and keynotes for companies around the world in addition to her established coaching and consulting practice. She is a contributing editor for *Strategy + Business* magazine and a member of the 100 Coaches Network and the New York and International Women's Forums. She lives in Chatham, NY.

Mr. Takahiro Honda is an International Coaching Federation Master Certified Coach (MCC) who has coached corporate executives for more than 2,500 hours of sessions, and he has delivered training more than 2,000 times. Mr. Honda mainly contributes to leadership improvement and human resource development for SoftBank Corp, Panasonic Corporation, Nisshin Food Products Co., Ltd, The Prudential Life Insurance Company of Japan Ltd, Sumitomo Mitsui Banking Corporation, etc. For 3 years as a representative of the Shinjuku branch of the Ginza coaching school, Mr. Honda has continued to rank in the first place (among the 40 places in Japan) for the number of participants attending. His belief is that everyone has a meaning of being born and a mission to be fulfilled. He is thanked by clients that "You were close to my heart and encouraged me for awareness"; "I learned not only the skills but also the principles and essences"; etc. Mr. Honda's books include *Practical and Effective One-On-One Meeting* (Nikkei Business Publications, Inc.), *How Will You Live in the "VUCA" Era* (SMBC Consulting Co., Ltd), *Time Management Basics and Practical Course* (PHP Institute), and *Selling High-priced Products Naturally! Sales to Move the Mind of the Customers* (PHP Institute).

Maya Hu-Chan is a globally recognized keynote speaker, Master Certified Coach, and bestselling author. She specializes in global leadership, cross-cultural management, diversity, equity, and inclusion. Ranked Top Leadership Coaches of 2021, Top 8 Global Solutions Thinkers by Thinkers50, World Top 30 Leadership Gurus, and Top 100 Thought Leaders in Management & Leadership, Maya has worked with thousands of leaders in global Fortune 500 companies, non-profits, and public sectors worldwide. Maya is the founder and president of Global Leadership Associates, a global consultancy that partners with organizations to build leadership capabilities and enable profound growth and change. Her latest book *Saving Face: How to Preserve Dignity and Build Trust* is Amazon #1 bestseller (Berrett-Koehler 2020). Her book *Global Leadership: The Next Generation* was a Harvard Business School Working Knowledge book. She is a contributing author of 11 business books and a columnist for INC.com. Born and raised in Taiwan and living in San Diego, California, Maya is fluent in Mandarin Chinese and English. She earned her master's degree from University of Pennsylvania and BA from National Chengchi University in Taiwan. Maya has lectured at the Brookings Institution, University of California, San Diego, University of Chicago, University of Southern California, and Tuck School of Business at Dartmouth College.

Jane Hyun Often called an "interpreter," Jane Hyun is the leading authority for leveraging culture and diversity to drive business growth and innovation. Named the "#1 Coach for Cultural Fluency in Leadership" at the Thinkers50/Marshall Goldsmith Global Coaches Awards in London, Jane is a dynamic speaker, consultant, and trusted coach to global Fortune 500 companies and an internationally recognized expert in cross-cultural effectiveness, inclusive leadership, and talent onboarding. She has helped individuals navigate change in high-stakes business environments and has coached thousands of leaders to increase their agility in the workplace. Her insights appear on *CNN, CNBC, Harvard Business Review,* Fast Company, *Wall Street Journal, Forbes,* and *Atlantic* on the topics of culture, leadership, and diversity. Jane has been an external advisor to the American Heart Association Diversity Council, and Operation Exodus, a non-profit that provides academic enrichment and transformative relationships to Latino youth in Washington Heights. She served as research director for The Conference Board's "Cultural Fluency: How Culture Shapes Leadership Styles in Asia." Jane serves as a coach for Columbia Business School's MBA and EMBA programs and has lectured at numerous MBA programs across the country. She is the author of the groundbreaking bestseller *Breaking the Bamboo Ceiling: Career Strategies for Asians.* She is the co-author of *Flex: The New Playbook for Managing Across Differences,* which examines the skill of switching between communication styles to leverage the power of diversity in teams. In addition to her work with multinational companies, Jane has held leadership posts at JPMorgan, Deloitte, and Resources Global. She holds a degree in Economics and International Studies from Cornell University and is passionate about helping individuals flourish in their workplaces and communities.

Dr. Terry Jackson is a dynamic executive advisor, thought leader, TEDx speaker, and organizational consultant. Terry is a member of the prestigious Marshall Goldsmith 100 Coaches. Terry was recently chosen by Thinkers50 as one of the Top 50 Leaders in Executive Coaching. Terry was named by Thinkers360 as a Top 20 Global Leader in the Future of Work and CIO Review Magazine named Terry's consulting company, JCG Consulting Group LLC, as one of the "Top 10 Most Promising Leadership Development Solution Providers 2019." He is also a consultant/speaker for the US State Department International Information Program. Terry also leads a division of a public company in which his emphasis was on Sales and Operations. He has also worked for such corporate giants as ExxonMobil, Bristol Meyers, and Norfolk Southern Corp. Terry earned his PhD in Management, with a concentration in Leadership and Organizational Change, in 2007. He started as a business coach in 2003, and in 2011 earned his certification as an executive coach through the Center for Executive Coaching. Terry has since earned the Marshall Goldsmith Stakeholder Centering Coaching certification. As an executive coach, Terry has helped executives and organizations execute more effectively to produce sustainable behavioral change to achieve their desired results. Terry has served as a business coach for startups and coached executives at Pinterest, Google, Intel, ExxonMobil, Norfolk Southern Corp, Valassis, DellEMC, New York Life, Pakistan Government, Amazon, McDonalds, and IBM. Terry published his latest book titled *Co-Creation Leadership: Helping Leaders Develop Their SuperPower of Co-Creation for The Greater Good of the Organization.* It is an actionable business journal for leaders. Terry is also the author of *Transformational Thinking: The First Step Toward Individual and Organizational Greatness.*

Whitney Johnson CEO of boutique consultancy Disruption Advisors, is one of the 50 leading business thinkers in the world (Thinkers50), and is an expert on smart growth leadership: how to grow your people to grow your company. The #1 Talent Coach, she was selected as a Top 15 Coach out of 16,000 applicants by Dr. Marshall Goldsmith, the world's leading executive coach. She is a Master Certified Coach in Stakeholder-Centered Coaching and has coached for Harvard Business School Executive Education. As an Institutional Investor-ranked analyst at Merrill Lynch, Whitney innovated an approach to momentum and growth that started with stocks and then applied it to people. In working with Harvard's legendary thought leader Clayton Christensen, she developed a similar adaptation to the concept of disruption: companies do not disrupt, people do. The Disruptive Innovation Fund in which she was a co-founder invested in and led the $8 million seed round for Korea's Coupang, currently valued at $50+ billion. In 2012, she began to focus exclusively on developing the IP of Personal Disruption as a mechanism for personal and organizational growth. She codifies the Personal Disruption framework in the bestselling books *Disrupt Yourself* and *Build an A Team and the forthcoming Smart Growth: How to Grow Your People to Grow Your Company,* published by Harvard Business Press.

Whitney has 1.8 million followers on LinkedIn, where she was selected as a Top Voice in 2020, and she hosts the weekly Disrupt Yourself podcast.

Atchara (Cara) Juicharern, PhD was named and awarded #1 Coach in Asia by Dr. Marshall Goldsmith – the world's most influential leadership thinker and executive coach. She has helped leading organizations in Thailand and other countries develop their leadership and innovative people development programs. She has also successfully coached leaders at all levels during their leadership transition and in terms of people management strategies. She regularly conducts studies on coaching culture and is frequently invited to speak on coaching trends and the future of leadership and coaching to international executives and HR forums as well as coaching conferences. Her "thought leadership" appeared in leading newspapers and business magazines. Atchara's bestselling book *Leader as Coach* is the first Thai-language book that introduced the notion of simplified coaching conversations to leaders and contains a foreword from Dr. Marshall Goldsmith. Atchara was interviewed by *GM Magazine* recently as the only coach recognized as a Thailand Top Influencer. She was also given the "Asia's Woman Leaders" award by CMO Asia. She was the first coach from Thailand who was nominated for The Thinkers50 Marshall Goldsmith Distinguished Achievement Award for Coaching and Mentoring. Atchara received her bachelor's degree in Education at Chulalongkorn University. She earned her master's degree in Arts at National Institute of Development Administration (NIDA), where she was awarded an outstanding academic record in 2001. She has a PhD in Management Development, an international program at NIDA. Atchara was also awarded a Distinguished Alumni Award in 2012. She is the Chief Executive Officer of the AcComm Group.

Carol Kauffman is on the faculty of Harvard Medical School and a visiting professor at Henley Business School. She is known globally as one of the top leaders in the field of leadership coaching. Thinkers 50 shortlisted her as one of the Top 8 coaches in the world due to her impact on the field of coaching. She is also a senior leadership advisor at Egon Zehnder and works with CEOs and their teams. Her work developing Leader as Coach won Harvard's Inaugural Award for the Culture of Excellence in Mentoring and her programs have been rolled out and scaled for thousands of leaders and their teams in both public and private sectors. At Harvard, Dr. Kauffman received a $2,000,000 grant to launch the Institute of Coaching, which awards grants for coaching research, brings science to coaching, and has a community of over 20,000 (InstituteofCoaching.org). She also chairs Harvard Medical School's annual coaching conference, their most widely attended event. She also launched their Leadership Forum, has chaired numerous conferences, and is the co-convener of the European School of Management and Technology Coaching Colloquia. Kauffman was also the founding editor in chief of the first coaching academic journal from a major publishing house, *Coaching: An International Journal of Theory, Research and Practice* (T&F). She has written numerous academic and professional articles and is currently under contract with Harvard Business Review Press for the book: *It's Your Move: The Art of High Stakes, High Risk Leadership*. Of all her activities, Carol most loves coaching her CEOs and C-level leaders to become their best selves and have the impact they want. She has accrued over 40,000 hours of experience. Dr. Kauffman is a board-certified psychologist and an examiner for the American Board of Professional Psychology. She lives in the Boston area with her husband and two adult children nearby. Her passion is for prehistoric cave art and has explored caves from France to Sulawesi. Her love of animals is core to her being; she has trained abused ones and been on nine safaris – and next up are the Sami reindeer and the wolves of Yellowstone. Please visit CarolKauffman.com and consider receiving the Marshall Goldsmith–inspired "Knowledge Philanthropy" newsletter.

Thomas Kolditz is the founding director, Doerr Institute for New Leaders at Rice University. The Doerr Institute, Tom's fifth successful leader development startup, was named the top university leader development program by the Association of Leadership Educators and the #4 Leader Development Program worldwide by Global Gurus. Prior to founding the institute, Tom designed the Leader Development Program at the Yale School of Management and chaired the Department of Behavioral Sciences and Leadership at West Point for 12 years. Brigadier General Kolditz has more than 35 years in leadership positions on four continents and received the Distinguished Service Medal, the Army's highest award for service. He is a fellow in the American Psychological Association and has published more than 75 articles and book chapters to date, including in the Proceedings of the National Academy of Sciences and the proceedings of the World Economic Forum. Tom has delivered more than 350 speeches worldwide. In 2017, he received the prestigious Warren Bennis Award for Excellence in Leadership. An accomplished leadership coach, he was listed as #6 in the Coaching category in 2018 by Global Gurus, and in 2019, #24 in Coaching by Thinkers50, a UK management ranking group, and was a finalist for the Thinkers50 Goldsmith Coaching Award in London. He holds a BA from Vanderbilt University, three master's degrees, and a PhD in Psychology from the University of Missouri. Tom Kolditz is the director of Doerr Institute for New Leaders at Rice University, named the top university program by the Association of Leadership Educators. A retired Army general holding a PhD, he received the Warren Bennis Award for Excellence in Leadership in 2017, and has ranked among the Top 25 global coaches for 3 years.

Dr. Oleg Konovalov is a global thought leader, author, business educator, consultant, and C-Suite coach. He has been named among the Top 8 global experts in leadership and shortlisted for the Distinguished Award in Leadership by Thinkers50 2021. He is on Global Gurus Top 30 in Leadership, has been recognized as #1 Global Thought Leader on Culture by Thinkers 360, and is #1 Global Leading Coach (Marshall Goldsmith Thinkers50). He is the author of game-changing books including *LEADEROLOGY*, which defines the beginning of the Renaissance period in modern management and leadership while helping leaders to reach a new level of success; *Corporate Superpower*, which is named a bible of culture management for modern leaders; and *Organisational Anatomy*, which discusses organizations and management from a biological perspective. Oleg is passionate to help companies to make a leap in performance. His work identifies leaders' and entrepreneurs' strategic needs and helps them to drive their companies to success. He always offers unique perspectives and approaches to enhance the role of people and improve performance and help leaders to attune their companies, culture, and leadership into a customer-centered business at the age of digitalization. Oleg received his doctoral degree from Durham University Business School. He is a visiting lecturer at a number of business schools, a Forbes contributor, and a high-in-demand speaker at major conferences around the world. Originally from Russia, he is based in Birmingham, UK, and Moscow, Russia.

Hortense le Gentil is the author of the widely acclaimed *"Aligned: Connecting Your True Self with the Leader You're Meant to Be."* She works with decision-makers around the world to help them lead with authenticity by finding and closing the gaps between the leader they are and the leader they want to be. Le Gentil is a certified Marshall Goldsmith Stakeholder Centered™ coach and is part of MG100 Coaches, Marshall Goldsmith's "Pay It Forward" project. In 2020, she was ranked #13 "World's Top Management Gurus" by Global Gurus Top 30 and in 2019 received a Marshall Goldsmith "Thinkers50 Top Coaches in the World" Award. Le Gentil's executive coaching is informed by her 30 years in business, working across a number of industries – including media consulting, advertising, and entrepreneurship

Dr. Mongezi C. Makhalima is a Chartered Executive Coach, Thinkers50 Top 50 Global coach & an organization development specialist with 30 years of working with organizations and leadership in corporates and NGOs. He is currently the Chairperson of the *Africa Board for Coaching, Consulting and Coaching Psychology (ABCCCP)* and also sits as a non-executive director on several boards in the NGO, film, and music sectors. Mongezi is also one of the founding members of the Special Interest Group on Consulting and Coaching psychology with the Society for Industrial and Organisational Psychologists of South Africa (SIOPSA). He is one of the global founding members of the International Society for Coaching Psychology (ISCP). Mongezi serves as a faculty member in the Faculty of Commerce, Law, and management of the University of the Witwatersrand as well as Wits Business School, teaching master's and advanced programs in leadership and coaching. He holds a BCom in Industrial Psychology and Business Management, an MBA through the University of the North West, an MA in Coaching Psychology with a focus on Work-based Learning from Middlesex University in the United Kingdom, and a PhD in Organizational Psychology. Mongezi has presented and written widely on the subject of coaching, mentoring, and leadership and works with clients globally and locally.

Pamela McLean PhD is the CEO of The Hudson Institute of Coaching, an organization with over 30 years of experience providing a full suite of coaching services inside organizations around the globe. Her organization was on the forefront of providing year-long coach certification programs for leaders and has certified well over 2,000 leadership and executive coaches around the globe. McLean brings more than three decades of experience as a clinical psychologist, a master coach, a coach supervisor, and a leader in the field of coaching. McLean authored *The Completely Revised Handbook of Coaching* (2012), examining key theories, and evidenced based research informing the field. McLean's latest book, *Self as Coach, Self as Leaders* (2019), examines the internal landscape of the leader and the coach and all that is required to be at our very best when working with others. Pam has served on Harvard's JFK Women's Leadership Board, the faculties of Saybrook University and Antioch University, and Editorial Board of IJCO. She lives in Santa Barbara, California, where she and her late husband raised three sons. Making a difference in our world matters to her, and she has served on the board of Planned Parenthood and the Human Rights Watch Committee most recently. Today, she enjoys all things related to writing, weekend cooking, pottery making, birdwatching, and traveling to new places around the globe.

Magdalena Nowicka Mook brings experience in fundraising, coaching, and consulting and association management. Currently, she offers her vision and strategic direction as the CEO and Executive Director of the International Coach Federation (ICF), where she acts as a partner to the ICF's Global Board of Directors. Magdalena has also held positions with the Council of State Governments, where she was the Assistant Director of National Policy and Director of Development. The US Department of Agriculture's Economic Research Service has also utilized Magdalena's international business acumen, bringing her in for coordinating technical assistance programs and implementing special projects in four European countries. Magdalena is a trained professional coach and systems' facilitator. Magdalena is a frequent speaker on subjects of trends in coaching and leadership development as well as regulation and ethics. Ms. Mook received her MS in Economics and International Trade from the Warsaw School of Economics, Poland. She also graduated from the Copenhagen Business School's Advanced Program in International Management and Consulting. She is a member of the Women's Foreign Policy Group, Forbes.com Council on Non-profits, and Association for Talent Development (ATD), and serves as the Chair of the International Section Council of ASAE. She is also a member of the Advisory Board for Institute of Organizational Mindfulness. In 2019, Magdalena was recognized as #1 Coach: Global Influence by Marshall Goldsmith Thinkers50 and was a finalist for the Thinkers50 Marshall Goldsmith Distinguished Award in Coaching and Mentoring.

Howard J. Morgan As an executive coach, Howard Morgan has led major organizational change initiatives in partnership with senior executives across all levels and industries. He was named as one of the coach top coaches globally, has been recognized as one of five coaches with "a proven track record of success," and has published several books. Howard has worked with over 1000 CEOs and Executive Team members from more than 50 countries covering a diverse industry base including Technology, Financial Services, Chemical, Media, Retail, and Real Estate. He has worked with leaders in a variety of cultures: from nascent startups to Fortune 50 organizations. His work with these teams and individuals has become focused in recent years on two main practice areas. He knows what it means to structure an organization, lead people, and manage a business to exceed quarterly objectives. This practical background, along with an understanding of the politics of leadership and the competitive pressures of today's global marketplace, is reflected in the roll-up-your-sleeves coaching style he utilizes with executives. He specializes in executive coaching as a strategic leadership and change management tool, leading to improved customer and employee satisfaction and overall corporate performance. Howard holds an MBA from Simon Fraser University and has completed advanced studies at the University of Michigan. He currently serves on three Boards of Directors located in the United States and Europe. He is a member of MG100.

Aaron Ngui is the Global Projects Head and Chief Editor for ITD World and involved in several initiatives, including developing the Let's Coach app and eLearning programs. He is involved in digital marketing and content creation for online and offline marketing channels. He supports other initiatives to realize the vision of making ITD World the #1 Global Leadership Development Expert. As a former bureau chief and journalist, his beats included crime, politics, society, and business over a decade of writing. He covered elections, human trafficking cases, humanitarian crises, environmental issues, and court cases involving public figures. Aaron netted the Main Award for English News (Print) from Universiti Sains Malaysia (USM) for a story on the Penang Transport Master Plan. He was recognized by Han Chiang College for the Most Outstanding Alumni and tapped for the Penang Green Journalism Awards judging panel. He holds a

Bachelor of Mass Communication from the University of Southern Queensland and a Diploma in Mass Communication from Han Chiang College. In his spare time, Aaron tries new recipes. Feedback from his wife and children is worked into subsequent efforts. He is either searching for the perfect bowl of noodles or nose-deep in a book.

Prof. Jonathan Passmore, D.Psych has held board level roles in government, not for profit and the commercial sector. He is a licensed psychologist, holds five degrees, and is an award-winning coach, author, and researcher. He has authored and edited over 30 books, including *Top Business Psychology Models*, *Becoming a Coach*, *The Coaches Handbook*, and *WeCoach*. He is also the editor of the eight-volume Wiley-Blackwell Series on Industrial Psychology. He has published over 100 scientific papers and book chapters, on coaching, leadership, and change and spoken at over 200 events worldwide. He believes in Open Science, sharing knowledge openly with other scientists and practitioners; thus, much of his work is available for free download from his website: jonathanpassmore.com, and the income from most of his titles' is donated to charitable causes such as The Railway Children and Water Aid. He has been shortlisted and received multiple awards, including Marshall Goldsmith Global Coaching Awards Thinkers50, Global Gurus List, Association of Business Psychologists, British Psychological Society, EMCC, and Association for Coaching. He has previously worked for PWC, IBM, and OPM as a change consultant and executive coach, with clients including government ministers, celebrities, and senior leaders in the public, private and non-profit sectors. He is now the professor of coaching and behavioral change at Henley Business School and Senior VP for the global coaching tech company CoachHub, which provides coaching for leaders and managers through a network of over 2500 coaches worldwide. He also runs a small private coaching practice, which specializes in providing coaching for senior leaders who have derailed, are suspended or have lost senior or board level roles, and are in crisis. The coaching is available free until the individual is able to pay. He is based in the United Kingdom but works out of offices in London, Berlin, and New York.

Jennifer Paylor is an influential and provocative business thought leader, and she holds a published patent for inventing a coaching system for guiding interactions. She is an accomplished student of people, organizational culture, human behavior, exponential growth, and leadership. Jennifer has applied her techniques to massive enterprises like IBM and delivered unprecedented results. Jennifer is currently the Head of Learning & Development, Talent, and Culture for Capgemini in North America. Jennifer is widely known for creating and operationalizing the largest internal corporate coaching practice in the world at IBM. Her diverse background includes expertise in large-scale culture hacking, talent management, corporate learning, technology & engineering, science-based leadership development, human-centered design, Agile transformation, and personally coaching teams of senior executives who are leading complex change and exponential growth in large enterprises. Jennifer is a celebrated member of Marshall Goldsmith's exclusive group of MG100 Coaches.

David B. Peterson, PhD has been recognized as a world-class executive coach and thought leader in leadership and executive development for over 25 years. In 2019, he was selected as the #1 Corporate Coach in the world. As the co-founder and chief transformation officer at 7 Paths Forward, LLC, he provides executive coaching and leadership development programs to top executives in companies ranging from Amazon and Apple to Waymo and Zoom, as well as highly regarded virtual training and development programs for leaders and executive coaches around the world. Previously, David was the head of Google's Executive Coaching & Leadership team, where he built one of the world's most innovative and high-impact coaching programs, and led the agile organization design team to help prepare Google to address emergent and disruptive leadership challenges, as well as coaching hundreds of Google's senior leaders on their most complex and emergent challenges. In addition to being a world-class coach, he is a highly regarded speaker and author – his books, *Leader as Coach* and *Development FIRST*, have sold over 1,000,000 copies. He is known for being on the cutting edge of the profession, challenging the conventional wisdom, and constantly exploring provocative and compelling new ideas to help coaches and leaders have greater impact. He earned his PhD in Counseling and Industrial/Organizational Psychology at the University of Minnesota. He is a fellow of the American Psychological Association, the Society of Consulting Psychology, the Society for Industrial and Organizational Psychology (SIOP), and the Harvard Institute of Coaching.

Jack J. Phillips, PhD chairman of ROI Institute, is a world-renowned expert on accountability, measurement, and evaluation. A former HR executive and bank president, Phillips provides consulting services for Fortune 500 companies and major global organizations. The author or editor of more than 100 books, he conducts workshops and presents at conferences throughout the world. Phillips has received several awards for his books and work. The Society for Human Resource Management presented him an award for one of his books and honored a Phillips ROI study with its highest award for creativity. The American Society for Training and Development gave him its highest award, Distinguished Contribution to Workplace Learning and Development, for his work on ROI. Jack and his wife Patti Phillips were the first recipients of the Center for Talent Reporting's Distinguished Contributor Award. This award recognized their outstanding and significant contributions in the measurement and management of human capital. In 2019, Jack and Patti were named two of the Top 50 coaches in the world by the Thinkers50 organization, and they were named finalists for the Marshall Goldsmith Distinguished Achievement Award for Coaching. Jack's work has been featured in *The Wall Street Journal*, *BusinessWeek*, and *Fortune* magazine. He has been interviewed by several television programs, including CNN. He has served on the boards of several businesses, non-profits, and associations, including the American Society for Training and Development, the National Management Association, and the International Society for Performance Improvement, where he served as president (2012–2013).

Patti P. Phillips, PhD is the CEO of ROI Institute, Inc., the leading source of ROI competency building, implementation support, networking, and research. Patti has helped organizations implement the ROI Methodology® in more than 70 countries worldwide. Her work as an educator, researcher, consultant, and coach contributes to the advancement of measurement, evaluation, and analytics and their use in driving organizational strategy. Patti serves as a member of the Board of Trustees of the United Nations Institute for Training and Research (UNITAR) and serves on the faculty of the UN System Staff College in Turin, Italy. She serves as the chair of the Institute for Corporate Productivity (i4cp) People Analytics Board, Principal Research Fellow for The Conference Board, board member of the International Federation for Training and Development Organizations (IFTDO), and board chair for the Center for Talent Reporting (CTR), and is an Association for Talent Development (ATD) Certification Institute Fellow. Patti, along with her husband Jack J. Phillips, contributes to a variety of journals and has authored or co-authored more than 75 books on the subject of measurement, evaluation, analytics, and ROI. In 2019, she and Jack received the Distinguished Contributor Award from CTR for their contribution to the measurement and management of human capital. The Thinkers50 organization recognized Patti and Jack as two of the initial Top 50 World Leaders in Coaching in November 2019. They were among the top finalists for the Marshall Goldsmith Distinguished Achievement Award in Coaching.

Dr. Christopher Rauen psychologist, Senior Coach (DBVC/IOBC), studied physics and psychology at the Universities of Münster and Osnabrück and obtained his doctorate degree in coaching education. He has worked as a business coach since 1996 and is a lecturer at several German universities as well as the head of the RAUEN coaching training, which is certified as an Educational Provider for Business Coaching (DBVC/IOBC). In 2003, he founded the Christopher Rauen GmbH, a full-service provider for coaching, which he still heads as the managing director. The Christopher Rauen GmbH also provides several Internet portals, e.g., CoachDB.com, a worldwide database for professional coaches. In addition to his work as a coach and CEO, Christopher Rauen has published several articles and six books that are among the standard reference work of German-language coaching literature, e.g., the *Handbuch Coaching* (Handbook Coaching) and the Coaching-Tools series. He is also the editor of the *German Coaching-Magazine*, *Coaching-Report*, and *Coaching-Newsletter*. In addition, he is the initiator and first Chairman of the Board of the German Association of Coaching e.V. (DBVC) and founding member and Chairman of the Board of Directors of the International Organization for Business Coaching (IOBC). The IOBC represents the highest standards in Business Coaching worldwide and connects coaches and coaching experts from business, research, and education/training. As CEO and Chairman, Christopher Rauen knows the required competencies for management and leadership from his own experience. His motto is "I don't believe in hopeless situations."

Dr. Marcia Reynolds, PsyD helps global organizations grow their leadership using coaching for accelerated results. Her clients include executives and emerging leaders in multinational corporations, non-profit organizations, and government agencies. She also speaks at coaching and leadership conferences around the world and has taught classes and coached leaders in 43 countries. She is recognized by Global Gurus as the #4 coach in the world and is one of 15 coaches inducted by the International Coach Federation into their Circle of Distinction. Prior to coaching, Marcia ran training departments for two global companies. She designed the culture change programs that helped the second company launch the most successful IPO in the United States in 1993. Marcia was a founding member and the fifth global president of the International Coaching Federation, and one of the first 25 people in the world to become a Master Certified Coach (MCC). She teaches coaching for schools in the United States, China, Russia, and the Philippines, and offers classes in coaching mastery globally both live and online. Excerpts from Marcia's books *Outsmart Your Brain*, *Wander Woman*, *The Discomfort Zone: How Leaders Turn Difficult Conversations into Breakthroughs*, and her latest international bestseller, *Coach the Person, Not the Problem* have appeared in business, coaching, and psychological publications worldwide. Marcia's doctorate is in organizational psychology, and she holds two master's degrees in communication and adult learning. She is passionate about how we can expand minds, transform lives, and spread success through coaching conversations.

Prof. Philippe Rosinski, MCC is considered the pioneer of intercultural and global coaching. He is the author of two seminal books, *Coaching Across Cultures* and *Global Coaching*. His integrated coaching approach leverages multiple perspectives (from the physical to the spiritual) to tackle complex challenges, enabling greater creativity, impact, fulfillment, and meaning. Philippe shares his passion for making the most of cultural differences and for learning from multiple disciplines, in order to help unleash the human multifaceted potential. For 30 years and across continents, Philippe has helped people and organizations thrive and make a positive difference in the world. Philippe is a world authority in executive coaching, team coaching, and global leadership development. He is the first European to have been designated Master Certified Coach by the International Coach Federation. He has also developed an integrative coaching supervision approach. Philippe is the principal of Rosinski & Company, a consultancy based in Belgium with partners around the globe, and a professor at the Kenichi Ohmae Graduate School of Business in Tokyo, Japan. He intervenes in several other academic institutions including HEC Paris, Henley Business School and the University of Cambridge. He is the co-author of 12 books, including *Evidence Based Coaching Handbook* and *Mastering Executive Coaching*, and the author of the *Cultural Orientations Framework (COF) Assessment*. A Master of Science from Stanford University, Philippe has received numerous awards including the Thinkers50 Marshall Goldsmith Leading Global Coaches Award (London, 2019), and has been listed among the Global Gurus Coaching Top 30 (2021).

Dr. Lance Secretan is the world's top authority on inspirational leadership, a trailblazing teacher, advisor, and expert on corporate culture, whose bestselling books, inspirational talks, and life-changing retreats have touched the hearts and minds of hundreds of thousands of people worldwide. He is the author of 21 books about leadership, inspiration, corporate culture, and entrepreneurship as well as an award-winning memoir, *A Love Story*. He is the former CEO of a Fortune 100 company, university professor, award-winning columnist, poet, author, and outdoor athlete. He coaches and advises leaders globally (he is ranked among both the Top 30 Most Influential Executive Coaches and the Top 30 Most Influential Leadership Experts globally) and guides leadership teams who wish to transform their culture into the most inspirational in their industries. Dr. Secretan is the recipient of many other awards, including the International Caring Award, whose previous winners include Pope Francis, the Dalai Lama, President Jimmy Carter, and Dr. Desmond Tutu. He is a forum Chair at MacKay CEO Forums, current Chair of the Pay it Forward Foundation, and former Chair of the Advisory Board of the Special Olympics World Winter Games. He is an expert skier, kayaker, and mountain biker, and he divides his time between Ontario, Canada, and the Colorado Rockies.

Caroline Stokes is a human capital entrepreneur, the founder of FORWARD, the author of *Elephants Before Unicorns: Emotionally Intelligent HR Strategies to Save Your Company* (Entrepreneur Press, 2019.) and host of The Emotionally Intelligent Recruiter podcast. As a recipient of the "Leading Global Coach" award by Thinkers50 Marshall Goldsmith Coaching Award, Caroline's firm has a genre-defining approach to executive search (leadership attraction), coaching (organizational and leadership development), and training (C-Suite and HR leaders) to evolve organizations and their leaders. FORWARD has worked with leaders from companies including Autodesk, Microsoft, EA, Disney, the BBC, Amazon, Samsung, Adobe, and Google, along with many startups and scaling organizations. Her business book, *Elephants Before Unicorns*, examines the role of emotional intelligence in the age of artificial intelligence in recruiting, retaining, and engaging talent. It has been awarded 5-star reviews by Amazon customers across the United Kingdom, the United States, and Canada. She regularly speaks and gives workshops around the world on the need for leaders to develop organizational EQ in the face of technological advancements. Caroline contributes articles to Harvard Business Review, Entrepreneur, and Forbes. Before founding FORWARD, Caroline spent her international career at Sony, Virgin, and Nokia, working in Sydney, London, and Dublin. A British-Canadian citizen, she was raised in Singapore and the United Kingdom and now lives in Vancouver, British Columbia.

Didem Tekay describes herself as a "Grow-Forward Architect," curating development paths for leaders, teams, and organizations for their progress. She works as transformation consultant and coach supporting transformation and development process of many companies in many different industries such as Financial Services, Life Sciences and Healthcare, FMCG, and Technology and Telecommunications for more than 20 years. She is a pioneer on curating participatory coaching interventions to inspire executive leaders and leadership teams in their crucial conversations. She has been listed in the Forbes Global Forty Over 40 Women to Watch 2015 list, which celebrates women who are reinventing, leaning in, and creating momentum that will be felt by those beyond their community and field in the world. She is also one of the 200 female mentees in the Women on Boards program, an initiative launched to ensure that more women are assigned to top decision-making positions at top corporations. She has Leading Global Coach Award from Marshall Goldsmith MG100 initiation. She is the author of the book *The Grow-Forward Manifesto*, navigating leaders how to foster self, team, and organizational growth with a development framework. She is the founder of Grow Women Circle, a space where women leaders encouraged to voice their visions, step up, grow forward, and lead through coaching. Tekay is now working with private sector leaders to commit and craft roadmaps acting on UN Sustainable Development Goals.

Mark C. Thompson is the world's #1 CEO Coach ranked by the American Management Association and, for the past 5 years, has been on two of the 30 Global Gurus lists for Leadership and for Executive Coaching. Forbes described him as having the "Midas Touch," with more than 83 engagements with boards and C-Suite executives for CEO leadership development, including World Bank CEO Jim Yong Kim, Hewlett Packard CEO Enrique Lores, Nuskin CEO Ryan Napierski, Qualcomm CEO Cristiano Amon, Zoox\Amazon CEO Aicha Evans, Pinterest co-founder Evan Sharp, Schwab founder Chuck Schwab, and Virgin founder Richard Branson. He is founding advisor, adjunct faculty, and alumni of the Stanford University Realtime Venture Design Lab, a co-chairman of the Harvard Institute of Coaching, and a *New York Times* bestselling author of *Admired, Success Built to Last: Creating a Life That Matters*, and *Now Build a Great Business*. The #1 CEO Coach, he was also selected as a Top 15 Coach out of 16,000 applicants by Dr. Marshall Goldsmith, the world's leading executive coach. He is a Master Certified Coach in Stakeholder-Centered Coaching and has coached for The World Business Forum, World Economic Forum, Stanford, Harvard, and John F. Kennedy Universities.

Brian O. Underhill PhD, PCC is an internationally recognized expert in the design and management of worldwide executive coaching implementations. He is the Founder and CEO of CoachSource, the world's largest purely executive coaching provider, with over 1,100 coaches in 100+ countries. Previously, he managed executive coaching operations for Marshall Goldsmith, the world's #1 coach. Brian is the co-editor of "Mastering Executive Coaching" (Routledge, 2019), the author of "Executive Coaching for Results: The Definitive Guide to Developing Organizational Leaders" (Berrett-Koehler: 2007), and the author of numerous articles and blogs in the coaching field. He is an internationally sought-after speaker, addressing The Conference Board, ICF, EMCC, and many regional coaching events. He has been nominated as a Thinkers50 Leading Global Coach in 2019. Brian has a PhD and an MS degree in organizational psychology from the California School of Professional Psychology (Los Angeles) and a BA in psychology from the University of Southern California. Brian is certified in the Hogan Assessments, Element B, Extended DISC and holds Advanced Certification in the Goldsmith Coaching Process. He is a founding fellow of the Institute of

Coaching Professional Association at McLean Hospital – a Harvard Medical School affiliate. He was named a 2020 Fellow of the Society of Consulting Psychology (APA – Division 13). He is a Professional Certified Coach (PCC) with the International Coach Federation. Brian resides in Silicon Valley where he enjoys cycling and racquetball, plays music as a worship musician, and spends time with his wife, Julie, and kids, Kaitlyn (20) and Evan (17).

Nankhonde Kasonde-van den Broek is an executive coach, organizational change architect, and entrepreneur. She is the lead consultant at Nankhonde Kasonde Consultancy, founder and CEO at ZANGA African Metrics, and a pioneer in the use of technology to develop African coaching solutions that understand the mosaic of cultural dimensions and the reality of leadership in an emerging market context. Following a decade working in international development and finance globally, she returned to Zambia to pursue her purpose and desire to contribute to her country's economy and the wider African development agenda. She has over 20 years of experience supporting multi-nationals, international organizations, and governments. She is an accomplished professional with a wealth of African, international, and multi-cultural experience in designing and leading large-scale change across multiple sectors. Her philosophy of "African cultural and context–centered design" in human capital development comes from her complex worldview and shapes her impact. Nankhonde is a member of the Africa List, a group of future African leaders in emerging markets. She is a Global Guru, World's Top 30 Coach for 2021. Nankhonde is a Marshall Goldsmith 50 Global Leading Coach and a member of the MG100. Nankhonde has made positive contributions to the landscape of executive coaching in Zambia and across the African continent in addition to her roles on corporate boards. Nankhonde is a graduate of the renowned HEC Paris Business School (France) and Oxford University (UK) joint Executive Specialized Master's in Consulting & Coaching for Change. In addition, she holds an MBA specializing in Project Management from the African Institute of Management (Dakar, Senegal), an MSc in Management from the University of Quebec at Chicoutimi (Quebec, Canada), and a BA in Management from Webster University (Geneva, Switzerland). She is a Professional Certified Coach (ICF), Organization and Relationship Systems Certified Coach (CRR/Global), and a Stakeholder-Centered Certified Coach (Marshall Goldsmith). She is fluent in English and French and is married with two children.

Frank Wagner, PhD As a behavioral coach, Frank brings a broad base of experience working with individuals from midlevel management through C-level positions. Frank's specialty is leadership behavior, with an emphasis on commitment, teamwork, influence across organizational boundaries, coaching, and faster strategic planning and execution. Along with Marshall Goldsmith, he was one of the first coaches practicing results-based coaching where fees are charged only when those who work with the leader determine improvement in leadership behavior after one year. Frank is the principal designer and oversees the training process in Marshall Goldsmith's method of Stakeholder-Centered Coaching®. He is the principal author of *The Coach's Playbook*, *The Leader as Coach Playbook*, and *The Leaders Guide to Encouraging Development*. He published the *Power of Total Commitment* in 1991, with a second edition in 2015. Frank's consulting career started at The Center for Leadership Studies with Paul Hersey in the late 1970s. He then became a partner and director at Keilty, Goldsmith & Boone before starting his own boutique coaching firm Stakeholder-Centered Coaching LTD. He is also a founding member of Marshall Goldsmith Partners. Frank has a PhD and an MBA from The Anderson School of Management, UCLA, where he also served as a Post-Doctoral Scholar. His undergraduate degree in Economics is from Santa Clara University.

Affiliations/Achievements

- Master Certified Coach – Stakeholder-Centered Coaching® (2006)
- Master Certified Executive Coach (MCEC) – Association of Corporate Executive Coaches (2017)
- Top 50 Global Coaches (2019)

Gary Wang Driven, passionate, and strongly committed, Gary takes great pride in his self-made background. The fact that he had to quit senior high school only after the first semester did not stop him from dreaming big. In the following 7 years, he completed high school, college, and graduate studies in English language all by himself while working as a highly effective high-school English teacher for 4 years. After 14 years with blue-chip companies such as Sony, DuPont, and Dell; assuming Country Manager and Division Manager roles in China;

and failing in his first venture effort in the e-commerce space, he discovered executive coaching in 2008 and has since built MindSpan into a brand and market leader in China, serving 450+ global and local clients, including 136 Fortune 500 companies in China and 18 other markets. MindSpan's client list includes leading companies such as Microsoft, Ford, J&J, IBM, Roche, Pfizer, Texas Instruments, Bayer, ABB, Bosch, Boehringer Ingelheim, MSD, Nike, Coca-Cola, 3M, Starbucks, Deloitte, BCG, Disney, GE, AIA, Standard Chartered, HSBC, DuPont, eBay, Organon, Medtronic, NUS, Huawei, Alibaba, Tencent, JD.com, and Midea. Gary advocates relentless pursuit of what life can offer: self-worth, experiences, relationships, and impact on others. He believes that three things lead to ultimate meaning and success: Initiative, Drive, and Generosity (his so-called "IDG Excellence" model). He is an avid runner, having run more than 185 marathons and half-marathons, both in and outside China. He lives with his wife and two daughters in Shanghai.

Karen Yanqun Wu is the founder and CEO of Co-wisdom Coaching Ltd, a leading brand on corporate coaching in China. She is an impactful leader in China coaching market as the co-founder and vice president of ICF Beijing Chapter and focuses on CEO coaching and leadership team coaching. She is teaching Leadership Development in BUPT-Leon EMBA program. Karen has PhD on Economic from Peking University. Karen is one of few Chinese coaches who has rich business management experience. She understands both business and people. She was Corporate Vice President of AMD, Chief Marketing Officer in AMD China and Account General Manager in Nokia. Karen is a visionary authority in executive coaching and team coaching, and her purpose is to transform leaders and organizations with coaching services. Her customers include CEO and senior executive leaders in MNC in China and fast-growing Internet companies. Karen has partnered with top global coaching firms to introduce world-class ICF credential ACTP programs, executive coaching program, and team coaching program to China. Co-wisdom has trained over 300 corporate coaches. She has developed models to enrich coaching services including LBW – Leadership Behavior Wheel, TGI – Team Greatness Index, and VUCAR model for coaching style leadership. She also developed an online executive platform with her 5A process, which has been reviewed as world-class project management by the clients. Karen lives in Beijing with her family, including three daughters.

Cathleen Wu is an experienced executive coach, team coach, and coaching trainer. She brings to her coaching a vast wealth of experience collected over 30 working years and is motivated by her passion for individual, team, and organization development and her deep belief that people are creative, resourceful, and full of potential. Cathleen is striving 100% of her efforts to coaching since 2012 and is providing excellent coaching services in sectors of FMCG, high-tech, automobile, pharmaceutical, chemical, financial, professional service, and industries. She works with corporate leaders from various functions, including Country and BU General Management, Sales & Marketing, Finance, Manufacturing, R&D, Logistics, and HR, at levels spanning from middle manager (Director) to top executive (GM, CEO, CXO, VP). Cathleen work with clients on diverse coaching topics from executive presence, career and role transition, influencing power, interpersonal relationships, stakeholder management, developing confidence and authority, cross-culture effectiveness, people engagement, team effectiveness, to organization change and transformation, strategic mindset, and entrepreneurship. To facilitate client's growth and breakthrough in these areas, Cathleen's coaching style is a mixture of supporting and challenging, strategic, and tactical, which is built on solid foundation of mutual trust and deep empathy. Cathleen is credentialed by ICF as MCC since 2020 and by Marshall Goldsmith as SCC. Prior to her coaching practice, Cathleen worked as a telecom engineer for 6 years in her early career, followed by 16 years as a corporate HR leader in various industries, including semiconductor, IT, electronics, FMCG, and professional services. She co-wrote the *Strategic Change: Leadership Matters* in 2004. Cathleen is based in Shanghai, China, and speaks Mandarin and English.

Index

Note: Page numbers followed by "*f*" refers to figures and "*t*" refers to tables